Lucy
Audubon

SOUTHERN BIOGRAPHY SERIES

Lucy dressed in English finery to sit for Frederick Cruikshank of
London. She had at last reaped her reward for the years of sacrifice
and separation.

Lucy Audubon

A Biography

CAROLYN E. DeLATTE

Updated Edition

With a Foreword by Christoph Irmscher

LOUISIANA STATE UNIVERSITY PRESS)|(BATON ROUGE

Published by Louisiana State University Press
Copyright © 1982, 2008 by Louisiana State University Press
All rights reserved
Manufactured in the United States of America

Updated Edition, 2008
First printing

Designer: Albert Crochet
Typeface: VIP Goudy Old Style
Typesetter: G & S Typesetters, Inc.
Printer: Thomson-Shore, Inc.

Excerpt in the Foreword from John James Audubon's letter to John Bachman, dated August 25, 1834, with appended note by Lucy Audubon, call number bMS Am 1482 (61), is published with the permission of the Houghton Library, Harvard University.

Library of Congress Cataloging-in-Publication Data

DeLatte, Carolyn E.
  Lucy Audubon, a biography.

  (Southern biography series)
  Bibliography: p.
  Includes index.
    1. Audubon, John James, 1785–1851. 2. Ornithologists—United States—Biography. 3. Artists—United States—Biography. 4. Audubon, Lucy Green Bakewell, 1788–1874. 5. Wives—Kentucky—Biography. 6. Wives—Louisiana—Biography. I. Title. II. Series.
  QL31.A9D44   598'.092'4 [B]   82-15205
  ISBN 978-0-8071-3381-1 (pap.)   AACR2

Contents

Illustrations

Foreword

On 1 April 1829, after three long years in England during which his relationship with his wife back in Louisiana had steadily deteriorated, John James Audubon boarded the packet ship *Columbia* in Portsmouth. He was headed for New York, hoping that his family, which had so long been disappointed by his failure to provide for them, would finally give him a warm welcome. After all, he had proved to everyone that his "Birds of America," his grand plan to paint, life-sized, all the birds in his adopted country that he could lay his hands on, wasn't just a quixotic fantasy. "I am well received where ever I am Known—every Object Known to me smiles as I meet it," he had written, with characteristic hyperbole, in his journal on 6 August 1826—lines that he knew Lucy Audubon would later read. Meanwhile, he had met the great Sir Walter Scott, and he had been elected to the Royal Society of Edinburgh. In a report to the Royal Academy in France, the world-famous naturalist Georges Cuvier had praised his work as "the most magnificent monument yet erected to ornithology" (*Le Moniteur*, 1828). His "business," as he called *The Birds of America* in a letter he sent Lucy shortly after his arrival in New York, was going well. Surely this would persuade Lucy to join him to "enliven his Spirits" in the future. He gave Lucy an ultimatum: "If a no comes; *I never will put the question again* and *we probably* never will meet again—if a 'Yes,' a kind 'Yes' comes bounding from thy heart, my heart will bound also" (10 May 1829; American Philosophical Society).

Before his departure, Audubon had left twenty-five drawings for his London engraver, Robert Havell, Jr., among them that of a swamp sparrow (*Spiza palustris*) perched on a sprig of mayapple. On the draw-ing, Audubon wrote in ink: "Mr. Havell will please have Lucy Audu-bon [sic] name on this plate instead of mine." The experts agree that it was Audubon himself, and not his wife Lucy, who painted the bird, and while some suggest that Lucy might have had a hand in drawing the leaves, there is really no proof at all that she did even that. (Bill Steiner, the foremost expert on Audubon's prints, believes the mayapple was the handiwork of Joseph Mason, Audubon's assistant.) Obviously, the plate was intended as a peace offering to Lucy, an attempt to draw her, if not by force then by art, into Audubon's monumental project.

I have always been puzzled by Audubon's choice of a swamp spar-row as a tribute to Lucy, a person who, with extraordinary courage, patience, and skill, had carried on as a teacher back home, catering to the needs of the spoiled offspring of Louisiana plantation owners, while Audubon was tooting his own horn in England. Swamp spar-rows, Audubon tells us in the text he wrote later to accompany the plate, are "a timid species, destitute of song, and merely uttering a single *cheep*, which is now and then heard during the day, but more frequently towards evening." These little birds, barely five inches in height, are not high-flyers; in fact, Audubon explains that they typi-cally alight in the middle of the rank weeds on the ground, rarely making it up to a tree. Like the mayapple, the plant featured in Audu-bon's watercolor, these birds aren't even particularly rare: Audubon had seen them in great numbers along the banks of the Mississippi River when he traveled to New Orleans in 1820.

Why didn't Audubon, who had a lot to make up for, pick a more spectacular bird species for Lucy, or at least one whose main purpose in life wasn't, as it would seem, to be eaten by "Sparrow Hawks, Pi-geon Hawks, and Hen-harriers"? One might point out here that the bird in the image is a male, so that it cannot have been intended as a direct representation of Lucy anyway. But consider the image itself (plate 64 of *Birds of America*): the small bird, dwarfed by the may-apple's blossom and its umbrella-shaped leaves, looks skeptically at us. Its lithe body, somewhat ordinary but nevertheless pretty with its brownish-black markings, the tiny head that is about to turn away from us—both indicate that this little bird keeps its own counsel. Did Audubon know that the mayapple's roots and leaves, though they can be used to cure warts, are poisonous? The (unrelated) English version

Swamp Sparrow,
FRINGILLA PALUSTRIS, wils.
Male.
May-apple. Polophyllum pellatum.

Drawn from Nature by Lucy Audubon.   Engraved, Printed & Coloured by R. Havell.

Swamp Sparrow, plate 64 of *Birds of America*

Courtesy Lilly Library, Indiana University, Bloomington, IN

of the plant, the true mandrake, was said to have human features; it was widely believed that, when pulled from the ground, its screams would cause a man to lose his mind. Suddenly it becomes clear that this drawing—of a self-sufficient bird surrounded by a lethal, yet potentially useful plant—was as good an image as any that Audubon could have chosen to declare his love for Lucy. Arguably, a more immediately domestic picture—such as the one of the male passenger pigeon being fed by its mate (plate 62 of *Birds of America*), often interpreted as a veiled comment on Audubon's relationship with his wife—would not have fit the bill.

Of course, Lucy wasn't a demure swamp sparrow by any means. Small and inconspicuous she was not. Like the man she fell in love with when he showed up at her father's Pennsylvania estate, Fatland Ford, she was tall and athletic, and while she wasn't perhaps classically beautiful, she impressed all those who met her with her intense gray eyes. A miniature made by Frederick Cruikshank in 1834, which serves as the frontispiece of this biography, shows a woman with rich dark hair and a high forehead, a prominent nose, and a small mouth pressed firmly shut—a mixture of schoolmarmish propriety and barely repressed sensuality.

Lucy Bakewell was to the manor born, as Audubon was not. Raised in Derbyshire, in "the comfortable and secure surroundings of wealth, social prestige, and intellectual stimulation" (p. 2 herein), she and the long-haired, handsome Audubon with the Roman nose must have made an odd, or, rather, oddly memorable pair. How appealing her British accent must have sounded in combination with her husband's soft, French-inflected English. While Lucy was a responsible housekeeper, able to oversee a household that, during the years they spent in Kentucky, included several slaves, she also had a distinct taste for adventure, a quality that stood her in good stead during her rocky marriage to Audubon. A skilled equestrian, she would uncomplainingly ride eight hundred miles on horseback from Kentucky to Pennsylvania, and she also had a good eye for the beauties of the American landscape (when she first caught a glimpse of the Ohio River, she called it "the finest river I ever saw," 64). When Audubon left her behind teaching school in Louisiana, she had better things to do than hanker after her wayward husband. At the time Audubon had

Mr. Havell sign the swamp sparrow plate with her name, Lucy seemed to have given up any hope of joining Audubon in England. She was, she told the roving Audubon in a letter written on 2 November 1828, *"comfortable in the extreme"* at William Garrett Johnson's plantation, Beech Grove (191). Don't pull me from the ground where I have created a life for myself, she seemed to be saying.

Unlike the rest of her genteel family, Lucy was, in DeLatte's words, "extraordinarily independent" (193). She was no feminist; she probably never even heard of the Seneca Falls Convention (223). Yet Lucy Bakewell Audubon had one advantage over many other women of her time: she knew precisely what she wanted. As often happens to good biographers, Carolyn DeLatte herself seems to take on some of her subject's characteristics as her biography progresses. Modestly but firmly, she turns her book into a plea for Lucy Audubon—an entirely unapologetic one. DeLatte, a New Orleans native who was chair of the Department of History at McNeese State University in Lake Charles, Louisiana, at the time of her death in 2004, declines to judge and dismiss, and seems content to describe and explain instead. Nevertheless, her flexible prose consistently illuminates her subject's strengths rather than weaknesses. For the most part, she is able to do without the fraudulent ventriloquizing and over-the-top emoting other biographers have employed when their sources don't tell them what people really thought or felt. When she slips into her character's skin, she does so unobtrusively and to great effect—thus, we are right there with Lucy when a gentle breeze cools her face as she is trying to find "a comfortable position in the little craft for her cumbersome body, now swollen awkwardly in the fifth month of pregnancy" (70). Or read how she evokes for us the "rippling waters" of Bayou Sara (165) and the way the leather crop felt in Lucy's fingers as she set out for one of her early morning rides (163). First published in 1982, *Lucy Audubon: A Biography* has aged well.

DeLatte is acutely aware of the depth of the sexual attraction Lucy and John James felt for each other, a topic treated either too coyly or too clinically by Audubon's own biographers, and lets the reader share in it without becoming crude. When Lucy worked as a schoolteacher on the Beech Woods plantation in West Feliciana Parish, Louisiana, Audubon managed to have a major falling-out with the mistress of the plantation, the formidable widow Jane Percy, and left. (At issue was the too–true-to-life portrait of her daughters.) Audubon stole back into Lucy's cottage at night, and then disaster struck: "Lost in their affection for each other," writes DeLatte, "neither of them heard the cottage door open" (140). Jane Percy, who had long envied Lucy her intense relationship with that brute of a man Audubon, had walked in on them during sex. Audubon was expelled from Beech Woods, a tremendously humiliating experience, the memory of which still lingered when he was in England, marketing his birds. Endorsing Lucy's move to Beech Grove, a more congenial place of work in West Feliciana Parish, Audubon grumbles in a letter to Lucy: "If I wanted to go to bed to thee there I would not be sent back 15 miles on foot to Bayou Sarah instead" (177). Partly inspired by DeLatte's book (which she mentions prominently in her acknowledgments), New York novelist Maureen Howard, in the Audubon segment of her brilliant narrative triptych *Big as Life* (2001), imagined an uncanny scene on Bayou Sara in which, under cover of darkness, a shocked yet helplessly attracted Jane Percy spies on Audubon and Lucy fooling around in a stream, with Lucy's wet shift clinging to her thin body as a naked Audubon, his great chest glowing in the moonlight like that of a mythic river god, throws her back into the water. Howard reminds us, too, that Louisiana's lush plantations weren't fun-filled vacation spots—and that, in the hierarchy of a place that assumed Anglo culture as the norm, Audubon would have seemed closer to the Creole slaves, with whom he could converse in patois.

We don't have many sources that would provide us with a window into Lucy Audubon's soul. There are the letters she wrote, of course, but she left no diary and wrote no autobiography, and the original manuscript of her one book, a memoir she and a friend had compiled from her husband's journals and other papers, did not survive the relentless editing of the British writer Robert Buchanan, who boiled it down to what he thought were the essentials. (The preface to the American edition of Buchanan's book mentions, tantalizingly, that Lucy's original text could have filled four volumes instead of one.) We know that Lucy, rising at four o'clock in the morning, acted as her husband's copyist when he was working on his *Ornithological Biography* in London and Edinburgh. By that time, she was thinking of *The*

Birds of America as "*our* great Book" (to Euphemia Gifford, 19 July 1831, Stark Museum, Orange, Texas). Unsurprisingly, the manuscripts that have survived her daughter Maria's bowdlerizing show that she was much more than a secretary, adding words, correcting faulty grammar, sometimes editing passages for clarity. None of the existing biographies—including this one—talk much about the part she played in her husband's literary successes. Her own letters are grammatically more stable than his, though they share with them—and the rest of his work—a chatty, often breathless quality, as if words would never quite suffice to capture the stream of ideas, images, and experiences rushing through her mind. Like Audubon, though to a lesser degree, Lucy often demonstrates a cavalier disregard for punctuation (why stop a sentence when the thoughts run on?) and cohesiveness. No topic sentences for this English lady: "Your father is very busy with two beautiful Eider Ducks," she informs their son Victor in a letter sent from Boston, and then goes on, "We wrote to you for some drawing paper of the second size precisely, the middle size of the drawings and a portfolio—Jackson is our president for four more years" (25 November 1832; Audubon Museum, Henderson, Kentucky). Frequently she invokes God, "the Author of all good"—a phrase that becomes almost an invocation for her, a magic spell intended to ban the noxious influence of the outside world (a "world of trouble and sorrow") on her family and her husband's work (see her letters to Victor, 10 October 1832, and Audubon, 1 April 1832, both at the Audubon Museum). By now, she no longer doubts the lasting value of Audubon's art and promotes it vigorously in letters to friends and subscribers. *The Birds of America* has become a family affair. On 10 March 1841, she writes to Victor, "It is my constant mental prayer that we love and live for each other" (Audubon Museum).

Audubon's letters have been printed and reprinted, but without Lucy's postscripts and annotations—to our detriment, since we are missing out on their conversations, as it were. A good example is a letter Audubon sent from London, on 25 August 1834, to John Bachman, the Lutheran minister and naturalist in Charleston who had become his close collaborator. About halfway through the letter, after much bragging about his own superior work on *Ornithological Biography*, Audubon gently mocks Lucy, his "Old Friend," who "mends our socks, Makes our Shirts, Reads to us at times, but drank No brandy Now a days—She has cast off her purchased Sham Curls, wears her own dear grey locks and looks all the better." Realizing that the reference to brandy (even if cast in the past tense) would get the teetotaling Dr. Bachman's attention, Lucy appended a hilarious stream-of-consciousness note in which she both denies and admits having had brandy before. Here Lucy simply protests too much:

> I take up my pen, to tell you how glad we were to hear from you at last and to beg you not to be uneasy about your *sober friend* and the *brandy* for none did I see until a few days ago, an old Lady called upon me and being ill asked for some brandy, and to my *cost* I sent and had a *decanter* filled, for you must be told that brandy and that very indifferent is eight dollars a gallon, so that even if we wished for it, we should not have it, but I am so completely *set against* it by being obliged to drink it when sick at Sea, that I shall not attempt to touch it again till I set out to return towards you.

Then, after thanking Bachman's "Ladies" for their favors, Lucy adds her own little broadside against Audubon by promising to send gifts when the times are better: "When the 'Birds of America' begin to return some of the sums they fly off with, I hope to send many a little remembrance amongst friends I love so well and think so much of" (Houghton Library, Harvard University).

Carolyn DeLatte was a meticulous researcher: for this biography, she looked at every scrap of paper related to the Audubons that she could find, from the deed books in the Court of the Chancery at Henderson, Kentucky, to the personal papers of Audubon's business associates. Thus it seems almost improper to mention one oversight—one for which, to boot, she can scarcely be blamed. But here it is, in the spirit of Dr. Dryasdust: like other modern Audubon biographers, with the exception of Shirley Streshinsky, DeLatte disregards the editorial damage wrought by Audubon's meddlesome granddaughter. As she was destroying the original journals, Maria Audubon simply conflated Audubon's homecoming to Lucy in November 1824, after his year-long trip to Pennsylvania, and the more momentous return from his long European sojourn five years later, in November 1829. Arriving early in the morning, Audubon rushed to surprise his wife (if we believe Maria, Lucy just happened to be teaching a piano lesson each time, in 1824 as well as in 1829). In the later account, a dramatic scene unfolded: "I pronounced her name gently, she saw me, and the next moment I held her in my arms. Her emotion was so great I feared I had acted rashly, but tears relieved our hearts, once more we were together" (see p. 211). Lucy's reconstruction of her husband's life, though no doubt also skewed by Buchanan's editing, gives us at least a glimpse of the original passage. Here it sounds less like a Harlequin romance novel and more like Audubon, who was never one to proceed gently where rashness would have done, too, and who would never exempt himself from the powerful emotions experienced by others: "I took passage on another steamer going down the Mississippi, and in a few days landed at Bayou Sara, and was soon at the house of Mr. Johnson, and came suddenly on my dear wife; *we were both overcome with emotion,* which found relief in tears" (my emphasis; *The Life of John James Audubon, Edited by his Widow* [New York: Putnam, 1869], 197).

DeLatte's account of Lucy essentially ends with Audubon's anticlimactic, graceless death, from an early form of Alzheimer's disease or dementia, at age sixty-five. Lucy survived him by more than two decades, and it is a pity that DeLatte, influenced perhaps by considerations of book length and marketability, chose to skip Lucy's twilight years. This curious omission reinforces an impression that the rest of the book successfully dispels—namely, that Lucy's life is worth telling only in relation to that of her more famous husband. DeLatte does provide a hasty summary of Lucy's slow decline into poverty and gloom in the years after her husband's death, during which she saw both her sons die: first Victor, who succumbed to a spinal injury in 1860, followed, a mere two years later, by a completely overwhelmed, mentally and physically drained John Woodhouse. Without money or the prospect of future income, Lucy returned to what she had done before in times of dire need—teaching. And while it is often said that Audubon inspired George Bird Grinnell to name the Audubon conservation society after him, it would probably be more accurate to say that Lucy was the one who provided the inspiration. She was Grinnell's tutor, and it was through *her*—a woman he affectionately called "Grandma"—and in *her* house, full to the ceiling with copies of *Ornithological Biography,* decaying bird skins, and muzzleloaders, that Grinnell first encountered Audubon's work.

Lucy's letters from those last years are stark, unforgiving in their honesty. Her mind seemed permanently turned toward what she had lost: "May the Merciful God preserve you dear friend," she wrote on 27 December 1863, to a friend, Mrs. Groes, "from the loneliness, the want of some one to look to for advice and consolation, I often feel" (Audubon Museum). When her income from private teaching failed to make a dent in the debts her sons had left, she was forced to give up Minniesland, the estate in upper Manhattan that Audubon had named after her ("Minnie" is a Scots term of endearment for "mother"). After a depressing period in a New York boardinghouse—we are a "doomed family," she lamented in a letter to a relative (227)—she went back to where she and Audubon had begun their incredible journey together, Kentucky. There, waiting for "the great change" she knew would come soon, she still became annoyed enough to notice that the ladies were "prone to much dress" (7 and 8 October 1869; Audubon Museum). She died on 18 June 1874, aged eighty-seven, in her youngest brother's house in Shelbyville, Kentucky. The final image we have of her in her eighties is hard to forget (228): rail-thin and toothless, she looks firmly at the camera, her mirthless face wrapped in a white bonnet, one gnarled hand in her lap, the other clutching the belt as if making sure it is tight enough. Her posture is as erect as ever—she was still refusing, as she had done for such a long time, to bow to the pressures of life. The same resilience that drew Audubon to her—had he known that only with this woman as a partner would he be able to accomplish the task he had set for himself, gain the fame that he had dreamed of?—is palpable in the letter about her family's financial doom, in which she also reflects on "this beautiful World" and her intense attachment to it: "I sat on Sunday night after Church on the Piazza contemplating the beautiful Moon & its Creator, and I cannot yet say I wish to leave it, notwithstanding all my disappointments and mortifications" (11 July 1865; see p. 229). By then, every reader of DeLatte's splendid biography will have realized that while Lucy might not have painted that alert little swamp sparrow, she had taught her man to see it the way he did: unflinchingly, honestly, with a sense for the wonder of a world that defies all our attempts to understand it fully, even if we use double-elephant-folio-sized sheets to paint it.

Christoph Irmscher

Preface (1982)

Although much has been written about John James Audubon, comparatively little attention has been given to his wife, Lucy Bakewell. Yet she was a strong and admirable person, a force in her own right, whose story deserves telling. I have concentrated on Lucy's early life, between 1807 and 1830, partly because this period of her life is far better documented than her later years. However, the early years are also the most significant ones. They witnessed a series of events that dramatically changed every facet of Lucy's life. From a genteel English girl, born to affluence and surrounded by comfort, there emerged a woman possessing the strength of character to cope with a turbulent marriage, grim poverty, and life on the rowdy American frontier.

Unfortunately, sources after 1830 are at best spotty and inadequate to give any detailed account of Lucy's doings. Indeed, after Audubon's death in 1851, Lucy's life recedes into near total obscurity. We hear of her only as she figured indirectly in the disposition of Audubon's works.

In striving to arrive at a balanced picture of Lucy, I found it helpful to examine her relationships with her family and with the acquaintances she made during the period under study. I was assisted by the plenitude of characters rich in human virtues, vices, and idiosyncrasies that marched through Lucy's life. They invested the story with a myriad of emotional conflicts ranging from love to hate, from the comic to the tragic. Of course her eccentric husband was the most intriguing figure.

Always I have attempted to appraise John James from Lucy's perspective. Therefore, I have focused upon Audubon only as a husband and father. His work, travel, personality, and character were treated only insofar as such matters affected his relationship with Lucy. It was Audubon's talents, ambitions, failures, and ironically, his successes that set the course for Lucy's troubled wanderings.

In pursuing Lucy on her incredible odyssey, I had to give careful attention to the various areas where she lived. Moving from one frontier area to another, Lucy reflected the conditions of frontier life, especially as they affected women. Her lengthy stays in Henderson, Kentucky, and in West Feliciana Parish, Louisiana, allowed a portrayal of daily life in those two communities in the early nineteenth century.

I am grateful to many who have aided me during the course of my research. My special thanks to the Howard-Tilton Memorial Library, Tulane University, New Orleans; the Department of Archives and Manuscripts, Louisiana State University, Baton Rouge; the American Philosophical Society, Philadelphia; and the Cincinnati Historical Society for their assistance and for permission to quote from materials in their collections. Excerpts from letters in the Audubon Collection at Princeton University are reprinted courtesy of the Princeton University Library. Thomas C. Pears III allowed me to quote from letters between Thomas and Sarah Pears. Elizabeth Kilbourne Dart not only granted access to the Kilbourne Collection but also graciously shared her considerable knowledge of the early history of West Feliciana. She showed me sites where Lucy had lived and the lay of the land in the Feliciana woods. Mary T. Winters permitted me to use pictures from the Tyler Collection at the Audubon Museum in Henderson. The National Audubon Society; the New-York Historical Society; the Zigler Museum, Jennings, Louisiana; and the Kentucky State Parks Department also provided information and assistance.

I am grateful to Thomas D. Clark for permission to quote from his book, *The Rampaging Frontier: Manners and Humors of Pioneer Days in the South and Middle West* (Indianapolis: Bobbs-Merrill, 1939). Dover Publications gave permission to use excerpts from

Maria R. Audubon (ed.), *Audubon and His Journals*, and Francis Hobart Herrick, *Audubon the Naturalist: A History of His Life and Time*. The Club of Odd Volumes permitted me to quote from *Journal of John James Audubon Made During His Trip to New Orleans in 1820–1821* and *The Letters of John James Audubon, 1826–1840*.

I appreciate the encouragement of William J. Cooper, Jr., and Joe Gray Taylor. I am particularly grateful to Jules F. Landry of Baton Rouge for providing financial assistance that made my research possible. Without his help and the encouragement and guidance of T. Harry Williams, this story might yet be untold.

Lucy
Audubon

CHAPTER I

To America

B y the late eighteenth century, England was experiencing a significant economic transformation. The Industrial Revolution was making radical changes in demography, agriculture, commerce, and transport. Within this climate of economic boom, William Bakewell left Derbyshire to set out on his own in the bustling mercantile world. Bakewell was descended from the ancient and aristocratic Peveril family, great landowners of the northern part of Derbyshire. One of the Peveril ladies had married a retainer of the court of William the Conqueror, Count Bassquelle. The name was later corrupted to Bakewell. Some members of this family moved to Dishley, Leicestershire, but William Bakewell was a direct descendant of John Bakewell of Derby. Orphaned at an early age, William was cared for, educated, and grew to manhood on the country estate of his uncle, Thomas Woodhouse, a wealthy bachelor of the old "fox hunting squire" type.[1]

Thomas Woodhouse arranged for his young nephew to enter the business world as a tea factor at Burton-on-Trent. William pursued this new enterprise with enthusiasm, and with bright prospects for a lucrative future, he married Lucy Green in February, 1786. It was a marriage of genuine affection for both William and Lucy. In this

---

1. Phyllis Deane, *The First Industrial Revolution* (Cambridge, 1969), 1–84; Julia Alves Clore, "Genealogy of the Audubon and Bakewell Families" (in Family Files, Henderson Public Library, Henderson, Ky.); Lucy Audubon (ed.), *The Life of John James Audubon, the Naturalist* (New York, 1869), 19; Francis Hobart Herrick, *Audubon, the Naturalist: A History of his Life and Time* (2 vols.; New York, 1968), I, 200; B. G. Bakewell, *The Family Book of Bakewell, Page, Campbell* (Pittsburgh, 1896), 25.

thriving hamlet surrounded by the natural beauties of the Trent vale, William and his young bride found life most agreeable. It was here that the first of the numerous Bakewell progeny, Lucy Green, was born on January 18, 1787.[2]

As fate would have it, William soon left the entrepreneurial life. Thomas Woodhouse died, leaving the whole of his considerable fortune to his nephew. Upon receiving word of his uncle's death, William gathered his wife and family for the return journey to the Derbyshire estate on the outskirts of Crich village. The estate comprised a mansion house and extensive outbuildings for the storage of equipment and produce. Apparently the land had not yet been enclosed and was farmed in discontinuous strips.[3]

Thus the Bakewells came to the life of leisurely affluence enjoyed by the country gentry in eighteenth-century England. William commanded the respect and admiration of this rural community. Management of the estate left a good deal of time for hunting and for philosophical and scientific pursuits. He spent many hours conducting experiments in a laboratory that he had constructed on the estate, and on occasion he visited the observatory that had been erected in 1789 one mile north of the village on "Crich Cliff, a lofty hill." Such notables as Joseph Priestley and Erasmus Darwin were friends of the family and frequent visitors. Indeed, before long William received appointment to the influential and prestigious post of justice of the peace.[4]

In the comfortable and secure surroundings of wealth, social prestige, and intellectual stimulation, Lucy Bakewell spent her childhood and early adolescence. Lucy's father, a man of few words, with high moral and ethical standards, had considerable influence

2. B. G. Bakewell, *The Family Book of Bakewell*, 25, 27; Alexander B. Adams, *John James Audubon: A Biography* (New York, 1966), 40; Stanley Clisby Arthur, *Audubon: An Intimate Life of the American Woodsman* (New Orleans, 1937), 34.

3. B. G. Bakewell, *The Family Book of Bakewell*, 25; Adams, *John James Audubon*, 40.

4. Samuel Lewis, *A Topographical Dictionary of England, Comprising the Several Counties, Cities, Boroughs, Corporate and Market Towns, Parishes, and Townships, and the Islands of Guernsey, Jersey, and Man, with Historical and Statistical Descriptions: Engravings of the Arms of the Cities, Bishoprics, Universities, Colleges, Corporate Towns, and Boroughs; and of the Seals of the Various Municipal Corporations* (5th ed., 4 vols.; London, 1844), I, 708; Alice Ford, *John James Audubon* (Norman, 1964), 47; B. G. Bakewell, *The Family Book of Bakewell*, 26; Adams, *John James Audubon*, 40.

upon the children. He was an extremely practical man, scientifically oriented and very much opposed to sentimentality. According to one story, when he found Lucy and Thomas, the eldest son in the family, crying over the book *Simple Susan*, he threw the book into the fire. Yet fortunately for Lucy, William, like his friends Darwin and Priestley, held advanced notions concerning the role of women in general and female education in particular. That is, although he shared the almost universal eighteenth-century belief in the innate inferiority of women, he embraced the most unorthodox idea that women were capable of imbibing and assimilating a solid academic education. In his view, education was necessary to make the woman a better companion and helpmate to the man she married.[5]

By the late eighteenth century, daughters of the gentry were customarily sent to nearby boarding schools, and apparently, William sent Lucy to such a school. There she would have received a smattering of French, geography, needlework, music, and dancing, but academic instruction at these schools was at best superficial. Heaviest emphasis was placed upon teaching the girls proper modes of dress and correct deportment, the educational staples of female instruction. Hence, serious study for Lucy came when she left her friends and school to return home. Her classroom was her father's library; her texts, the exceptionally fine collection of books amassed by William, who obviously placed great value on intellectual pursuits. He supervised his children's education, hired their tutors, and demanding much study of them, he encouraged them to excel. Lucy's mother, too, contributed to this learning process. As a young

5. B. G. Bakewell, *The Family Book of Bakewell*, 26; William Bakewell to Miss Gifford, November 18, 1801, in John James Audubon Collection, Department of Archives, Princeton University Library, Princeton, N.J. For more complete treatises on eighteenth-century views regarding female education, see Mary Sumner Benson, *Women in Eighteenth-Century America: A Study of Opinion and Social Usage* (New York, 1935); Page Smith, *Daughters of the Promised Land: Women in American History, Being an Examination of the Strange History of the Female Sex from the Beginning to the Present with Special Attention to the Woman of America, Illustrated by Curious Anecdotes and Quotations by Divers Authors, Ancient and Modern* (Boston, 1970), 95–101; Thomas Woody, *A History of Woman's Education in the United States* (2 vols.; New York, 1966), I. For a bitter condemnation of eighteenth-century notions about female education, see Mary Wollstonecraft, *Thoughts on the Education of Daughters with Reflections on Female Conduct in the Important Duties of Life* (New York, 1974), 24–35.

girl Mrs. Bakewell had been exposed to the excellent tutelage of her father, Dr. Richard Green. An apothecary and surgeon, Dr. Green served as sheriff, bailiff, and alderman of Lichfield, and he was widely recognized as an antiquary and collector. He was also a kinsman and correspondent of the celebrated Dr. Samuel Johnson.[6]

Information about the details of Lucy's childhood is scarce. We know that she was fond of music and took lessons in voice and pianoforte. Trained to an outdoor life, Lucy ranged through the surrounding woods where she enjoyed riding, boating, and swimming. The care and instruction of her younger brothers and sisters also engaged her attention. She was fond of gardening, and the beautiful walled gardens on the Derbyshire estate provided ample opportunity to pursue this fancy. It is reported that her most treasured possessions were Darwin's *Loves of the Plants* and *Botanic Garden*.[7]

In later years Lucy frequently spoke with nostalgia of the beautiful Peak district of Derbyshire in which she spent her youth. Travel accounts described the area as "beautifully situated," and "commanding a splendid and extensive prospect." The imposing contrast of soaring mountain peaks and sloping wooded vales never failed to impress visitors.[8]

Living amid the natural beauties of the area, Lucy developed a fondness for the outdoors and physical activity. At an early age she became an accomplished equestrian.[9] Her father took pride in owning fine horses and excellent hunting dogs, and Lucy frequently experienced the enthusiasm and exhilaration of a cross-country ride to the hounds.

6. William Bakewell to Miss Gifford, November 18, 1801, in Audubon Collection; Doris Mary Stention, *The English Woman in History* (New York, 1957), 278; William Mathews (ed.), *The Diary of Dudley Ryder, 1715–1716* (London, 1939), 84; G. E. Fussell and K. R. Fussell, *The English Countrywoman: A Farmhouse Social History, A.D. 1500–1900* (New York, 1971), 138; Margaret Phillips and William S. Tomkinson, *English Women in Life and Letters* (London, 1927), 164–65, 172–74; David Staars, *The English Woman: Studies in Her Psychic Evolution*, trans. and abr. J. M. E. Brownlow (London, 1909), 138–39, 141, 148–153; B. G. Bakewell, *The Family Book of Bakewell*, 25–26.

7. B. G. Bakewell, *The Family Book of Bakewell*, 25–26; Ford, *John James Audubon*, 47.

8. Lewis, *A Topographical Dictionary of England*, I, 708; John Byng Torrington, *The Torrington Diaries, Containing the Tours Through England and Wales of John Byng (Later Fifth Viscount Torrington) Between the Years 1781 and 1794*, ed. C. Bruyn Andrews (4 vols.; New York, 1970), II, 198–199.

9. B. G. Bakewell, *The Family Book of Bakewell*, 26; Lucy Audubon to Miss Gifford, January 5, 1812, in Audubon Collection.

The hunt was an important gathering in rural England. These sporting events meant a day of socializing with friends and neighbors who gathered to participate in the chase or to remain at the estate awaiting the return of the riders. All joined in the evening festivities that usually ended the day. Indeed, Lucy's life in the country could not be considered dull. The Bakewells had many neighbors within easy distance, and visiting and inviting friends to visit were major preoccupations. Lucy especially enjoyed spending the day in Crich, a large village only a short distance from her home. There, she could visit well-supplied shops, stores, and markets offering everything from the latest styles in caps, dresses, and shoes to London newspapers. One traveler gave this description: "Crossing Cromford Bridge, I kept a gloomy, pleasant road thro' woods, and by the river side, till the country . . . brought me to Crich Chase, whence is a very noble prospect of a wooded, and well cultivated country. Crich is a large village, whose church, with a high steeple, must be a great land mark."[10]

Throughout the area were ruins of manors and monasteries that had been destroyed during the Civil War. The marble works, lead mines, limestone quarries, booming cotton-textile industry, and the availability of coal accounted for the growing population in the area. Neither in her own life nor in that which she observed did Lucy have any intimate contact with poverty. John Byng Torrington, a London traveler, observed with astonishment that "owing either to plenty of coals or employment, we have never been teiz'd by beggars!!"[11]

In view of the Bakewells' comfortable and stimulating surroundings it is difficult to understand their decision to leave England for America. According to family tradition, William's political views caused the move. The story has it that through association with liberals and radicals, such as Priestley and Darwin, he had become increasingly advanced in his thinking. Consequently, he came to view America as a mecca of intellectual and political freedom. This explanation is supported by some evidence. The government de-

10. Staars, *The English Woman*, 131–133; Lucy Audubon to Miss Gifford, April 1, 1821, in Audubon Collection; Torrington, *The Torrington Diaries*, II, 198.
11. Torrington, *The Torrington Diaries*, II, 42.

manded his resignation as justice of the peace apparently because it regarded him as a dissenter.[12] By the mid-1790s the French Revolution had become so terrifying to the dominant aristocracy that any nonconformity was regarded as a threat. Statutes suspending *habeas corpus*, restricting public gatherings, and limiting freedoms of speech and of the press were only a few examples of parliamentary reactions to the French Revolution. In addition to the general instability generated by the revolution and the ensuing war with France, taxes were particularly burdensome to the landed class, who bore most of the expenditures of the war. Yet it is unlikely that ideology and excessive taxation were the only factors in William's decision to move to America. He was too much of an aristocrat to be truly radical.

William was probably influenced by the emigration of family and friends to America. His brother Benjamin, an international merchant operating from London, suffered a severe financial reverse as a consequence of the dislocation of trade with France. Benjamin came to believe that his losses could be recouped only by establishing a trading base in America. William thought well enough of his younger brother's scheme to invest in Benjamin's mercantile venture in New York. In 1793 Benjamin, his wife, and his infant son emigrated to America. William's sister, Sarah Bakewell Atterbury, her husband Job, and their many children also settled in America, and a number of Bakewell's friends, including Joseph Priestley, made the journey across the Atlantic. Priestley settled in western Pennsylvania in 1794. He hoped that William and others in sympathy with his religious and political views might settle near him. Lucy's father did buy a tract of land from Priestley, but he never joined the proposed colony.[13]

Benjamin Bakewell's report of the success of the infant counting-house venture in New York and the numerous opportunities for for-

12. B. G. Bakewell, *The Family Book of Bakewell*, 26.

13. Benjamin Bakewell to Miss Gifford, July 28, August 25, 1788, May 10, 1790, March 22, 1791, November 28, 1792, and December 16, 1794, Benjamin Bakewell to Reverend Richard Gifford, April 15, July 2, 1793, William Bakewell to Miss Gifford, November 18, 1801, all in Audubon Collection; Ford, *John James Audubon*, 46.

tune in America impressed William.[14] For someone with capital to invest, America seemed a land of vast opportunity. Bakewell was presented with the attractive possibility of increasing his fortune while escaping the turmoil of wartime England.

The practical-minded William planned well for the move to America. He was especially interested in Benjamin's proposal that they form a partnership and open an ale brewery in New Haven, Connecticut. William, accompanied by his eldest son, left England in 1798 and traveled to New Haven to check firsthand the prospects for a successful life for himself and family before liquidating his holdings in England.[15] The partnership was struck, and the brewery purchased. At the end of nine months William was sufficiently impressed with the prospects for economic success in America to return to England and begin preparations to move his family to a new life.

It is understandable that Mrs. Bakewell viewed her husband's decision with considerable anxiety. To uproot the family and sell the estate for an uncertain future in an alien and, reportedly, backward country was difficult for her to accept. It is likely that Lucy, as the eldest daughter, sympathized with her mother's feelings, but there is no indication that she shared her mother's doubts. At fourteen, Lucy had never known anything but comfort and security. She had a youngster's confidence in her father's judgment and probably envisioned the journey as a great adventure.

Since those early days at Burton-on-Trent the Bakewell family had grown. The family that arrived in New York in the fall of 1801 included six children. Besides Lucy there were Thomas Woodhouse, Eliza, Sarah, Ann, and William Gifford.[16] Awaiting their arrival were aunts, uncles, and numerous cousins.

After a few weeks, the Bakewells left New York for their new home in New Haven. According to William, "We left N York . . .

14. Benjamin Bakewell to Miss Gifford, December 16, 1794, Benjamin Bakewell to Richard Gifford, July 2, 1793, William Bakewell to Miss Gifford, November 18, 1801, all in Audubon Collection.

15. B. G. Bakewell, *The Family Book of Bakewell,* 25.

16. *Ibid.,* 27–28; William Bakewell to Miss Gifford, November 18, 1801, in Audubon Collection.

in consequence of the yellow fever having appeared & though few persons died compared to former years yet as the reports were much magnified & the alarm very great we came to N Haven to be out of danger." Entranced with the pleasures of country living, William purchased a farm and secured as tenants an English family from Melbourn. Thomas, writing to his cousin in the summer of 1802, described the farm as "a very pleasant place." With a child's enthusiasm, he mentioned that he and his brothers and sisters bathed "almost every day in the salt water which is but a few yards down a declivity from the front of our house." He took particular delight in describing the numerous strange insects and the peculiar noises that filled the air by night. Lucy, too, greeted life in this new country eagerly. She described the farm as a combination of orchard and pastureland. "We have had a great many Peaches from the Farm this year but not so many Apples as last Autumn. We have a great number of Sheep but not many Cattle."[17]

Family correspondence indicates that the numerous Bakewell cousins and assorted relations maintained close ties in America. Visits between New York and New Haven were frequent for the time. Equally important, contact with England still had a significant impact upon their daily lives. On numerous occasions Lucy expressed gratitude for various goods, newspapers, and other reading materials sent from Derbyshire by her cousin, Miss Gifford. One of these letters provides an early impression of Lucy's personality. She demonstrates a good deal of youthful inquisitiveness and a sophisticated, typically English wit.

> My Aunt Atterbury returen'd last week from a journey to Albany she is much pleased with her jaunt; her health too is better. She saw . . . a Sect of people, whose religeon consists in jumping backward and forwards with all their might for half an hour without ceasing. They are called "The Jumpers" & are all dressed alike. When first they begin to jump they all join and make a noise that is between a groan and a loud laugh. They have a bucket of water and a cup to drink out of in the

17. William Bakewell to Miss Gifford, November 18, 1801, Thomas Bakewell to Miss Gifford, November 22, 1802, Lucy Bakewell to Miss Gifford, October 16, 1803, all in Audubon Collection.

room. My Aunt says they all look very pale & thin; that I suppose is owing to the great exercise of jumping three times a day in the Summer.[18]

It is evident that New Haven did not fulfill the expectations of Lucy's father. In the summer of 1803 he journeyed to the Shenandoah Valley, with which he was so highly delighted that, Benjamin reported, "he has concluded on removing there & commencing Virginia Farmer." Benjamin's assumption was premature, but it is true that William was looking for a place to sink roots. New Haven was obviously unsuited to commercial farming. William and his son Thomas traveled through Virginia, Maryland, and Pennsylvania seeking rich farm land. Then, acting upon the advice of Brigadier General Andrew Porter, William purchased Vaux Hill plantation a short distance from Norristown, Pennsylvania. He and Thomas returned home with news of their purchase and in October of 1803 set out once again to take possession of the farm. Lucy wrote to her cousin about the purchase and the impending move, but she did not reveal her thoughts at the prospect of a new home.[19]

William had already determined upon moving when misfortune struck in the winter of 1803. His hopes for a profitable return on monies invested in the ale brewery were dashed when the brewery burned to the ground. The Bakewell brothers decided not to rebuild. Benjamin was busy with the countinghouse in New York, and William had already determined to turn to what he knew best, cultivating the land.[20]

In 1804, two years after the Bakewells arrived in America, the family moved to yet another beginning in Pennsylvania. There is little surviving evidence to indicate Lucy's impressions of her first two years in America. However, in view of her life in England, she

18. William Bakewell to Miss Gifford, November 22, 1802, Lucy Bakewell to Miss Gifford, October 16, 1803, both in Audubon Collection.

19. Benjamin Bakewell to Miss Gifford, May 31, 1803, Lucy Bakewell to Miss Gifford, October 16, 1803, both in Audubon Collection; B. G. Bakewell, *The Family Book of Bakewell*, 26.

20. B. G. Bakewell, *The Family Book of Bakewell*, 25–26; Benjamin Bakewell to Miss Gifford, May 31, 1803, Lucy Bakewell to Miss Gifford, October 16, 1803, both in Audubon Collection.

probably found these years unsettling. She was old enough to know that this new country had not fulfilled her father's expectations. Yet she was young enough to be excited by the new and strange and confident that her father could handle any situation.

The sight of their new home must have been sufficient to warm the spirits of the Bakewells, perhaps even those of Mrs. Bakewell, who was depressed at the ill fortune that had characterized their brief stay in New Haven. The Vaux Hill mansion was a spacious and handsome Greek Revival building. Besides the elaborate dwelling, there were two large stone barns, a washhouse, a springhouse, a servant tenement, and in the best English tradition, a walled garden. The estate must have reminded the Bakewells of their old home in Crich. From the balcony they had a splendid view of the lush rolling countryside. The estate encompassed broad acres of farmland so rich that earlier settlers had referred to the area as "the fatlands of Egypt Road."[21] Presumably, William took his cue from them when he renamed the plantation Fatland Ford.

Several weeks were spent readying the main house and surrounding buildings. The plantation bustled with activity as the Bakewells settled in and Fatland Ford woke to become again a going enterprise. As was customary when a new family arrived, neighbors began to call to introduce themselves and make the new family welcome. The Pawlings, Porters, and other families put in appearances. But oddly enough, Lucy did not meet her nearest neighbor. Mill Grove, the estate of Captain Jean Audubon was only half a mile away. For years it had been run by the Thomas family, but recently, the Bakewells were told, John James Audubon, the captain's son had arrived from France and was in residence. Audubon may have come to Fatland Ford to inquire about purchasing a horse only two days after the Bakewells arrived. If such a visit did occur, it is apparent that William was the only Bakewell he met. In the bustle of moving the encounter would have been brief and evidently unrewarding for Audubon because in ensuing weeks he did not return to meet and extend the customary welcome to the new family. Not one to stand on protocol, William called at Mill Grove. When Mrs.

21. Ford, *John James Audubon*, 43–44.

Thomas explained that young Audubon was off in the woods, William left an invitation for the young man to join him on a shooting expedition.[22]

In New Haven the Bakewells had been able to visit frequently with their many nearby relatives and friends. By comparison, Fatland Ford was lonely and isolated. Mrs. Bakewell had frequently been ill since arriving in America. Lucy had yet to meet someone her own age at Fatland Ford. She spent long days sewing, reading, and instructing her younger brothers and sisters. Some time was spent at the pianoforte practicing music. The endless prattle of Thomas singing the praises of the woods, of hunting, and of hounds would have wearied Lucy, who was soon to be eighteen. Fatland Ford had none of the social life that a young woman of Lucy's class would have enjoyed in England. There were few young people in the vicinity, and the inclement winter weather made the plantation even lonelier.

For William Bakewell life at Fatland Ford held much promise. The fertile land would yield good crops and a satisfactory profit. In addition, the surrounding countryside was virtually a male paradise. The woods around Perkiomen Creek abounded with game, and William and Tom were avid hunters. Reportedly they had the best-trained pointer dogs in the area. It was during a hunting foray shortly after New Year's that William came upon the elusive Audubon in the woods, and they continued the hunt together. Audubon stammered an apology for not calling and William extended yet another invitation to visit Fatland Ford.[23]

When William returned home, he told the family of the meeting. If for no other motive than curiosity, Lucy listened with interest as her father told of the meeting, the apology, and the successful hunt. It was unlikely that William's account satisfied his young daughter's curiosity about why Audubon had failed to return her father's call. She could hardly have realized that her neighbor shared

22. William Bakewell Journal (MS in possession of Susan Lewis Shaffer, Cincinnati), cited in Ford, *John James Audubon,* 43–44; Maria R. Audubon (ed.), *Audubon and His Journals* (2 vols.; New York, 1960), I, 17; Robert Buchanan, *Life and Adventures of Audubon, the Naturalist* (New York, 1924), 11.
23. Mary Fluker Bradford, *Audubon* (New Orleans, 1897), 17; Ford, *John James Audubon,* 44; Maria R. Audubon (ed.), *Audubon and His Journals,* I, 18.

the traditional French abhorrence for the English, which was particularly intense in the early years of the nineteenth century. In later years Audubon remembered his earlier prejudice:

> A few months after my arrival at Mill Grove, I was informed one day that an English family had purchased the plantation next to mine, that the name of the owner was Bakewell, and moreover that he had several very handsome and interesting daughters, and beautiful pointer dogs. I listened, but cared not a jot about them at the time. . . . Now this gentleman was an Englishman, and I such a foolish boy that, entertaining the greatest prejudices against all of his nationality, I did not return his visit. . . .
>
> Mrs. Thomas, good soul, more than once spoke to me on the subject, as well as her worthy husband, but all to no import; English was English to me, my poor childish mind was settled on that, and as I wished to know none of the race the call remained unacknowledged.[24]

Yet on that morning in the woods William must have shaken Audubon's confidence in the validity of his anti-English bias, for shortly after this encounter John James called at Fatland Ford.

There was nothing unusual about that winter morning for Lucy. As on countless other occasions she was seated snugly before the fireplace sewing when the servant showed the young Frenchman into the parlor. "She rose on my entrance, offered me a seat, and assured me of the gratification her father would feel on his return, which, she added, would be in a few moments, as she would despatch a servant for him. . . . There I sat, my gaze riveted, as it were, on the young girl before me, who, half working, half talking, essayed to make the time pleasant to me."[25]

Here seated before her was the young man whose past conduct towards her family had been most impolite. She had heard of his carefree and extravagant manner of living, certain aspects of which were indeed peculiar even by the standards of early nineteenth century rural life. Yet Lucy was too poised and polished a hostess to let slip the slightest curiosity. The young man's appearance most assuredly made an impression. The long flowing locks reaching to his shoulders were an unusual hairstyle for the day. Nevertheless, he

---

24. Maria R. Audubon (ed.), *Audubon and His Journals*, I, 17.
25. *Ibid.*, I, 18.

Audubon's good looks and his long, flowing locks are evident in this engraving by John Sartain after a painting by Frederick Cruikshank.

was handsome, and dressed in the latest fashion he was quite the dandy. His manner of speaking was also strange, for he had a heavy French accent and used the Quaker idioms *thee* and *thou*. Lucy made her guest so comfortable that he quickly forgot his original misgivings about his past conduct. Soon they were exchanging impressions of this new country. Lucy spoke of England and her life in Derbyshire. In turn, Audubon spoke of the Loire valley and his life in France. The young man was at his charming best. Lucy found the fervor, excitement, and enthusiasm of his rhetoric unique and refreshing. Audubon could see from the pianoforte and song books in the corner that the Bakewells shared his appreciation of music. In the midst of the conversation the younger Bakewells bounced in and out of the parlor. Callers were rare enough to produce a stir in any household.[26]

William and Thomas returned to the house to greet their guest, and the younger Bakewells were controlled long enough for a formal introduction. Lucy's mother was ill and confined to bed, so she did not meet Audubon on this occasion. Thomas, who was approaching seventeen, was obviously delighted to meet the young Frenchman who was so enthusiastic about hunting. The conversation soon turned to guns, dogs, and horses. Although normally enthusiastic about these subjects, on this day Audubon had other interests in mind. When Lucy left the room to see that luncheon was prepared, the Frenchman's gaze followed her. "She now arose from her seat a second time, and her form, to which I had previously paid but partial attention, showed both grace and beauty; and my heart followed every one of her steps."[27]

It is understandable that Audubon found Lucy attractive. She was not beautiful. Her nose was a bit too long and low-bridged and her lips too thin, giving her, in later years, a rather severe look. However, she was of imposing stature, tall and willowy with a tiny

26. John Burroughs, *John James Audubon* (Boston, 1902), 15–17; Edward Muschamp, *Audacious Audubon: The Story of a Great Pioneer, Artist, Naturalist, and Man* (New York, 1929), 39, 46; Maria R. Audubon (ed.), *Audubon and His Journals*, I, 16; Ford, *John James Audubon*, 45. Evidently Audubon picked up the Quaker idioms from the Fisher family with whom he stayed for a short time in Philadelphia.

27. Maria R. Audubon (ed.), *Audubon and His Journals*, I, 18.

waistline, and her dark smoke-gray eyes set off her coloring. Her appearance was striking, but Audubon was also attracted by her soft and chipper English accent and her Anglo-Saxon reserve and shyness.[28]

When the meal ended, Lucy watched as William, Thomas, and Audubon gathered guns and dogs to set out for the woods. The first meeting was over. Audubon left a clear description of his thoughts and feelings on that occasion. By his account Lucy emerges as a very sensitive person able to soothe his initial uneasiness over his past discourtesy. By the time the visit was over Audubon was very definitely comfortable with the Bakewells, and he was particularly taken with Lucy. "Lucy, I was pleased to believe, looked upon me with some favor, and I turned more especially to her on leaving. I felt that certain '*je ne sais quoi*' which intimated that, at least, she was not indifferent to me."[29] Lucy left no record that she was similarly smitten. Even if she had written one, she would not have indulged in profuse emotional statements. They were as foreign to her makeup as they were natural to Audubon's.

28. Ford, *John James Audubon*, 45.
29. Maria R. Audubon (ed.), *Audubon and His Journals*, I, 18.

CHAPTER II

The Courtship

One day in February, when the ice was hardening on Perkiomen Creek and the Pennsylvania countryside glistened white with snow, William announced that he had accepted an invitation for the entire family to dine at Mill Grove. Not only would Lucy have an opportunity to see Audubon once again but the meeting would be a welcome break in the routine of rural life. In a whirl of preparation Lucy turned her attention to such crucial feminine matters as the arrangement of her hair and the choice of a dress. The food, at least, must have met Lucy's expectations. Those present dined on pheasants and partridges trapped and prepared by the Thomas family. Audubon left an account of what followed the dinner: "After dinner we all repaired to the ice on the creek, and there in comfortable sledges, each fair one was propelled by an ardent skater. Tales of love may be extremely stupid to the majority, so that I will not expatiate on these days, but to me, my dear sons, and under such circumstances as then, and, thank God, now exist, every moment was to me one of delight."[1] Although Audubon's description is overflowing with sentimentality, an impression emerges from it that Lucy was as happy as he was on this occasion. The "ardent skater" who propelled her was, of course, John James.

After this meeting Audubon became a frequent visitor at Fatland Ford. Several times a week he came to take English lessons from Lucy. In turn John James taught her French. Most frequently the language lessons turned into musical sessions. Both were talented

1. Maria R. Audubon (ed.), *Audubon and His Journals*, I, 19.

This painting of Mill Grove by Thomas Birch shows Perkiomen Creek where Audubon and Lucy skated during their courtship.

musicians. Lucy played the pianoforte and John James, the fiddle. At times Lucy's mother and sisters joined in the singing. There were many other skating parties on Perkiomen Creek, and surely Lucy came to think that her young man had no equal as a skater. She heard from her brother Tom that he was also a skilled marksman and hunter. Indeed, Audubon was recognized throughout the area as a superb athlete, and he demonstrated his ability at every opportunity.[2]

Sometimes Lucy visited Mill Grove. On one such occasion, when Lucy was visiting there with her family and some guests from New York, Audubon revealed his tendency to enhance himself in the eyes of others—including Lucy—at the expense of the truth. Pointing to a George Washington portrait above the mantel in the sitting room, John James claimed that Washington had given it to his father, "Admiral" Audubon at the "battle of Valley Forge." He also showed the party what he called his museum, which Lucy now saw for the first time. Scattered about an unoccupied bedroom were a number of stuffed birds, rodents, and several crayon representations of birds. John James told the guests that he had studied under the famous Jacques Louis David of France. On yet another occasion Audubon wrote: "In Pennsylvania . . . my father, in his desire of proving my friend through life, gave me what Americans call a beautiful 'plantation.'"[3]

In his anxiety to impress his guests, particularly Lucy, Audubon's comments strayed from the truth. His father had never attained the rank of admiral, nor had he met or received a gift from Washington. Undoubtedly, Audubon had heard that Washington had stayed at Mill Grove on several occasions while fleeing from the British and decided that his father's involvement in the American war should be recognized by his visitors. Accounts differ as to whether John

2. Alice Ford (ed.), *Audubon, by Himself: A Profile of John James Audubon* (Garden City, N.Y., 1969), 10–11; Ford, *John James Audubon*, 48; Adams, *John James Audubon*, 54–55; Lucy Audubon (ed.), *The Life of John James Audubon*, 19–20.

3. Maria R. Audubon (ed.), *Audubon and His Journals*, I, 10; Ford, *John James Audubon*, 47; John James Audubon, *Ornithological Biography; or, An Account of the Habits of the Birds of the United States of America; Accompanied by Descriptions of the Objects Represented in the Work Entitled "The Birds of America," and Interspersed with Delineations of American Scenery and Manners* (5 vols.; Edinburgh, 1831–39), I, ix.

James ever studied under the famous French artist David. If he did, it was obviously only for a very short period. And finally, his father had never given him Mill Grove.

We do not know what Lucy thought of Audubon at this time. He was obviously a handsome young man who commanded great charm and who was very much at home in the company of women. There is little doubt that she was very much in love with him. Influenced by Audubon's accounts of himself, Lucy also believed that the young Frenchman came from a socially prominent and wealthy family. Although not formally educated, he had studied under one of the most renowned artists of Europe. His father was wealthy enough to have established him as the owner of Mill Grove. These supposed material advantages would have been important factors to Lucy. She had been raised in aristocratic surroundings, and she might not have succumbed to his charm had a basis for social equality not been assumed initially.

To William, too, Audubon's seeming affluence was important. He would not have permitted the young man to call upon Lucy had he suspected that Audubon was not what he seemed to be. William revealed this bias in his reaction to a young friend of Audubon's, Jean de Colmesnil, a refugee from Santo Domingo. By Audubon's generous description, "He was very poor. . . . handsome in form, and possessed of talents far above my own. . . . and at one time he thought himself welcome to my Lucy." Indeed, while he was Audubon's guest at Mill Grove, Colmesnil was well received by the Bakewells—until he began to pay court to Lucy. William found the attentions of this refugee unacceptable, and he instructed the boy to stay away from his daughter.[4] A poor man, no matter how talented, was apparently not fit for a Bakewell.

Audubon was not what he seemed to the Bakewells, however. His father, Jean Audubon, a lusty, swashbuckling sailor who sailed the triangle between Europe, North America, and the West Indies in pursuit of profit and prize, was descended from a long line of merchant marine captains. Born in Les Sables d'Olonne, one of

4. Maria R. Audubon (ed.), *Audubon and His Journals*, I, 20; Ford, *John James Audubon*, 48–49.

twenty-one children, he made his first voyage at the age of thirteen aboard his father's ship. During the Seven Years' War, Jean, along with other crew members, was captured and spent five years in an English prison. By the 1770s Audubon was commanding merchant vessels plying the sea between France and Santo Domingo. In 1772 when he was twenty-eight years old, he married Anne Moynet, the widow of a prosperous merchant and many years his senior. Jean seldom saw his wife, for the sea claimed most of his time.[5]

In 1779 during the American Revolution, while traveling from Les Cayes, Santo Domingo, to Nantes, his ship, *Le Comte d'Artois*, was attacked by four British corsairs and two galleys. Audubon fought savagely against superior odds until most of his crew were either dead or disabled. Then, in a desperate attempt to prevent the English from seizing his ship and cargo as prize, the captain tried to blow up the vessel. The plan was foiled, however, and Captain Audubon was taken prisoner while attempting to escape in the shallop. This time he spent thirteen months imprisoned in New York in the hands of the occupation forces.

When Jean was released in June of 1780, he immediately joined the French navy, securing command of the corvette, *Queen Charlotte*, in Count de Grasse's fleet. In a switch of fortune, he had an opportunity to witness the British surrender at Yorktown. Jean remained in the thick of the American war, first commanding a merchant vessel in which he had a financial interest and later accepting command of an American armed vessel, the *Queen*. On a voyage to France, Jean's ship was once again attacked by the British. However, this time the enemy was a lone privateer. After a pitched battle at close quarters, Audubon stood on the quarterdeck and watched with great satisfaction as the enemy ship sank to the bottom of the Atlantic.

When the war was over Jean resigned the commission he held in the United States and returned to Nantes. Anxious to build a fortune, he decided to give up the sea and to turn colonial merchant and planter in the West Indies. From his many travels he knew that

5. Unless otherwise indicated, the account of Jean Audubon was taken from Herrick, *Audubon, the Naturalist*, I, 27–89.

Les Cayes was the ideal place to amass riches. Once there Jean did indeed become a wealthy man, evidently acquiring more than one plantation. His letters make references to his sugarcane plantations and his sugar refinery. He also had large interests in the slave trade, from which he derived further profits, and his mercantile endeavors in foreign exchange augmented his fortune even further.

It was on a voyage from France to Les Cayes that Audubon met the "extraordinarily beautiful" Mademoiselle Rabin, a fellow passenger. According to the passenger list, Jeanne Rabin was twenty-five years of age, a "chambermaid, of Les Touches parish." Before the ship docked Audubon had persuaded Jeanne to accompany him to his plantation instead of entering the service of a distinguished French lawyer as she had initially planned, although by some accounts she did work for a retired lawyer, Jacques Pallon de la Bouverie, for a short time before moving to Captain Audubon's plantation. Already in residence in Audubon's household was Catherine Bouffard, called "Sanitte," a graceful and beautiful quadroon who served as the captain's housekeeper and mistress. Such arrangements were not unusual in the islands, where white women were scarce. Jean and Sanitte's firstborn, a little girl named Marie-Madeleine, was also living there.[6]

Jeanne Rabin evidently supplanted Sanitte in Audubon's affections, for very soon Mademoiselle Rabin was expecting a child. Early in April, 1785, Dr. Sanson was summoned to the Audubon plantation to minister to Jeanne, who was seriously ill and due soon to deliver. On April 24 the physical strength of the delicate young Frenchwoman was drained even further when she went into labor. For two days Jeanne lay in the sultry tropical heat, soaked in sweat, exhausted and only partially conscious, struggling to give birth to the child who seemed most reluctant to leave the womb. At last Jean Rabin, the future John James Audubon, was born. His mother lived only six months after his birth, during which time she was almost constantly confined to bed. Since Jeanne was unable to nurse and care for her robust son, this task was probably assigned to a slave woman on the Audubon plantation. In November, Made-

6. Ford, *John James Audubon*, 8, 12, 13.

moiselle Rabin died. Shortly afterward Audubon resumed the liaison with Sanitte, who cared for the young Jean Rabin, and in 1787 she gave birth to another little girl, named Rose.[7]

In late 1788 Audubon purchased a merchantman, took on a load of sugar and set sail for New York, where he hoped that the sale of his cargo would return a handsome profit. It would seem, also, that he hoped to collect some debts due him in America. Always watchful for opportunities to engage in profitable investments, he learned while in the city that a plantation outside Norristown, Pennsylvania, was for sale. It was Mill Grove, and Audubon journeyed there to look at the place. At Mill Grove he was greeted by the Quaker tenant, William Thomas, who convinced him that the farm was a worthy investment. Audubon then came to terms with the owner, one Henry Augustin Prevost.[8]

Another reason for the Mill Grove purchase was Captain Audubon's increasing apprehension over black unrest in the islands. When he returned to Les Cayes he enlisted as a soldier in the national guard that the planters had formed to meet any emergencies that might arise from the blacks, who were clamoring for freedom and equality. News of sporadic clashes among whites, blacks, and mulattoes in the northern provinces increased in frequency, and the white populace grew more fearful of the slaves, who outnumbered them greatly at this time. The white exodus back to France began.[9]

In July, 1790, Jean returned to Philadelphia to conclude the bargain with Prevost on Mill Grove. He then secured passage on *La Victoire* for Nantes. The wealthy planter-merchant was never again to see Les Cayes nor the considerable fortune he had amassed over the years.

Hardly had he arrived in France when he learned that the revolt he dreaded had broken out in Les Cayes. Audubon took immediate

7. *Ibid.*, 14, 15; M. Audubon, merchant, to Sanson, Physician at Cayes, medical bill for the period December 29, 1783–October 19, 1785, copy of original, reproduced in Herrick, *Audubon, the Naturalist*, II, 319–27, I, 56.

8. Ford, *John James Audubon*, 18–19.

9. For a complete account, see C. L. R. James, *The Black Jacobins: Toussaint L'Ouverture and the San Domingo Revolution* (New York, 1938); Noel Deerr, *The History of Sugar* (2 vols.; London, 1949–50), II, 317–60.

steps to rescue his white son and Rose, whose pale skin could secure her entrance into France. Audubon's wife Anne, who had agreed with the plan of rescue, accepted the children as her own. She showed special affection for the seven-year-old Jean and attempted to gratify his every whim. Jean and Rose were legally adopted by the Audubons in 1794.[10]

During the 1790s Jean Audubon was caught up in the revolution at home. He served as a commissioner and member of the Department of Loire-Inférieure and as a member of the Council of the Navy. He sat on various Republican committees and in the commune of Nantes where citizen Audubon had a reputation as an ardent patriot. In 1793 he returned to sea and received command of the *Cerberus*. From the deck of this lugger, he fought his last battle against the British. After three hours of fighting the British privateer *Brilliant* limped away in the fog, making an opportune escape. In January, 1801, his health failing, Audubon retired from the navy on a modest pension, which was augmented by rents from a small amount of property in France.

Audubon did try to salvage his economic interests in the islands. He gave one Jean François Blanchard, a friend in Les Cayes, the power of attorney to act on his behalf in collecting rents on stores and houses on the island. These efforts produced few results. France was too preoccupied with internal affairs and the war on the continent to put down the revolt in the West Indies. It was not until 1802 that Napoleon moved to destroy the virtual autonomy of Santo Domingo then controlled by the brilliant leader Toussaint L'Ouverture. A French expeditionary force under General Leclerc, Napoleon's brother-in-law, fell victim to guerrilla warfare and a deadly epidemic of yellow fever and failed to reestablish French rule in the island.[11] With Leclerc's failure, Jean Audubon's fortune was forever lost.

At this point Jean received a letter from his agent in America,

10. Arthur, *Audubon*, 24; Muschamp, *Audacious Audubon*, 15–16; Act of Adoption of Fourgere (John James Audubon) and Muguet (Rose Audubon), Nantes, March 7, 1794, reproduced in Herrick, *Audubon, the Naturalist*, II, 328.

11. Herrick, *Audubon, the Naturalist*, I, 85–87; Leo Gershoy, *The French Revolution and Napoleon* (New York, 1964), 384–85. For a more complete account, see James, *The Black Jacobins*.

Miers Fisher, who advised Audubon that he had reduced the rent of William Thomas because of the repairs he had effected at Mill Grove, but more importantly because of the word Thomas sent regarding the discovery of "a very rich lead mine." [12] Intrigued by this news, Audubon in the summer of 1803 sent François Dacosta, an acquaintance who had some knowledge of mineralogy, to Pennsylvania to act as his overseer. The discovery of the mine might solve Jean's economic problems. The promise of gain to be derived from the Pennsylvania property also suggested to Jean that he could place his son on the estate. Heretofore, the boy had shown no interest in any profession.

The young Jean Audubon was not interested in a seafaring career. Indeed, no serious enterprise seemed to hold any attraction for the boy. He had spent a short period in a military school, but he did not pursue his studies seriously and failed the examination for officer's training. In America he could learn something of farm management and perhaps gain some knowledge about mineralogy. Sending the boy to America would also get him out of the reach of the recruiters who were in hot pursuit of all eligible young men since the peace of Amiens was on the verge of crumbling. Using his influence with naval friends, the captain secured a passport for his son that gave his name as John James Audubon and Louisiana, which had been recently purchased by the United States, as his birthplace. [13] Thus, John James came to America and into Lucy's life.

As the ice melted and spring came to the Pennsylvania countryside, Audubon and Lucy went for daily walks in the woods. On these excursions Lucy learned of his consuming interest in nature. On one of these walks he showed her a sheltered rock cave above Perkiomen Creek that was the nesting place of some phoebes and their newly hatched young. Lucy was amazed to see that he could handle the birds freely. Encouraged by Audubon, Lucy too fondled

    12. Ford, John James Audubon, 36.
    13. Donald C. Peattie (ed.), Audubon's America: The Narratives and Experiences of John James Audubon (Boston, 1940), 7; Ford, John James Audubon, 36–37; Arthur, Audubon, 22–23; Gershoy, The French Revolution, 262, 268; William Bakewell to Miss Gifford, October 12, 1804, in Audubon Collection.

the fledglings. During the nesting period Lucy and John James were daily visitors to the cave. It is likely that she took part in the banding experiment that John James conceived to discover if the same birds would return next season. Perhaps Audubon first proposed marriage to Lucy in the cave surrounded by the phoebes.[14]

Lucy's father regarded her growing attachment to the Frenchman with alarm. William regarded Audubon as an immature boy who was not ready to assume the responsibilities of marriage. Audubon had displayed no interest in any serious enterprise. Indeed, the only interests the youth seemed to have were in dressing extravagantly, riding, shooting, dancing, skating, and drawing. These were hardly pursuits that would enable him to support a wife and family. At length, William became so concerned that he warned his daughter not to see Audubon so often. When she disregarded his admonition and continued her excursions to the cave, William decided to take more direct action. He sent Lucy to New York to visit her Aunt Atterbury for a month.[15]

William was the only member of the family who opposed the Audubon courtship. The other Bakewells liked the young man. Brother Tom admired John James because of his skill in sports and imitated the slightly older youth in all activities. Lucy's mother also admired John James, probably because he had deliberately directed so much of his Gallic charm at her. He continued to pay attention to her while Lucy was gone, calling daily on the pretext he had come to help Tom with the chores. Sometimes Mrs. Bakewell would slip him a message that Lucy had enclosed in a letter to her mother.[16]

After staying with her aunt for about a month, Lucy returned to Pennsylvania in time for the wheat harvest. To her surprise and delight John James was at Fatland Ford helping with the work. William, acceding to the pleas of his wife, had relented and allowed Audubon to continue calling. Again the festive evenings of song and dance resumed at Fatland Ford. William dismissed these gather-

14. Ford, *John James Audubon*, 49.
15. William Bakewell to Miss Gifford, October 12, 1804, in Audubon Collection; Ford, *John James Audubon*, 49.
16. Ford, *John James Audubon*, 49–50.

ings as "noisyish." To these sessions came a newcomer, Ferdinand
Rozier, the son of a close friend of Captain Audubon's, who was
visiting John James. Rozier, who had served for some years in the
French merchant marine, was interested only in making money. He
showed no desire to learn English and, indeed, felt uncomfortable in the company of English-speaking people. To Lucy, Rozier
seemed crude and tedious, but in later years she would find him ob-
jectionable on grounds other than bad manners.[17]

Lucy's delight in the round of gaiety was rudely broken when her
father informed her that he was still opposed to her marrying Audubon. To add to her dismay John James confided to her that his
father was also opposed to their marriage, apparently because he
thought that the Bakewells did not have an acceptable economic or
social status. How much of what he represented as his father's opinion was accurate and how much was his own rendition of that opinion is hard to say. At the time, John James's future was threatened by a complicated struggle among Captain Audubon, William
Thomas, and François Dacosta over the control of Mill Grove. He
may not have understood the issues at stake and may have misrepresented the facts to Lucy.

The problem arose when the mine discovered on Mill Grove was
opened in November, 1804, and promised to yield great wealth.
John James believed himself to be the owner of Mill Grove, or at
least assumed that he would inherit the farm on his father's death.
Neither Thomas nor Dacosta had any legal claim to the property,
but Dacosta moved quickly to rectify this situation. He persuaded
Captain Audubon to sell him a half interest in Mill Grove.[18]
Thomas, too, wanted to purchase a share in Mill Grove, and when
he was unsuccessful, he went to John James to complain that Dacosta was trying to shut them both out of the expected profits.

Expensive to operate, the mine gobbled up capital, and Dacosta
appealed to Captain Audubon for additional funds. But having lost
his island fortune, the captain had no money of his own to send
Dacosta. However, he was able to borrow sixteen thousand francs

17. William Bakewell Journal, quoted in Ford, *John James Audubon*, 50, 52; Arthur, *Audubon*, 64; Adams, *Audubon*, 128–129; Peattie (ed.), *Audubon's America*, 11.
18. New York *Herald*, November 17, 1804; Herrick, *Audubon, the Naturalist*, I, 114.

from his friend Claude François Rozier, who was willing to put up the money but insisted upon securing the loan with a mortgage on one-half of the value of Mill Grove. Thus, half of the farm was owned by Dacosta and the other half was mortgaged. Captain Audubon still hoped the mine would prove profitable, and he constantly reminded Dacosta that, if it were successful, a place was to be reserved in the management of the enterprise for his son.[19]

John James may not have known about these complicated dealings or may not have understood them. He referred to Dacosta as "my tutor," to Thomas as "our tenant," and to Mrs. Thomas as "my tenant's wife." In his journal he wrote of giving orders on the farm: "I gave strict orders that no one should go near the cave, much less enter, or indeed destroy any nest on the plantation."[20] He did not seem to understand that his authority at Mill Grove was almost nonexistent.

Apart from the dispute over authority and future profits at Mill Grove, Lucy became a central figure in the hostilities that developed between Dacosta and John James. In later years John James left this account for his sons: "Mr. Da Costa . . . took it into his head that my affection for your mother was rash and inconsiderate. He spoke triflingly of her and of her parents, and one day said to me that for a man of my rank and expectations to marry Lucy Bakewell was out of the question."[21] To Lucy, John James spoke of Dacosta as a "cunning wretch" who was lying to his father about the Bakewells and trying to steal Mill Grove. Neither Lucy nor John James knew that the initiative for Dacosta's opposition to marriage came from Captain Audubon:

> Remember, my dear Sir, I expect that if your plan succeeds, my son will find a place in the works, which will enable him to provide for himself, in order to spare me from expenses that I can, with difficulty, support. . . . My son speaks to me about his marriage. If you would have the kindness to inform me about his intended, as well as about her par-

19. Herrick, *Audubon, the Naturalist*, I, 115; Jean Audubon to Francis Dacosta, 1804–1805, cited in Herrick, *Audubon, the Naturalist*, I, 117.
20. Maria R. Audubon (ed.), *Audubon and His Journals*, I, 16, 21, 27; Ford (ed.), *Audubon, by Himself*, 8.
21. Maria R. Audubon (ed.), *Audubon and His Journals*, I, 21.

ents, their manners, their conduct, their means, and why they are in
that country, whether it was in consequence of misfortune that they left
Europe, you will be doing me a signal service, and I beg you, moreover,
to oppose this marriage until I may give my consent to it. Tell these
good people that my son is not at all rich, and that I can give him
nothing if he marries in this condition.[22]

Lucy's father was also involved in this web of confusion, for
Dacosta approached him at once and informed him of Captain Audubon's objections to the marriage and of young Audubon's inconsequential standing at Mill Grove. At the same time Lucy and John
James were telling William that Dacosta was a villain. Lucy's ap-
peals, supported by those of her mother, seem to have made an impression on William. He wrote to his relations in England, "Mrs B.
was expressing the pleasure it would give her to have *Lucy settle near*
her. A Mr. Audubon a young man from France . . . has solicited
Lucy's hand but as I made it a point that his Father shd be informed
first . . . indeed they are both young enough til he hears from
France. The young man was sent here to be out of the way of the
requisition for the invasion of England & boards with the tenant."
William assured his relatives in England that the young man's father
had at one time owned a great deal of property in the West Indies
and that Mill Grove, while not equal in value to Fatland Ford, nevertheless had "a flour mill & a saw mill on it."[23]

While Lucy's father mellowed regarding John James, Audubon's
father became more vexed and more critical of his son's judgment
and what he assumed to be the Bakewells' influence upon him. Jean
Audubon had concluded that the Bakewells were fortune hunters
who were attempting to ensnare his son in the mistaken belief that
John James was heir to considerable wealth. Reports from Dacosta
and a father's natural inclination to blame others for the miscon-
duct of his child brought Jean Audubon to this incredibly inaccurate appraisal of Lucy's family.

Armed with the Captain's permission to oppose the Audubon-

22. Jean Audubon to Francis Dacosta, 1804–1805, cited in Herrick, *Audubon, the Naturalist*, I, 117–118.
23. William Bakewell to Miss Gifford, October 12, 1804, in Audubon Collection.

Bakewell marriage and to report on the situation, Dacosta took the opportunity to criticize the obnoxious and arrogant behavior of John James. Responding to Dacosta, Jean wrote, "I am [vexed] Sir; one cannot be more vexed at the fact that you should have reason to complain about the conduct of my son, for the whole thing, when well considered, is due only to bad advice, and lack of experience; they have goaded his self-esteem, and perhaps he has been immature enough to boast in the house to which he goes, that this plantation should fall to him, to him alone. You have every means to destroy this presumption; . . . this, if you will have the kindness, is what you may say to the would-be father-in-law, that I do not wish my son to marry so young."[24]

John James and Lucy suspected that Dacosta was sending reports to Jean Audubon that undermined their chances for a future together. Indeed, at the very time that Dacosta's complaints were on their way to France, Lucy and John James agreed he should go to France to obtain permission to marry and to secure his position at Mill Grove.

While Lucy was considering her uncertain future, she suffered a sad loss at home. On September 20, 1804, her mother became ill. It was a severe case of dysentery, and a physician was summoned. He bled Mrs. Bakewell and prescribed medication, but nothing could alleviate the intense pain she suffered. William described her ordeal in a letter to his English cousin and added, "The neighbours were as civil as people could be on this occasion. Some from an idea of the contagious nature of the disease were afraid of coming; but had this been the case we must have survived it, for Lucy & I were almost incessantly with her . . . without any inconvience."[25] Mrs. Bakewell died on the last day of September.

Lucy assisted her father in choosing the site for the family burial ground. They selected a plot near the garden where Lucy and her mother had spent so much time. Lucy's thoughts turned inward to the family in general but most especially to her father. A shadow of

24. Jean Audubon to Francis Dacosta, cited in Herrick, *Audubon, the Naturalist*, I, 118–19. Dacosta sent reports to Jean Audubon on November 12, and December 5, 1804.
25. William Bakewell to Miss Gifford, October 12, 1804, in Audubon Collection.

gloom fell upon Fatland Ford as William retreated to the darkness of his study where he spent most of his time writing a suitable epitaph for his wife and determining where he would plant the weeping willow trees to her memory.[26]

During the family crisis Lucy had little time for John James, who was preparing to leave for France. Then in December he became seriously ill, and Lucy insisted that he be brought to Fatland Ford so that she could care for him properly. He was delirious, and his fever was so extreme that for a time his life hung in the balance. After ten days the crisis passed, but John James had to remain in bed through Christmas and into the New Year. His illness strengthened his relationship with Lucy, making him more dependent on her. Lucy was nurse, companion, and instructor. She read to him by the hour, and most important, she kept her eyes and ears keenly alert to the activities of Dacosta and reported them to John James.[27]

In February, Lucy saw John James off for New York where he hoped to take an early ship to France. In order to facilitate his stay in the city, she had written to her numerous relatives in New York of his coming and had secured a letter of introduction from her father to Uncle Benjamin, which John James carried with him. Hardly had he arrived at Uncle Benjamin's, however, when he sent Lucy an urgent plea for help. The supposed letter of credit that Dacosta had given John James in Philadelphia turned out to be a letter suggesting to the banker in New York that the young Frenchman be sent either home to Mill Grove or, perhaps, to China. John James had departed from the bank in a fit of rage and had announced to Mrs. Sarah Palmer, Lucy's aunt, that he meant to return to Philadelphia and murder Dacosta. But as he later wrote in his journal, "women have great power over me at any time. . . . Mrs. Palmer quieted me . . . and . . . persuaded me to relinquish the direful plan." Distressed at the news, Lucy persuaded her father to send Benjamin instructions to advance the young man's fare with a promise of repayment. Benjamin advanced John James $150, which Lucy's father immediately made good, and Audubon got off

26. *Ibid.*
27. William Bakewell to Miss Gifford, July 19, 1805, in Audubon Collection; Ford, *John James Audubon*, 54.

to France.[28] It would be more than a year before Lucy would see him again.

During his absence, Lucy turned her attention to the household at Fatland Ford. She accepted this responsibility with pride and strength of character that would grow with the years, and she obviously enjoyed her new role as the first lady of the household. Lucy conveyed this satisfaction in a letter to her English cousin. "I have not been from home since the loss of my Mamma; indeed I do not Know how it is possible for me to be spared." She emphasized that differences of time and place did not alter the problems of running a large household: "You wished to know how our servants went on. The Hollander is improved, but the Swiss whom we thought the best is become worse. I have much ado to make her milk the cows clean and I am often obliged to go with her. How people forget their former situations when they came here they were thankful for linsey gowns and now though my Papa bought each of them a printed cotton, yet nothing would do but a white dimity and they have each out of some money given them bought one."[29]

In the same letter Lucy described how she spent her leisure time. She thanked her English cousin "for the magazines and newspapers, Miss Edgeworth's tales &c, which in our retired situation have afforded us and our neighbours much information and amusement." Ties with England were still important. Reading materials were eagerly sought after and exchanged among neighbors and friends. With the day's work completed, Lucy spent the evening hours reading, sometimes to her younger brother and sisters, sometimes to her father. She was also an excellent seamstress and spent many hours sewing. In June, Lucy prepared for the visit of her Aunt Atterbury and her cousins, who spent a month at Fatland Ford. Their visit meant more chores for Lucy but also agreeable company. William, too, enjoyed the visit but noted that his sister "has been so much accustomed to a Town life that she is out of her element in the country."[30]

28. Maria R. Audubon (ed.), *Audubon and His Journals*, 22–23; William Bakewell, Accounts, cited in Herrick, *Audubon, the Naturalist*, II, 336.

29. Lucy Bakewell to Miss Gifford, September 2, 1805, in Audubon Collection.

30. *Ibid.*; William Bakewell to Miss Gifford, July 19, 1805, in Audubon Collection.

By the summer of 1805 Lucy had come to accept the possibility that her father might remarry. Although she, Tom, and Eliza were approaching an age when they could fend for themselves, Sarah, Anne, and young William needed the care of a mother. Moreover William needed a companion his own age. His eventual choice fell upon Rebecca Smith, daughter of land speculator Robert Smith of Philadelphia. Accounts describe Rebecca as an austere, critical, and cold woman of thirty-eight years, a woman who would always remain a spinster by temperament. William and Rebecca were married on December 10, 1805, at the Second Presbyterian Church in Philadelphia.[31]

After the marriage, life at Fatland Ford became increasingly difficult for Lucy. She had been accustomed to running the affairs of the household, but Rebecca quickly asserted her authority as the mistress of Fatland Ford. Lucy's life was lonely on other accounts. Her brother Tom had gone to his Uncle Benjamin's in New York to begin a life of his own in the export-import business.[32] Most distressing to her, she had had only a few letters from John James.

Audubon did write to her father in May, 1805. A rather strange letter, it is one of the few written by John James that reveal his rather colorful mismanagement of English. "I am here in the Snears of the eagle, he will pluck Me a little and then I Shall Sails on a Sheep have good Wind all the way and as Soon a land under My My feet My compagnon of fortune Shall Carry Me Very Swiftly Toward you." The letter ran on in similar vein. William forwarded the note to a cousin in England with the comment: "I enclose you a short letter I lately recd. from Mr. Audubon who is at his Father's near Nantes. You must make it out as you can for I cannot exactly understand it. . . . His 'companion of fortune' is an ass of the Spanish kind which I desired him to procure me for breeding mules. I do not understand his snares of the eagle but suppose it is that the government are wishing to put him in requisition for the army."[33]

31. Ford, *John James Audubon*, 62.
32. Benjamin Bakewell to Miss Gifford, May 6, 1806, in Audubon Collection.
33. John James Audubon to William Bakewell, May 20, 1805, William Bakewell to Miss Gifford, July 19, 1805, both in Audubon Collection.

Audubon finally arrived in New York in May, 1806, and renewed his acquaintance with Benjamin and Tom before departing for Pennsylvania. Benjamin's appraisal of Lucy's young man is interesting. "Mr. Audubon (Lucy's Beau) arrived from France a few days ago to the great satisfaction of his & her friends, as from the difficulty of leaving France which all young men now find we were apprehensive he would be retained. He is a very agreeable young man, but volatile as almost all Frenchmen are."[34]

Even the fact that Rozier had accompanied John James on the return could not abate Lucy's excitement at seeing him again. She was also delighted to see Tom, who had returned to help with the harvest. Soon she and Audubon were once again walking in the woods, swimming in the mill pond, and riding horses through meadow and woods. Lucy listened admiringly as John James told how he avoided recruitment and the numerous intrigues employed by his father that allowed him and Rozier to escape and get through naval customs.[35]

In a more serious vein, John James explained to Lucy that Captain Audubon and Rozier's father had arranged for the two young men to operate Mill Grove as partners. Lucy could not have been too pleased at the news that Audubon's future was to be tied to Rozier's. Yet if the partnership proved profitable Rozier and John James were to have equal shares in one-half of Mill Grove. Dacosta was, of course, owner of the other half. According to the provisions of the partnership both young men were to remain at least six months at Mill Grove "to gather from the country information of a kind that would be advantageous to us; we shall then apply ourselves to some commercial occupation, whether inland or maritime."[36] This partnership was Jean Audubon's final effort to secure his son's future.

The reception given John James by Lucy's father was something less than enthusiastic. "Don't like their being here in idleness. Mr.

---

34. Benjamin Bakewell to Miss Gifford, May 6, 1806, in Audubon Collection.
35. Maria R. Audubon (ed.), *Audubon and His Journals*, 24–26.
36. Articles of Association of John Audubon and Ferdinand Rozier, reproduced in Herrick, *Audubon, the Naturalist*, II, 345–49, 347.

Audubon did not bring his father's permission to marry nor the $150.00 lent him." The Frenchman also found that he had lost a valuable ally in the Bakewell household. Whereas Lucy's mother had approved of and aided John James in his courtship of Lucy, Rebecca Bakewell found the young man obnoxious. His wit and charm held no fascination for the fastidious Rebecca, who made her disapproval obvious to Lucy, William, and John James.[37] This newest development served to further widen the breach between Lucy and her stepmother.

William's fear that Lucy and her suitor would remain idle proved correct. They took their ease that summer. While Fatland Ford bustled with the activity of reaping and hauling of wheat, barley, and oats, Lucy and John James lounged in the sun. Thomas Pears, a young man who was at Fatland Ford to study farming before marrying Lucy's cousin, Sarah Palmer, reported that Lucy and Audubon were constantly together. Indeed Lucy and John James enjoyed teasing Pears because he worked so hard. Audubon told Pears that he intended to go to New York and become a prosperous international merchant, an occupation that would preclude having to work in the hot sun for a living. Pears repeated this remark to Sarah Palmer, who responded with a shrewd analysis. Sarah wrote, "I am sorry to hear that Mr. Audubon is going to turn merchant . . . for I do not think he will like it at all." Remembering her visit to Fatland Ford the previous year, Sarah told her fiancé that Lucy was too fond of country living and the liberty that such a life afforded to be content married to a merchant and living in New York City.[38]

While Lucy and Audubon whiled the summer away, Rozier, who had a keen business sense, arranged for a settlement of the property at Mill Grove. By the terms of the agreement, Dacosta retained 113½ acres including the mine and the buildings. Audubon and Rozier retained 171 acres and the difference in value between the

---

37. William Bakewell Journal, cited in Ford, *John James Audubon*, 62; Sarah Pears to Thomas Pears, October 23, 1814, in Thomas Pears Papers, privately owned by Thomas Pears III, Pittsburgh; Adams, *John James Audubon*, 93.

38. Thomas Pears to Sarah Palmer, July 4, 1806, Sarah Pears to Thomas Pears, undated excerpt, both in Pears Papers; Ford, *John James Audubon*, 63–64.

two. Dacosta was to pay eight hundred dollars with interest in three years and another four thousand dollars from the profits of the mine.[39]

This issue settled, Lucy encouraged John James to accept her father's advice and take a clerkship in her Uncle Benjamin's foreign exchange firm in New York. John James intended to engage in some investments of his own, and Lucy hoped that he would apply himself so as to secure their future. Yet it was a precarious time to become involved in the import-export business. The wars of the French Revolution and Jefferson's embargo were ruining many veteran merchants, and novices had little chance. Audubon, working out of New York, and Ferdinand, operating from Philadelphia, did not do well. According to John James, "The very first venture which I undertook was in indigo; it cost me several hundred pounds, the whole of which was lost. Rozier was no more fortunate than I, for he shipped a cargo of hams to the West Indies, and not more than one-fifth of the cost was returned."[40]

This initial failure must certainly have disturbed Lucy who saw a life and family of her own slip further into the future. Nor could she have been encouraged by the knowledge that Audubon's father had yet to yield to his son's constant entreaties to marry her. But when John James returned to Fatland Ford in the spring of 1807, he assured Lucy that his father would soon realize the "prudency" of his choice, and he revealed to her a new venture which gave Lucy hope for the future. Rozier had proposed that he and Audubon move west of the mountains and open a retail store in Louisville. Needing capital, John James turned to Lucy's Uncle Benjamin, who gave the partners a note for $3,647.29 payable within eight months.[41]

Shortly afterward Benjamin's business was forced into receiver-

39. Ferdinand Rozier to Claude François Rozier, September 12, 1806, reproduced in Herrick, *Audubon, the Naturalist*, I, 150.

40. Maria R. Audubon (ed.), *Audubon and His Journals*, I, 28. John James Audubon to Jean Audubon, April 24, 1807, in John James Audubon Papers, Department of Archives, Tulane University Library, New Orleans.

41. Accounts of John James Audubon and Ferdinand Rozier with the estate of Benjamin Bakewell, Document no. 11, in Herrick, *Audubon, the Naturalist*, II, 355; John James Audubon to Jean Audubon, April 24, 1807, in Audubon Papers.

ship. Lucy's uncle was so distressed over this humiliation that William feared for his health. He and Lucy journeyed to New York to see what could be done. Benjamin turned over his property to Page and Kinder, two of his friends who would dispose of it so as to avoid further losses. Lucy's uncle would eventually move to Pittsburgh and become involved in a glass-manufacturing enterprise.

There are no records of Lucy's activities at Fatland Ford while John James and Rozier were establishing and supplying the store in Louisville. Yet one wonders if John James gave her an accurate account of his business affairs in his correspondence. It would seem that business in Louisville was not as profitable as the partners had hoped. But then Lucy would probably have cared little about such mundane matters as sales or credit. She was twenty-one years of age and Audubon was twenty-three and both were more interested in marriage than in business.

During these years, Lucy appears in many ways a typical early-nineteenth-century woman. She was anxious to marry, to establish and manage her own household, and to assume the wifely responsibilities of caring for a husband and children. These she considered the primary functions of a woman. Yet Lucy, unlike most women of her day, did not regard herself, nor did her father or John James regard her, as having no function outside the home. In the management of Fatland Ford and in taking her along when he ventured to New York to assist Benjamin, William Bakewell had showed considerable regard for his daughter's intelligence and judgment. In the various intrigues over the mine and in considerations about his future in the countinghouse and the Louisville store, Audubon sought and respected Lucy's advice. Neither in her mind nor in Audubon's did marriage mean that she would merely adorn his house, bear his children, make life pleasant for him, and yield to his always superior judgment. Audubon already viewed her as a companion and an invaluable advisor in all matters.

In the spring of 1808 when Audubon came back to Fatland Ford, he was as charming and witty as ever and now as determined to marry Lucy as she was to marry him. William had to give reluctant consent. On April 5, 1808, friends and neighbors gathered in the parlor at Fatland Ford. The Reverend William Latta performed the Presbyterian nuptial service, and Lucy Green Bakewell became Mrs. John James Audubon.[42]

42. Norristown *Weekly Register*, April 6, 1808; William Bakewell to Miss Gifford, April 17, 1808, in Audubon Collection.

CHAPTER III

The Frontier and a Partner of Destiny

⌒⁓

The days immediately following the wedding were busy ones for the new Mrs. Audubon, who was preparing to go with John James to Kentucky, and for the entire Bakewell family. In a whirl of laughter and tears, Eliza, Sarah, and Ann scurried about helping Lucy pack. Lighthearted because of Lucy's bubbling exhilaration, they were nonetheless sad that their older sister would soon be separated from them by so great a distance. Since the death of their mother Lucy had become in many respects a maternal figure to the younger children.[1] Rebecca Bakewell had always resented William's affection for his children, and on occasions when her jealousy proved too exacting, it had always been Lucy who intervened on their behalf. With Lucy gone, there would be no one to blunt the sharp edge of Rebecca's tongue.

William, too, looked upon Lucy's departure and her husband's decision to locate in Kentucky as a "formidable undertaking & I wish it had suited for her to be nearer us, but smaller circumstances must give way to greater."[2] Of course, the "greater" circumstances were his daughter's happiness, her expectations for the future, and her duty as a wife to go where her husband wished to go.

The packing completed, on April 8 Lucy and John James bade the Bakewells adieu and set out from Fatland Ford on the long and hazardous journey to the frontier. The carriage was loaded with

1. Lucy Bakewell to Miss Gifford, September 2, 1805, in Audubon Collection.
2. William Bakewell to Miss Gifford, April 17, 1808, in Audubon Collection.

Lucy's furniture, "all such kind as are not too bulky for carriage," and a considerable quantity of merchandise that John James had purchased for the Louisville store.[3] The first stop on the journey was Philadelphia, where the newlyweds took a stage for Pittsburgh.

On the trip from Philadelphia to Louisville, Lucy had her first encounter with physical hardship. She displayed a remarkable degree of stamina, mastering, even minimizing the difficulties:

> I wish my Dear Cousin, you could have enjoyed the variety beautiful prospects we did on our journey without partaking of the fatigues. However considering the length of it I must not complain. We travelled something more than three hundred miles by land and seven hundred by water. You will form some idea of the roads when I tell you that the first day we travel seventy miles; set out at four in the morning and arrive at the inns about seven in the evening; and every day afterwards travelling the same number of hours we only go between thirty and forty, unfortunately we had rain most of the way as I intended to walk a great deal for whilst the stage is going either up or down the mountains they move as slowly forwards as possible, but the great stones beneath the wheels make the stage rock about most dreadfully. After the two first days we commence climbing the mountains.[4]

Spring rains varying between loitering mists and sudden torrential downpours made their appearance nearly every day during Lucy's overland journey to Pittsburgh. Narrow roads strewn with stones, boulders, and ankle-deep dust when dry quickly turned to "horrid bog" when wet. Crossing the Alleghenies under these conditions nearly cost Lucy her life. Because of the precarious rocking of the coach, most passengers preferred to ascend the slopes on foot. Walking was not only a safer but a quicker method of reaching the summits. However, one rainy day Lucy chose to remain in the coach rather than climb to the crest of a particular slope. John James, who was walking at the time, kept a record of the incident for his children. "We met with a sad accident, that nearly cost the life of your mother. The coach upset on the mountains, and she was severely, but fortunately not fatally hurt."[5] The stage was dragged

---

3. *Ibid.*
4. Lucy Audubon to Miss Gifford, May 27, 1808, in Audubon Collection.
5. *Ibid.*; Ferdinand Rozier Diary, in possession of Welton A. Rozier, Sr., St. Louis, Mo., cited in Herrick, *Audubon, the Naturalist*, I, 187–92; Maria R. Audubon (ed.), *Audubon and His Journals*, I, 28.

on its side for a considerable distance before the driver regained
control of the horses. Battered and bruised, Lucy was helped from
the coach. After much heaving and lifting, the passengers righted
the stage, the horses were reharnessed and hitched, and the cumbersome vehicle moved forward inching its way through the mire.
Inside the coach John James comforted his bride who now found the
rocking not only uncomfortable but definitely painful.

Lucy probably owed her life to the skill of the coachman. These
wagoners, uniformly condemned by travelers as crude and coarse,
vulgar and profane, were nonetheless admired for their skill in ma-
neuvering horses and coaches over nearly impassable roads. One
traveler called the passage over the mountains "a continuance of
miracles."[6] Yet, for all of its hazards, the road west was thronged
with too many colorful frontiersmen and too much unfamiliar traffic
for Lucy's attention to be long diverted by physical discomfort.

It seemed that the entire country was on the move westward.
Seldom were the Audubons out of sight of travelers, either before
them or behind them. Another traveler described the kind of traffic
Lucy would have seen:

> Apropos of travelling—A European, who had not experienced it,
> could form no proper idea of the manner of it in this country. The trav-
> ellers are, wagonners, carrying produce to, and bring back foreign goods
> from the different shipping ports . . . Packers with from one to twenty
> horses, selling or trucking their wares through the country;—Country-
> men, sometimes alone, sometimes in large companies, carrying salt . . .
> for the curing of their beef, pork, venison, &c.;—Families removing
> further back into the country, some with cows, oxen, horses, sheep,
> and hogs, and all their farming implements and domestick utensils, and
> some without; some with wagons, some with carts and some on foot.

The large numbers of children who crowded most wagons and the
accompanying sounds of their excited prattle, laughter, and crying
gave the westward trek an air of youthful vitality. Indeed, one trav-

---

6. Thomas Hulme, "A Journal Made During a Tour in the Western Countries of Amer-
ica, September 30, 1818–August 8, 1819," in Reuben G. Thwaites (ed.), *Early Western
Travels, 1748–1846* (32 vols.; Cleveland, 1904–1907), X, 36; Henry Bradshaw Fearon,
*Sketches of America: A Narrative of a Journey of Five Thousand Miles Through the Eastern and
Western States* (New York, 1969), 189; Francis S. Philbrick, *The Rise of the West, 1754–1830*
(New York, 1965), 310.

eler counted twenty people, mostly "young citizens," in a single wagon.[7] However, the sights along the road paled by comparison to the unusual people and the astonishing conditions at the inns where the Audubons stopped for food and rest.

They stopped at many of the same taverns and inns that Audubon and Rozier had visited on their trip the previous year. In most instances even Rozier, whose prior experience as a merchant sailor prepared him for the primitive facilities encountered at the inns, complained of dirt, poor food, and the drunkards who frequently loitered about these establishments.[8]

Other wayfarers who trekked over the mountains by the same route left more vivid descriptions of the frontier inns. These establishments were little more than hastily constructed log cabins, usually consisting of one large room downstairs, which served as a tavern, a dining room, and a sleeping room for late arrivals. Upstairs each room was crowded with beds, and the traveler never knew when his coach pulled into the tavern yard how many bedfellows he would have to share his too-soft feather mattress with before morning. "Of one thing he could be certain: there would be no dearth of bedfellows, of both humans and insects." It was not uncommon for the bedbugs and fleas to cover weary wayfarers only seconds after they crawled into bed seeking much-needed sleep. Complaints about filthy sheets and hungry fleas were met with snarling scowls from innkeepers who knew that by nightfall their establishments would be filled to overflowing, and that travelers had little choice but to accept the facilities they found.[9]

7. Morris Birkbeck, Notes on a Journey in America (Ann Arbor, Mich., 1966), 34, 35, 59, 62; Fortescue Cuming, "Sketches of a Tour to the Western Country Through the States of Ohio and Kentucky; a Voyage Down the Ohio and Mississippi Rivers, and a Trip Through the Mississippi Territory, and Part of West Florida. Commenced at Philadelphia in the Winter of 1807, and Concluded in 1809," in Reuben G. Thwaites (ed.), Early Western Travels, 1748–1846 (32 vols.; Cleveland, 1904–1907), IV, 62.

8. Rozier Diary, reproduced in Herrick, Audubon, the Naturalist, I, 187–92.

9. Thomas D. Clark, The Rampaging Frontier: Manners and Humors of Pioneer Days in the South and Middle West (New York, 1939), 103; Birkbeck, Notes on a Journey in America, 36–37; Charles August Murray, Travels in North America During the Years 1834, 1835, and 1836 Including a Summer Residence with the Pawnee Tribe of Indians and a Visit to Cuba and the Azore Islands (2 vols., New York, 1974), I, 192–93; Basil Hall, Travels in North America in the Years 1827 and 1828 (3 vols.; New York, 1974), III, 392; James Flint, "Letters from America, Containing Observations on the Climate and Agriculture of the Western States, the Man-

Lucy quickly ascertained that the journey would permit no false modesty. Concepts of propriety were lost on the rough frontier, and a certain egalitarianism invaded all aspects of life, including separation of the sexes. Women had to sleep either in the common dormitory rooms or the woods, and of the two, the inns were preferable. One female traveler who arrived too late to get a bed upstairs related the unpleasant experience of sleeping on the barroom floor downstairs surrounded by wagoners who were profane beyond description. Another wayfarer described a similar scene: "We were permitted to stop, on condition of all three sleeping in one bed, which was said to be a large and a good one. Two-thirds of the barroom floor was covered by the beds of weary travellers, lying closely side by side, and the remaining part occupied by people engaged in drinking, and noisy conversation." [10]

If Lucy thought the nightly noise and perpetual disturbance of restless bedfellows barely tolerable, she soon learned that Saturday nights at these frontier inns defied description. The inns were public gathering places, and Saturday nights brought scenes of "most dredful riot, and . . . horrible excess." The sound of a scraping, whining fiddle signaled that a frolic was beginning, and the vexed traveler knew that there would be no rest for him that night. [11] Tunes from the fiddle and the shuffling and stomping of the dancers below were frequently interrupted by the roaring din of a fight. Combatants hurled profane and vulgar epithets at each other and generally did their best to maim their opponent or batter him senseless. Knives flashed, parts of noses and ears were bitten off, and eyes

---

ners of the People, the Prospects of Emigrants, &c., &c.," in Reuben G. Thwaites (ed.), *Early Western Travels, 1748–1846* (32 vols.; Cleveland, 1904–1907), IX, 77; Fearon, *Sketches of America*, 191–92.

10. Clark, *The Rampaging Frontier*, 103, 104; Eleanor Flexner, *Century of Struggle: The Woman's Rights Movement in the United States* (Cambridge, 1959), 9; James Flint, "Letters from America," 77; Murray, *Travels in North America*, I, 192.

11. Francois Andre Michaux, "Travels to the West of the Alleghany Mountains in the States of Ohio, Kentucky, and Tennessea [sic], and Back to Charleston, by the Upper Carolines; Comprising the Most Interesting Details on the Present State of Agriculture, and the Natural Produce of Those Countries: Together with Particulars Relative to the Commerce That Exists Between the Above Mentioned States, and Those Situated East of the Mountains and Low Louisiana, Undertaken in the Year 1802, Under the Auspices of His Excellency M. Chaptal, Minister of Interior," in Reuben G. Thwaites (ed.), *Early Western Travels, 1748–1846* (32 vols.; Cleveland, 1904–1907), III, 144; Clark, *The Rampaging Frontier*, 103.

were gouged out. When a fight ended, the whiskey would flow, the fiddle would whine out another tune, and the singing and dancing would begin again with renewed vigor.

The bedlam of a Saturday night and the unorthodox sleeping conditions seemed to suit the alien frontiersmen with whom Lucy came into contact in these inns. They also amused themselves in somewhat sedater fashion. Travelers universally complained about frontiersmen who never tired of plying wayfarers with questions. Everywhere visitors, both native and foreign, met with an eternal stream of questions. Everybody at the inns delighted in taking a turn at quizzing each sojourner, asking name, occupation, destination, and all manner of more personal questions.[12] Lucy's chipper English accent and Audubon's patois of French and English definitely marked them as "furrin" and meant that westerners took particular pleasure in quizzing them. The thorough cross-examination would eventually turn up the news that the Audubons were newlyweds, and these frontier wags, who prided themselves upon having a coarse quip ready for all occasions, would make the most of this bit of information.

Evidently, Lucy was better able to ignore these rowdies than were other Englishwomen who visited the western inns. Lucy was also silent about tobacco chewing, though she found this habit particularly loathsome. If there was one trait that all frontiersmen seemed to have in common, it was the chewing of tobacco and the incessant spitting that the chewing required. Most other women complained because chewers with poor aims spat in any direction, frequently spattering their frocks with the yellowish brown spittle. The women were hard pressed to dodge these soggy missiles, which descended upon them while they were seated at the table or standing before the fireplace. It was difficult to tell which was worse—having the tobacco strewn along the bottom of their dresses or having projectiles sailing overhead drop bits of slime upon their heads.[13]

Meals at the inns also provoked negative comments from other

12. Murray, *Travels in North America*, I, 190; Clark, *The Rampaging Frontier*, 103.
13. Frances Trollope, *Domestic Manners of the Americans; Edited, with a History of Mrs. Trollope's Adventures in America* by Donald Smalley (New York, 1949), 16, 18; Clark, *The Rampaging Frontier*, 104; Arthur, *Audubon*, 363; Herrick, *Audubon, the Naturalist*, I, 396–97;

females, although Lucy appears to have accepted the mealtime bedlam in stride. Frances Trollope lamented the total absence of the
usual courtesies of the table. She believed herself surrounded by
barbarian hordes as she watched the voracious manner in which the
food was seized and devoured. She noted "the strange uncouth
phrases and pronunciation; the loathesome spitting, from the con-
tamination of which it was absolutely impossible to protect our
dresses; the frightful manner of feeding with their knives, till the
whole blade seemed to enter into the mouth; and still more frightful
manner of cleaning the teeth afterward with a pocketknife."[14]

Unfortunately, the quality of the food seldom deserved such
rapacious appetites. The meals were heavy and abounded with
grease; the coffee was too black and too thick; and the tea was indifferent. Indeed, at some inns there was no food to be had. Some
innkeepers offered wayfarers only whiskey, and it never occurred to
them that a guest might want anything else. Thus, with many travelers, Americans gained the reputation of having a mania for whiskey.[15] Whether or not Lucy concurred in this belief is not known.

By day or night the western inns fomented discomfort, indiges-
tion, and chaos. This was especially true in the mornings. Well before dawn the inns began to bustle with activity as weary guests,
deprived of rest the previous night, prepared for another day of hazardous travel. One traveler described a typical morning scene that
Lucy probably witnessed again and again: "At half past five all were
in bustle, preparing for the road: Some settling bill with the hostess, others waiting to settle: Some round a long wooden trough
at the pump, washing, or drying themselves with their pocket-
handkerchiefs: Some Americans drinking their morning's bitters,
(spirits with rue, wormwood, or other vegetable infusion:) Some
women catching children who had escaped naked from bed, others
packing up bed clothes, or putting them into waggons: Waggoners

---

Howard Corning (ed.), *The Letters of John James Audubon, 1826–1840* (2 vols.; Boston,
1930), I, 176. In later years Audubon began to use snuff. He promised Lucy that he would
quit—a promise he made many times.

14. Trollope, *Domestic Manners,* 18.

15. Michaux, "Travels to the West of the Alleghany Mountains," 144; Cuming,
"Sketches of a Tour to the Western Country," 62; Fearon, *Sketches of America,* 192.

harnessing their horses; &c."[16] Amidst such confusion Lucy would continue her journey each morning.

Yet from Lucy there was neither complaint nor even mention of the crude shelter, the rowdy people, and the moldy food she found along the route. Although she was a young lady of genteel sensibilities, unprepared for the rough, uncivilized people she encountered, Lucy's silence in regard to such matters suggests that she was frail neither in body nor in spirit. The unpolished frontiersmen were strange, and the country more rugged than any she had ever seen. However, the novelty, the spirit of adventure, and the happiness of just being a bride dwarfed the more barbarous aspects of the trip. Lucy did not allow discomforts to mar the present or dim her expectations for the future.

Arriving in Pittsburgh, Lucy alighted from the coach sore and exhausted. Accommodations at the Jefferson Hotel were the best that the newlyweds had encountered since leaving Philadelphia. The first order of business was a bath and much needed sleep. Once she was sufficiently rested to look about, Lucy found Pittsburgh a most disagreeable place. "High mountains on all sides environ Pittsburgh," she wrote, "and a thick fog is almost constantly over the town; which is rendered still more disagreable by the dust from a dirty sort of coal that is universally burnt. Coal is found at the surface of the earth in the neighbourhood of this place, which is really the blackest looking place I ever saw." Other travelers also commented on Pittsburgh's coal-besmirched air. "This great consumption of a coal abounding in sulphur, and its smoke condensing into a vast quantity of lampblack, gives the outside of the houses a dirty and disagreeable appearance."[17]

However, Pittsburgh hummed with such activity that English visitors called the fledgling city the "Birmingham of the West." In March, 1808, the city consisted of "seventeen streets and four lanes or alleys . . . two hundred and thirty-six brick houses, of which forty-seven were built in the last twelve months, and three hundred

16. James Flint, "Letters from America," 77–78.
17. Lucy Audubon to Miss Gifford, May 27, 1808, in Audubon Collection; Cuming, "Sketches of a Tour to the Western Country," 77; Birkbeck, *Notes on a Journey in America*, 39; Murray, *Travels in North America*, I, 197.

and sixty-one wooden ones, seventy of which were added last year. There are fifty stores generally well assorted and supplied, and which divide the retail business of the town and adjacent country in tolerably good proportion." The city had grown rapidly because it was a major embarkation point for people and goods traveling west to the Ohio and Mississippi Valleys. Many more settlers floated west than trudged over the Wilderness Road, and most Pittsburgh merchants were in some way occupied with providing travelers with provisions for the journey downriver. At the waterfront in Pittsburgh, folks could purchase provisions, farming utensils, and a variety of crude and clumsy craft—flatboats, arks, broadhorns, rafts, and keelboats. Those who chose to purchase their own craft for the journey also bought a copy of Zadak Cramer's river guidebook, *The Navigator*, which warned the greenhorn wayfarer of the hazards presented by the river itself and by the banditti who plied the river preying upon unwary pilgrims.[18] The Audubons, because they had neither animals nor farming equipment nor a large family to transport, merely purchased passage on a craft going downriver, leaving the navigation to professional rivermen, well-acquainted with the journey's dangers.

Lucy accompanied John James down to the dock to look for places on a craft going to Louisville. The waterfront was a "veritable" hell "because rivermen who had wrestled with every conceivable hardship on the river relaxed by taking in stride the fastest entertainment . . . offered."[19] But once she got past the saloons and brothels, Lucy was intrigued by the throng of shouting humanity, the noisy livestock, the variety of cargoes, and the chaos of loading and unloading the many boats. Because of the great number of

18. Thomas Nuttall, "Journal of Travels into the Arkansa [sic] Territory, During the Year 1819, with Occasional Observations on the Manners of the Aborigines," in Reuben G. Thwaites (ed.), *Early Western Travels, 1748–1846* (32 vols.; Cleveland, 1904–1907), XIII, 45, 47–48; Cuming, "Sketches of a Tour to the Western Country," 245–55; Lucy Audubon to Miss Gifford, May 27, 1808, in Audubon Collection; Boynton Merrill, Jr., *Jefferson's Nephews: A Frontier Tragedy* (Princeton, 1976), 98–102.

19. Clark, *The Rampaging Frontier*, 87; Edmund Flagg, "The Far West: or, A Tour Beyond the Mountains. Embracing Outlines of Western Life and Scenery; Sketches of the Prairies, Rivers, Ancient Mounds, Early Settlements of the French, etc. etc." Part I, in Reuben G. Thwaites (ed.), *Early Western Travels, 1748–1846* (32 vols.; Cleveland, 1904–1907), XXVI, 62; Birkbeck, *Notes on a Journey in America*, 85.

people looking for transport, Audubon was unable to book immediate passage. Indeed, he and Lucy were probably not in any great hurry to leave Pittsburgh. This was their first opportunity since the wedding to be alone in relatively comfortable surroundings. The two-week stay in Pittsburgh provided Lucy and John James some semblance of a honeymoon.

By day Lucy and John James toured the city. Lucy particularly enjoyed shopping for merchandise to stock the store in Louisville. These shopping excursions took her to the heart of Pittsburgh's economic existence, which she described to Miss Gifford: "There are many nail manufactories carried on here, which supply the inland states of this Country, also iron castings, tin ware and glass manufactured. There is great trade carried on between Pittsburgh and New Orleans by means of the rivers Ohio and Mississippi; as well as many other places situated on the banks of those rivers."[20]

After two weeks Lucy and John James secured passage on a flatboat. Quarters were extremely cramped. Lucy shared the boat with goats, cows, hogs, sheep, and horses, in addition to a strange assortment of people. Wagons, carriages, and farming equipment were also squeezed on the deck.[21] Lucy was too engrossed in her new surroundings to consider such mundane matters as discomfort. Demonstrating a keen ability to grasp detail and a high degree of intellectual curiosity about anything unfamiliar, Lucy wrote the following bit of descriptive commentary to her cousin:

> The seven hundred miles by water was performed without much fatigue though not without some disagreables. Our conveyance was a large square or rather oblong boat; but perfectly flat on all sides; and just high enough to admit a person walking upright. There are no sails made use of owing to the many turns in the river which brings the wind from every quarter in the course of an hour or two. The boat is carried along by the current, and in general without the least motion. . . . There are not many extensive prospects on the river as the shores are in general bounded by high rocks covered with wood. However I was gratified by

20. Lucy Audubon to Miss Gifford, May 27, 1808, in Audubon Collection; Birkbeck, *Notes on a Journey in America*, 39.
21. Constance Rourke, *Audubon* (New York, 1936), 45–46. For more information concerning river traffic, see Timothy Flint, *Recollections of the Last Ten Years in the Valley of the Mississippi*, ed. George R. Brooks (Carbondale, 1968), 12–14.

the sight of a great variety of foliage and flowers. There are many small towns on the way some of which we stopped at. Mr. Audubon regretted he had not his drawing impliments with him, as he would have taken some views for you.[22]

All passengers had to provide their own food, bedding, and other personal necessities. In Pittsburgh, Lucy had procured bread, beer, and hams for the journey. Poultry, eggs, and milk were purchased from farmhouses along the banks of the river. With the exception of these brief stops for provisions, the boat moved steadily on, generally traveling all night.[23]

Sometime during the first week of May, Lucy and John James arrived in Louisville. Weary and travel stained, Audubon walked Lucy to Gwathway's hotel, the Indian Queen. Here he introduced her to the proprietor and other guests. Women were an unusual sight in the combination hotel and tavern, especially prim and proper easterners such as Mrs. Audubon. Lucy found the people very accommodating, insisting that we "are as private as we please"—an interesting comment considering that she had to pass through dormitories lined with beds for the transient guests to reach their rather cramped private quarters.[24]

By her own account, Lucy was committed to nineteenth-century ideas of womanly fulfillment. After three weeks in Louisville and more than a month of married life, she was happy and content. Carrying out the traditional duties of a wife gave her much satisfaction, and she took pride in her home-centered accomplishments. She wrote to her cousin that she found her duties to be "light and be they what they may I hope I shall ever cheerfully perform them." She was quite prepared to do what was expected of her even if it were difficult. With John James, Lucy was still the radiant bride, more convinced than ever that he was the ideal husband. Anxious to express her contentment, Lucy wrote to Miss Gifford, "I wish you were acquainted with the partner of my destiny. It is useless to say more of him to you at so great a distance, than that he has a most

22. Lucy Audubon to Miss Gifford, May 27, 1808, in Audubon Collection.
23. Ibid.
24. Ford, John James Audubon, 74; Adams, John James Audubon, 96; Lucy Audubon to Miss Gifford, May 27, 1808, in Audubon Collection; Fearon, Sketches of America, 246–49.

excellent disposition which adds very much to the happiness of married life."[25]

Lucy was as enchanted with this new country as she was with her volatile Frenchman. A contemporary account details the more pleasant aspects of the town: "Louisville is most delightfully situated on an elevated plain to which the ascent from the creek and river is gradual, being just slope enough to admit of hanging gardens with terraces." The town, according to this traveler, consisted "of one principal and very handsome street, about half mile long, tolerably compactly built, and the houses generally superiour to any I have seen in the western country with the exception of Lexington. Most are of handsome brick, and some are three stories, with a parapet wall on top in the modern European taste, which in front gives them the appearance of having flat roofs." Lucy, also, found Louisville a "very pleasantly situated place. The country round is rather flat, but the land is very fertile. . . . Most of the houses here have gardens adjoining, and some of them are very prettily laid out."[26]

Lucy did find that in Louisville the pace of living was slower than that to which she had been accustomed. Compared to the lively household at Fatland Ford, she had to adjust to living, at least temporarily, at the Indian Queen. The townspeople were attentive and the Gwathways were very accommodating, but nevertheless, the hours often seemed to drag while John James was gone during the day. With so much time and so little to do, she quickly perceived the intellectual and cultural lag so characteristic of frontier life. "I am very sorry," Lucy wrote to Miss Gifford, "there is no Library here or book store of any kind for I have very few of my own and as Mr. Audubon is constantly at the store I should often enjoy a book very much whilst I am alone."[27]

25. Lucy Audubon to Miss Gifford, May 27, 1808, in Audubon Collection. See also Smith, *Daughters of the Promised Land*, 54; Staars, *The English Woman*, 35–36; Anne Firor Scott, *The Southern Lady: From Pedestal to Politics, 1830–1930* (Chicago, 1970), 4; Woody, *A History of Woman's Education*, I, 39; Barbara J. Harris, *Beyond Her Sphere: Women and the Professions in American History* (Westport, Conn., 1978), 22.

26. Cuming, "Sketches of a Tour to the Western Country," 258, 259; Lucy Audubon to Miss Gifford, May 27, 1808, in Audubon Collection.

27. Lucy Audubon to Miss Gifford, May 27, 1808, in Audubon Collection.

Newcomers in the West, especially women, often felt a tinge of loneliness. This was particularly true for Lucy, whose naturally reserved personality frequently gave others the impression that she was "uppity" or arrogant and discouraged them from approaching her. Her bearing, speech, and manners could easily make people feel uneasy and inferior even though Lucy did not intend to produce that effect.[28] People simply mistook her self-assurance for snobbishness. Lucy knew who she was and felt no need to seek approval since her sense of security, of status, had never been threatened. But she never allowed her self-confidence to develop into rigidity or attempted to isolate herself from the rest of the community. In her own fashion she was remarkably flexible and adaptable.

Lucy soon became a willing participant in the social life of Louisville. Obviously pleased with the respect and admiration given his wife, John James wrote, "The country was settled by planters and farmers of the most benevolent and hospitable nature; and my young wife, who possessed talents far above par, was regarded as a gem, and received by them all with the greatest pleasure."[29] Keeping in mind Audubon's tendency to exaggerate, it is nonetheless obvious that the young Mrs. Audubon did not for long spend her time cooped up in the Indian Queen.

Lucy and John James frequently rode to Shippingport just below the falls of the Ohio, where she met Mr. and Mrs. James Berthoud and their son Nicholas, who would become lasting friends. Members of the French nobility, the Berthouds had fled France in the 1790s to escape the guillotine. Berthoud's real name was Bon Herve de Belisle, Marquis de Saint-Pierre. He assumed the name Berthoud in honor of a loyal coachman who helped the family escape France. In 1803 Berthoud purchased the town of Shippingport from its original proprietor, Colonel John Campbell. The handsome Berthoud home was widely known to travelers, especially Europeans, who knew that they would be graciously received by the family and that after several days of good food, rest, and pleasant conversation they could continue their journey much refreshed.[30]

28. Muschamp, *Audacious Audubon*, 144.
29. Maria R. Audubon (ed.), *Audubon and His Journals*, I, 29; Bradford, *Audubon*, 27.
30. Hulme, "A Journal," 43–44; Arthur, *Audubon*, 88–90.

In addition to being a large shipper, James Berthoud was associated with the Tarascon brothers of Louisville in one of the finest rope walks in the United States. Lucy also met the Tarascons, French emigrés like Berthoud, and Dr. William Galt, a physician and capable botanist who lived in Louisville. All would become fast friends of the Audubons.

Lucy was associating not only with the well-to-do but also with people of the lower classes. John James described an Independence Day celebration in which he and Lucy participated and the egalitarian spirit that prevailed:

> The whole neighborhood joined in, with no need of an invitation where everyone—from the Governor to the ploughmen—was welcome. . . .
>
> A carpet of green grass formed a clearing that was like a sylvan pavillion. Wagons moved slowly along, bearing provisions from the farms . . . hams, venison, and ox, and turkeys and other fowl. Flagons of every kind of beverage were to be seen. *La Belle Rivière*, the Ohio, had provided the finny tribe. There were melons, peaches, plums, and pears enough to have stocked a market. In a word, the land of abundance, Kentucky, had supplied a feast for her children.

Lucy joined in the merriment. She helped the other ladies, setting out "dishes, glasses, punch bowls, and bottles of rich wine, not forgetting barrels of 'Old Monongahela' for the crowd." She watched the shooting contests and was proud of her husband's skill. She joined in the singing of Yankee Doodle and tapped her foot to the rhythm of fifes and drums. When the meal was over, Lucy joined the other ladies in genial conversation and small talk, while the men got down to serious drinking, exchanging tall tales about their exploits in the wilds, or speculating about the prospects for the year's crop.[31]

Before long the first trills of the reels and cotillions began. Lucy was as fond of dancing as John James, and she was as skilled and graceful. By his own account, Audubon was the life of the party. He led the dances, played his fiddle, flirted with the ladies, and was popular with the men.[32] He neglected to mention that Lucy, too, danced the evening away. It is not likely that a woman who could

31. Ford (ed.), *Audubon, by Himself*, 17–18.
32. *Ibid.*; Adams, *John James Audubon*, 98.

dance in a meadow beside Beargrass Creek was merely tolerating an unhappy existence. Lucy was no stuffy easterner.

Even so, Louisville was a riverfront town on the western frontier, and it is somewhat surprising that Lucy was able to accommodate herself to the roughness that characterized life there. Audubon's re-action to life in Louisville was the most significant factor in helping Lucy to adapt. Frontier ways, manners, and values captivated John James. Sporting was the lifeblood of the town, and folks measured a man by his ability to shoot. Indeed, "every man who wore britches, and who amounted to anything, had to shoot straight and hit the mark." In addition, a man was expected to consume enormous quantities of whiskey and to tolerate not the slightest insult without fighting. "The 'best' man in the settlement was one, who, in the Kentucky sense of the word, had either whipped or could whip ev-erybody in the community."[33]

Audubon was easily able to measure up to these standards, and he quickly won the admiration and respect of the young men of the town. Considered a gentleman of leisure and property, John James was a skilled marksman and swordsman, and his expertise as a hunter in the wilds earned him the esteem of these rowdy western-ers. Indeed, he became an acknowledged leader of the town's young bloods, who took especial delight in perpetrating crude practical jokes upon unsuspecting easterners.

It was in Louisville that Lucy's husband first demonstrated a re-markable aptitude for inventing bizarre schemes to keep his young admirers amused. One such scheme involved a gentleman who col-lected geraniums.[34] Following Audubon's lead, the fun-loving men of the town presented the geranium fancier with a rare botanical specimen known as the "rat-tail-Niger" geranium. The stem of the plant was shriveled and wrinkled, but the young men assured the victim that by following their directions the plant could be revived. They instructed him to give the plant great quantities of sunshine and water. Hardly had the victim begun following these directions when he noticed that the geranium set forth a strange odor that

33. Clark, *The Rampaging Frontier*, 30, 88.
34. *Ibid.*, 211–12.

became more pronounced and more nauseating each day. Along with the sickening fragrance the victim noticed a further shriveling of the stem. Upon close examination the geranium fancier discovered that his rare specimen was nothing more than an oversized gray rat planted in the dirt with its tail tied to a stick. Audubon took great pleasure in relating the hoax to Lucy, giving her an insight into exactly how fun loving her "partner of destiny" was. Such frivolity was relatively harmless, but other aspects of life in Louisville had more serious consequences.

The Indian Queen was a cut above the ordinary western inns, but even so, Lucy lived above a tavern and public gathering place. She frequently heard the uproarious din of the merrymakers below, many of whom were her husband's companions in fun and hunting. The Louisville young bloods came to the tavern armed with the standard equipment of young men in the West—dirks, pistols, and swords concealed in walking canes. A minor altercation over a card game or any number of other insignificant incidents might quickly turn the merrymaking into a knock-down-and-drag-out fight in which eyes, ears, and noses were removed in true gouger style. Such scenes were so frequent that Lucy could not have avoided witnessing a few.

In time Lucy also became accustomed to the especially loud revelry of Saturday nights in Louisville. In addition to the numerous street fights and the din coming from the notorious waterfront establishments, Louisville's only street frequently became a racetrack for all the dandies gathered in town who wanted to test the speed of their prize mounts against those of their neighbors. The races were attended by shouting, shooting, drinking, and betting.

Amid this gaiety and love of sport, John James was in his element, and Lucy soon realized that he was not spending his time behind the counter at the store. Nor were his trips into the surrounding neighborhood primarily directed at procuring business. On the few occasions that Lucy went to the store, she found Rozier complaining that his partner's accounts were in total chaos. He grumbled further because Audubon took Nathaniel Wells Pope, the young clerk who worked in the store, with him into the woods. It is not likely that Lucy realized the validity of Rozier's complaints.

She curtly dismissed his grumblings and staunchly defended John James.[35]

Audubon never tried to deceive Lucy. She knew better than Rozier that the portfolio containing bird drawings was growing ever fatter. Indeed, many times John James returned from the woods after dark bursting with excitement because he had spied some strange winged creature or observed some new behavior. It was not in her husband to keep anything from her, either inadvertently or by design. He had an insatiable need for approval and recognition in all that he did, in all that he thought. Thus, Lucy was well acquainted with his activities.

It is unlikely that she objected strenuously to her husband's excursions into the woods. From an economic standpoint, there was little reason for complaint. She and John James were young, they had funds in reserve, and they lacked for nothing. Audubon still had a share in Mill Grove. Lucy realized that business was not good; yet these were, after all, difficult times for all businessmen. The failure of her Uncle Benjamin's firm in New York provided sufficient evidence of that. Nor is it likely that Audubon's attention to the business would have influenced the success or failure of the mercantile enterprise in Louisville. The markup on goods yielded tremendous profits on each item, but Audubon & Rozier Company did not sell in sufficient volume to provide an adequate return on their investment.[36]

Lucy did experience some disappointments, but her practical approach to matters that did not meet her expectations enabled her to put them in perspective. Evidently, Lucy had assumed when she arrived in Louisville that her residence at the Indian Queen would be only temporary. She wrote to Miss Gifford, "I cannot quite tell how I shall like Louisville as I have only been here three weeks and have not yet got a house."[37] Yet almost one year after her arrival, the

35. Maria R. Audubon (ed.), *Audubon and His Journals*, I, 29–30; Peattie (ed.), *Audubon's America*, 11; John Chancellor, *Audubon: A Biography* (New York, 1978), 66; Donald Peattie, *Singing in the Wilderness: A Salute to John James Audubon* (New York, 1935), 132.

36. Maria R. Audubon (ed.), *Audubon and His Journals*, I, 29–30; Adams, *John James Audubon*, 108; Ford (ed.), *Audubon, by Himself*, 25; Peattie (ed.), *Audubon's America*, 11; William Bakewell to Miss Gifford, April 17, 1808, in Audubon Collection; Peattie, *Singing in the Wilderness*, 132.

37. Lucy Audubon to Miss Gifford, May 27, 1808, in Audubon Collection.

riverfront hotel was still her home. Youthful optimism about the future and extravagant expenditures on fine horses, guns, and other items tempered Lucy's desire to own a home of her own.

In the winter of 1809 Lucy became pregnant. She reflected all the joy and anticipation of an expectant mother, taking particular delight in Audubon's exuberant reaction to the news that he was soon to be a father. When he was home he showered Lucy with every attention. Nevertheless, the months before the baby came went by slowly for Lucy. During the nineteenth century, the pregnant woman's activities were greatly curtailed. Expectant mothers were confined away from the eyes of the world. Thus, Lucy seldom ventured from the inn, and her lodgings were too small to allow visitors. She spent most of her time making clothes for the baby.

Lucy saw comparatively little of John James, who spent most of his days wandering in the woods. Sometimes he even accepted an invitation to hunt raccoons, a sport that involved spending the entire night under the stars. Frequently he left Louisville to procure additional merchandise for the store, sometimes being gone a day, sometimes weeks. While he was away Lucy, alone in their small quarters at the Indian Queen, was often awakened by the hurly-burly merriment of travelers spurred on by strong whiskey. If she ever complained to John James, he probably drew on his reservoir of charm and affection to soothe his young wife. Evidently, when he was with her his attentions were so intense that other considerations lost importance.[38]

On June 12, 1809, John James summoned Dr. Galt to the Indian Queen to attend Lucy. Later in the day she gave birth to Victor Gifford Audubon. Lucy named the baby after her cousin in Derby, England, and she generally called him Gifford rather than Victor. No doubt, Lucy heard the celebration in the tavern below that was touched off in honor of Gifford's birth. Her husband was there proudly accepting the toasts and congratulations of their friends.[39]

John James was the proudest of fathers. He hovered about the bed and simply could not do enough for Lucy and his son. He carried

38. Ford (ed.), *Audubon, by Himself,* 19–23; Adams, *John James Audubon,* 99; Peattie, *Singing in the Wilderness,* 132.
39. Adams, *John James Audubon,* 101.

Victor Gifford Audubon, whom Lucy called Gifford.

the child downstairs at the first opportunity, making boasts perhaps even more extreme than is usual for a new father. For more than a month he was content to stay in Louisville without excursions into the woods. Nor did he have time for the popular competitive shooting contests he so dearly loved. "Driving the nail," "snuffing the candle" and "business trips," took second place to his wife and son.[40]

By the end of July, Rozier forced John James to turn his attention to their rapidly deteriorating economic situation. They agreed that if the business was to survive, additional funds would have to be found.[41] With this end in view, Audubon left Louisville for Pittsburgh, where he purchased additional goods and arranged for extended credit. He then rode to Fatland Ford to confer with Lucy's father. Audubon also asked him to handle the sale of the portion of Mill Grove that belonged to him and Rozier.

Hardly had John James returned to Louisville when Lucy's father began to have serious doubts about selling Mill Grove. It occurred to him that, once this property was disposed of, his daughter and grandson would have nothing in reserve in the event of hard times. Moreover, William complained that the whole business was causing him a great deal of trouble and anxiety. Selling the property required time and money. In the spring of 1810 Lucy signed a statement relinquishing all claim to her husband's Pennsylvania property, and William was then able to conclude the sale. He deducted his expenses and a small commission and deposited the money from the transaction with Kinder's firm in the account of Audubon & Rozier.[42]

It would certainly have been remarkable if the Audubons had realized that the funds deposited with the Kinder firm were the last reserves available to them, for neither John James nor Lucy was conditioned to thinking in terms of financial difficulties. The very idea of impoverishment was foreign to them. Audubon considered himself a successful businessman with leisure time to pursue a life

40. *Ibid.*, 101; Ford (ed.), *Audubon, by Himself*, 19–23.
41. Adams, *John James Audubon*, 108; Herrick, *Audubon, the Naturalist*, I, 198.
42. William Bakewell to John James Audubon and Ferdinand Rozier, April 10, 1810, in Herrick, *Audubon, the Naturalist*, I, 199–200.

free from all restraint, and Lucy mirrored his thoughts. At Mill Grove her husband had been a young squire; in Louisville he was a successful merchant.

Once the proceeds from the sale of Mill Grove were available to Audubon & Rozier Company, Rozier came to believe that these new funds might be better employed elsewhere. He had concluded that Louisville was not the most advantageous location for a store because competition was too intense. In any event, since the store was still not successful after two years in operation, it was time for a change. At Rozier's urging, the partners decided to move 125 miles down the Ohio to a small hamlet originally called Red Banks that had been renamed Henderson, Kentucky.[43]

Henderson was part of the 200,000 acres of land in Kentucky that the Virginia House of Delegates granted to Richard Henderson's Transylvania Company in December, 1778.[44] The town did not meet the expectations of its promoters who had anticipated creating a thriving riverfront metropolis. Audubon, himself described Henderson as a town "of about twenty houses, and inhabited by a people whose doom is fixed."[45] Another observer described the settlement a bit more objectively: "It contains about twenty wooden houses and cabins, including two stores and two large tobacco warehouses. . . . About five hundred hogsheads of tobacco are shipped here every year, and the place now begins to thrive a little, since several wealthy people have settled in the neighbourhood, and on Green River."[46]

Nor did the town's reputation make it a particularly desirable place to live. For six years it had served as a base of operations for Samuel Mason and his band of cutthroat river pirates. Remnants of the town's notorious past were preserved as a reminder to others with criminal tendencies. Beside the roads leading into town, trav-

43. Maria R. Audubon (ed.), *Audubon and His Journals,* I, 30; Ford (ed.), *Audubon, by Himself,* 28; Peattie (ed.), *Audubon's America,* 11; Herrick, *Audubon, the Naturalist,* I, 236.

44. Workers of the Writers' Program of the Work Projects Administration in the State of Kentucky (comps.), *Henderson: A Guide to Audubon's Home Town in Kentucky* (New York, 1941), 25.

45. Quoted in Adams, *John James Audubon,* 112.

46. Cuming, "Sketches of a Tour to the Western Country," 267.

elers gazed upon the remains of the river banditti in Henderson, two sun-bleached skulls dangling from the tops of poles.[47]

Lucy's first impression of this forlorn little river community must have called to mind Ruth's promise, "Whither thou goest, I will go." The one-room abandoned log cabin that was to be her home was little comfort.[48] While John James and Rozier unloaded furniture and merchandise, Lucy stood holding Gifford, looking about the dirty little cabin. In that moment she must have doubted the sanity of her "partner of destiny."

However, in short order Lucy recovered from the shock. She placed Gifford in his cradle, and began to scrub, clean, and unpack. At least, for the first time, she would be able to use her mother's china and silverware, which had come to her when she married. How this finery contrasted with the rough logs and exposed beams of the cabin! Soon the small dwelling was clean, the musty odor gone, curtains hung at the windows, and the furniture pleasantly arranged.

The myth that he and Lucy were destitute at this time must be laid at the feet of John James. He wrote in his journal that the finest piece of furniture they had was the cradle. This may have been so in his estimation, but his reports of financial disaster were premature.

Very soon the Audubons made new friends. Lucy was pleased and somewhat relieved to meet Dr. Adam Rankin and his wife Elizabeth Speed Rankin. The Rankins, large property owners ranked among Henderson's first citizens, lived on what Audubon described as a large farm, Meadow Brook, some three miles distant from Henderson.[49] In Elizabeth, Lucy found someone whose conversation and company she could enjoy. The Audubons were frequent visitors and overnight guests in the spacious Rankin home.

Business prospects in Henderson proved so poor that even John James, the eternal optimist, had doubts about the wisdom of the

47. Adams, *John James Audubon,* 112–13; Maria R. Audubon (ed.), *Audubon and His Journals,* II, 232–33.
48. Maria R. Audubon (ed.), *Audubon and His Journals,* II, 209; Peattie, *Singing in the Wilderness,* 144. Audubon's memory of Lucy's initial response is obviously faulty.
49. Ford (ed.), *Audubon, by Himself,* 44.

move. He later wrote in his journal: "We took there the remainder
of our stock on hand, but found the country so very new, and so
thinly populated that the commonest goods only were called for."[50]
This, of course, suited Audubon well enough. He soon returned to
hunting, fishing, and drawing in the woods while Rozier stood behind the counter.

However, after his experience in Louisville, Rozier was determined not to linger too long in a location that failed to meet his
economic expectations. He convinced Audubon that they should
try their luck at Ste. Genevieve, a small French community farther
downriver. Rozier had never been at home in the English-speaking
settlements. His inability to master the language hindered his capa-
bilities as a merchant.[51]

When Lucy learned of Rozier's latest scheme, she opposed it. She
would not pack once again and move downriver on the chance
of finding a suitable location, when the new place might prove as
economically unrewarding as Henderson. Indeed, Lucy's opposition
went even deeper. At the core of her displeasure was Rozier. She
was tired of what she considered to be Rozier's constant interference
with their lives. It had been Rozier's decision to come west, to leave
Louisville for Henderson, and now he wanted to move yet another
time. She most surely resented what seemed to be Rozier's domination of her husband.[52]

Elizabeth Rankin provided Lucy with an affable way of placating
John James, who did not want to leave her alone in Henderson but
who was nevertheless anxious to see the new country downriver
and to hunt in other woods. When Elizabeth heard of the proposed
trip, she insisted that Lucy and Gifford stay with her. As a further inducement, she asked Lucy to assist with the education of the
Rankin children. Elizabeth knew that such a task would appeal to
Lucy and make her feel useful and also that her children would
benefit greatly under the instruction of Lucy Audubon. Lucy ac-

---

50. Maria R. Audubon (ed.), *Audubon and His Journals*, I, 30.
51. *Ibid.*, 30–31.
52. On Lucy's antipathy for Rozier, see Herrick, *Audubon, the Naturalist*; Ford, *John James Audubon*; Arthur, *Audubon*; Adams, *John James Audubon*; Peattie (ed.), *Audubon's America*; L. Clark Keating, *Audubon: The Kentucky Years* (Lexington, 1976).

cepted the invitation, and in December, 1810, John James escorted her and Gifford through a snowstorm to the warmth of the Rankin farm. He returned to Henderson, loaded the boat with merchandise and provisions, and set out with Rozier, Pope, and two crewmen for Ste. Genevieve.[53]

Lucy settled down for a comfortable winter. She set aside time in the morning and evening for the instruction of the Rankin children. Her teaching experience with the Rankins was both enjoyable and intellectually rewarding. She and Elizabeth spent many hours in agreeable and genial conversation, and she also took part in the Christmas parties and sleigh rides. On occasion she would use one of the fine horses owned by the Rankins to take a refreshing ride about the large farm. No doubt the pleasant company and surroundings at Meadow Brook made Lucy nostalgic about Fatland Ford and the security she had known there. Perhaps, for the first time, Lucy felt that she and John James were not establishing a firm basis for the future. Audubon's absence of almost five months must have heightened her apprehension. Indeed, as the months passed, Lucy became fearful that Rozier had once again had his way with her husband, and that soon she would be on the move again.

John James and Rozier had other worries, for the journey was a difficult one. When ice on the river prohibited further travel, they made camp on the bank. Audubon was delighted, for it gave him an opportunity to observe the Shawnee and Osage Indians and to spend many hours stalking game through the forest. He was mischievously gleeful over Rozier's discomfort and "gloom" at the delay. Rozier was discredited as a "tenderfoot," and he endured much harassment.[54] Soon tempers flared between the two Frenchmen, and each blamed the other for their failure during five years of partnership.

The longevity of the partnership was more surprising than its impending dissolution. Audubon and Rozier had always been ill-suited partners. Rozier was serious minded, hard working, and determined to make his fortune. He worked while Audubon hunted, drew,

53. Keating, *Audubon: The Kentucky Years*, 42; Ford (ed.), *Audubon, by Himself*, 44.

54. Maria R. Audubon (ed.), *Audubon and His Journals*, II, 222–25; Adams, *John James Audubon*, 118–29; Herrick, *Audubon, the Naturalist*, I, 238–241.

fished, and took any excuse to go on business trips that turned out
to be excursions into the wilds. Up to this time Rozier had only
complained about the eccentricities of his immature partner. But
while waiting for the ice in the river to melt, the two Frenchmen
were thrown into constant and prolonged contact that fully revealed their incompatibility. The break would probably have come
sooner had Rozier seen Audubon in the store as frequently as he had
demanded.[55]

When John James returned to Meadow Brook in April, Lucy was
relieved and happy at the news that the partnership had been dissolved. Audubon accepted a portion of the value of the merchandise in cash, the rest in notes payable at some time in the future.
John James told Lucy that he had refused to remain in Ste. Genevieve because of his concern for his wife and son. It would have
been necessary to leave Lucy and Gifford in Henderson, he explained, because the village downriver was small and dirty. "Its population was then composed of low French Canadians, uneducated
and uncouth. . . . Rozier, on the contrary, liked it; he found plenty
of French with whom to converse." Actually, Ste. Genevieve was
far more populous than Henderson and ripe for a mercantile venture. The goods that John James and Rozier transported received a
hearty welcome from the residents. The three hundred barrels of
Monongahela whiskey, which had cost the merchants only twenty-
five cents a gallon, were selling well at two dollars a gallon.[56] However, even had Lucy known that business prospects in Ste. Genevieve were good, it is not likely that she would have favored a
continuation of the partnership that she found so disagreeable.

Much more to her liking was Audubon's announcement that he
was going to Louisville to procure merchandise to open a store of
his own in Henderson. The Rankins were not anxious to lose Lucy
either as companion or as teacher, and they considered John James

55. Adams, *John James Audubon*, 129–30; Herrick, *Audubon, the Naturalist*, I, 238,
241–42.
56. Maria R. Audubon (ed.), *Audubon and His Journals*, I, 31; Adams, *John James Audubon*, 128–29; Muschamp, *Audacious Audubon*, 69; Herrick, *Audubon, the Naturalist*, I,
241–42.

a charming and lively addition to the household. Therefore, they sincerely pressed the Audubons to remain at Meadow Brook until the new store should prove profitable, an invitation they willingly accepted.[57]

During the summer of 1811, John James procured goods in Louisville and opened the store in Henderson, but he spent most of his time with Lucy. They took part in the social life at Meadow Brook, rode horses, swam in the river, and strolled through the woods. Taking advantage of the leisurely summer, Lucy urged John James to take her and Gifford to Fatland Ford for a visit. Audubon received this idea enthusiastically, and with little preparation Lucy, Gifford, and John James left Meadow Brook for Fatland Ford. When the Audubons reached Louisville, they learned that Lucy's brother Tom was on his way south from New York.[58] Both Lucy and John James were anxious to see Tom, so they waited in Louisville rather than chance missing him on the way. While waiting, the Audubons visited the Berthouds and other friends, and Lucy found herself once again in her honeymoon abode at the Indian Queen.

Tom's arrival was delayed until the fall. Evidently, he had written to the Audubons during the summer, giving some indication that perhaps he could point the way to prosperity in the future. For several years Tom had been working for the Kinder firm in New York. He was now going to strike out on his own, establish a firm in New Orleans, and act as a consignee for the Liverpool firm of Martin, Hope, & Thomley.[59] He would become their cotton factor and seek consignments of various other products to the company.

When Tom arrived in Louisville, he and John James roamed the woods just as they had years before on Perkiomen Creek. At night Lucy would join them to discuss their plans for the future. Tom invited Audubon to become his partner in the new business. According to Tom, "the French qualities of Mr. A. in language & nationality, it was thought wd be an advantage in so Frenchified place

57. Keating, *Audubon: The Kentucky Years*, 48–49.
58. Lucy Audubon to Miss Gifford, January 5, 1812, in Audubon Collection.
59. Thomas W. Bakewell, "Audubon & Bakewell, Partners: Sketch of the Life of Thomas Woodhouse Bakewell Written by Himself," *Cardinal*, IV, No. 2 (1935), 36.

as New Orleans, & concluded that Mr. A. shd join me there, after waiting(?) up in Kentucky for consignments to the new house of Audubon & Bakewell."[60] Lucy was delighted. A partnership between Tom and John James would be ideal, certainly far different from the tense situation that had always existed with Rozier. More importantly, ties with her family would once again be established. Equally pleasing was the prospect of living in the thriving metropolis of New Orleans.[61]

It was not until the fourth of November that Lucy and John James mounted their horses to resume the long journey to Fatland Ford. It was Audubon's idea to make the trip on horseback. He was so proud of their horses, particularly Barro, who had cost him the majority of his income for the year, that he would hear of no other mode of transport. Interestingly, Lucy did not object. She was, after all, an excellent equestrian, and her experience with stagecoaches had been most unpleasant. Gifford rode before his father in some sort of carriage attached to Audubon's saddle.

Perhaps more than any other event this trip demonstrated the remarkable stamina of Lucy Audubon. In retrospect, she herself was surprised. "Now the difficulties, and fatigue are over," she wrote, "I can scarcely reallize that I have rode on horse back nearly eight hundred miles." It should also be noted that the Audubons covered this great distance during the winter. They crossed numerous rivers and creeks, often having to swim the horses over and getting cold and wet as a result. Lucy traced the route taken in a letter to her English cousin: "Should you have a wish to see our rout on the Map you will find it by commencing at the Falls of the Ohio and looking for the Towns I mention which are the principal ones we passed through Lexington, Paris, Limestone, Chilicothee; on the Scioto river, Trainsville on the Muskingam; Wheeling on the Ohio, Washington; and Pittsburgh in Pennsylvania at the junction of the Alleghany and Monogahela rivers, which is also the head of the Ohio which is the finest river I ever saw."[62]

Always perceptive and sensitive to her surroundings, Lucy's cor-

60. *Ibid.*
61. Lucy Audubon to Miss Gifford, January 5, 1812, in Audubon Collection.
62. *Ibid.*

respondence depicts the contrast between the beautiful and the terrible that characterized the frontier. "The Country from Louisville to Pittsburgh is flat rich woodlands; there are some cultivated farms which diversify the scene a little; but [the] chief part of the road is through thick woods, where the Sun scarcely ever penetrates."[63]

The Audubons stopped in Pittsburgh and spent four days with Lucy's Uncle Benjamin. Pleased to see her favorite uncle, Lucy's joy bounded to greater heights at the news of Benjamin's newly won prosperity. Since the failure of his countinghouse in New York, Benjamin had moved his family west to Pittsburgh where he had opened a flint-glass manufactory. Not only was her uncle's business profitable but the Bakewell glass works had quickly become a show case of western industry. Daily, travelers appeared, asking to be shown through the Bakewell establishment. Europeans always seemed surprised to find such delicate beauty being produced amid the smoke and filth that blanketed Pittsburgh. Many found it incredible that there should be a market among the rowdy westerners for the fragile works of art that Bakewell produced. One visitor to the glass manufactory made this observation: "The day after my arrival I went through the flint-glass works of Mr. Bakewell, and was surprised to see the beauty of this manufacture, in the interior of the United States, in which the expensive decorations of cutting and engraving (amidst every discouragement incident to a want of taste and wealth) were carried to such perfection. The productions of this manufacture find their way to New Orleans, and even to some of the islands of the West Indies."[64] The fact that her uncle had recouped his fortune only served to make a good visit better.

Lucy delighted in the warmth and affection that Benjamin showered upon her and his grandnephew. Benjamin thought Lucy looked much the worse for the wear and tear of a journey that he considered too difficult for a young woman. He felt that Gifford had "endured the fatigue better than his mother." Indeed, he was much impressed with the small lad, who, although he had ridden six hun-

63. *Ibid.*
64. Hulme, "A Journal," 37; Nuttall, "Journal of Travels," 45; Una Pope-Hennessy (ed.), *The Aristocratic Journey: Being the Outspoken Letters of Mrs. Basil Hall Written on a Fourteen Months Sojourn in America 1827–1828* (New York, 1931), 289.

dred miles already, "appeared very willing to proceed."[65] With obvious family pride Benjamin concluded that Gifford was an exact
replica of Lucy at the same age.

After four days of much-needed rest, the Audubons left Benjamin's comfortable home and continued the trek to Fatland Ford.
The difficult and dangerous task of crossing the mountains lay before them. "From Pittsburgh we cross the . . . Mountains, which
are really most dreadful roads at all seasons of the year and a continued shelving of rocks and stumps or roots of trees. From the top
of the last Mountain there is a most beautiful view of a level well
cultivated Country, and from having travelled so far through woods
where the eye can scarcely see fifty yards the scene is peculiarly
pleasing," Lucy wrote. Relieved to be out of the mountains, she
viewed the countryside ninety miles from Philadelphia with a sigh
of relief that "there is no perceptable rise in the whole way."[66]

This ride is convincing evidence that Lucy was a woman not only
of great physical stamina but also of great determination. Her great
desire to see her family made the physical hardships tolerable. "You
will easily conceive," Lucy wrote her cousin, "I must have suffered
from, cold and fatigue considerably at that season, but the prospect
before me of seeing my family and friends after an absence of nearly
four years, buoyed up my spirits, and enabled me to indure more
than in any common cause I perhaps should have done."[67]

After a total of twenty-four days of riding, the Audubons arrived at Fatland Ford. Lucy found that members of her family had
changed, at least in appearance. Her father looked old and tired,
while "Sisters Sarah and Ann are very much grown since I left
them." There was some distressing news concerning Eliza who was
"going through a course of Medicine for a blindness in one of her
eyes. We have felt much alarm about her, but I hope she will recover the use of it entirely, as it is even now better."[68] Her youngest
brother Will had developed into a husky young man who fell immediately under the influence of the charming John James.

65. Benjamin Bakewell to Miss Gifford, December 22, 1811, in Audubon Collection.
66. Lucy Audubon to Miss Gifford, January 5, 1812, in Audubon Collection.
67. *Ibid.*
68. *Ibid.*

Gifford was, of course, the toast of the household. Lucy's father was proud of the stout lad who was his first grandchild. Her sisters vied with each other for the privilege of dressing and feeding their nephew. They considered themselves less fortunate, however, when they had to chase him about the house and farm trying to keep him out of the mischief he was always inclined to get into.

Lucy's father was very anxious that the commission business being undertaken by his son and Audubon succeed. He therefore agreed to grant the loan that Lucy and John James solicited for Tom. For his part, Audubon also needed funds for the new business. He still had the note on Dacosta that provided him and Rozier an equal share of the profits from the mine. He found, however, that Dacosta had sold his share of Mill Grove two years before to one Robert Hobard. Audubon attempted to see both Dacosta and Hobard, but he was unsuccessful. He informed Rozier of his activities. "I am very much afraid that we will never get anything out of this bad bargain. However, before my departure, I will do my best. I saw the interior of the mine, which has, I assure you, a bad appearance. They are not working there at the present moment."[69]

The Audubons were anxious to get the new business going. They decided that John James ought to proceed at once to New Orleans to assist Tom in launching the enterprise while Lucy and Gifford remained at Fatland Ford. Audubon promised to return for his family in the spring.

Since their marriage no scheme had evoked as much enthusiasm from Lucy and John James as did the commission house in New Orleans. Several weeks after Audubon left Fatland Ford, Lucy was already anticipating her departure. She wrote to her cousin in England, "I hope dear cousin you will soon write to me, and if you please direct your letter for me to the care of Audubon & Bakewell New Orleans, where I shall be in the spring and will write to you from thence." Audubon's optimism was described by Vincent Nolte, a New Orleans merchant whom John James met on the road between Harrisburg and Pittsburgh and with whom he traveled

---

69. John James Audubon to Ferdinand Rozier, December 9, 1811, reproduced in John James Audubon, "Four Audubon Letters," *Cardinal*, IV, No. 7 (January, 1938), 171.

west. Nolte found Audubon to be an "original." He invited Audubon to travel on his flatboat but learned little of Audubon's plans until they stopped to eat at an inn in Limestone, Kentucky. The Frenchman suddenly jumped from his seat at the table and proclaimed: "Now I am going to lay the foundation of my establishment." The startled guests watched as Audubon proceeded to the door of the tavern waving his arms and alternately searching his pockets. When he found the card he was looking for, he tacked it to the tavern door. It read: "*Audubon & Bakewell, Commission Merchants (Pork, Lard, and Flour)*, New Orleans."[70]

The bright hopes of the Audubons were soon discouraged. At Fatland Ford Lucy learned from her father and letters from Uncle Benjamin that the country seemed determined to rush into a war with England. Her fears were confirmed when Tom wrote from New Orleans that war was almost a certainty, and that he was unable even to launch the new business with hostilities pending. Evidently, John James, who had not yet left Kentucky for New Orleans, was receiving the same discouraging missives from Tom. After receiving this adverse news and trying unsuccessfully to collect monies still due him from Rozier, John James decided to return to Fatland Ford instead of continuing to New Orleans.[71]

In March, 1812, Audubon arrived at Fatland Ford, where he and Lucy remained for almost four months. It seems that they were waiting for the international situation to determine the direction of their future, hoping that the war fever would subside. While they lingered, Audubon hunted and drew. Lucy frequently sat beside him while he sketched, reading at intervals from Scott and Edgeworth.[72] Unfortunately, these peaceful moments were won at the cost of enduring Rebecca Bakewell's obvious displeasure with their lengthy stay.

On June 18, 1812, the wait was over. War with England was de-

70. Lucy Audubon to Miss Gifford, January 5, 1812, in Audubon Collection; Vincent Nolte, *Fifty Years in Both Hemispheres; or, Reminiscences of the Life of a Former Merchant* (New York, 1854), 177–78.
71. John James Audubon to Ferdinand Rozier, January 29, 1812, reproduced in Audubon, "Four Audubon Letters," 173; Keating, *Audubon: The Kentucky Years*, 55–56.
72. Ford, *John James Audubon*, 86; Keating, *Audubon: The Kentucky Years*, 55–56.

clared. There would be no commission house in New Orleans. Without any apparent direction or definite ideas of what to do, the Audubons decided to return to the place that they knew—Henderson, Kentucky.

When John James helped Lucy into the carriage at Fatland Ford to begin their journey to Kentucky, she was no longer the romantic and sheltered young lady of 1808. She had matured in years and in her outlook on life. In the summer of 1812 Lucy was twenty-five years old and expecting another child. She knew that there was little to return to in Henderson, neither a home nor a profitable business. She knew, too, that they would have to depend upon the hospitality of the Rankins for a place in which to live and to give birth to her child. Fully aware of all these matters, Lucy, nevertheless, neither despaired nor found fault with her husband. On the contrary, John James embodied her hope and consolation in disappointment.

CHAPTER IV

The Mighty Fall

 ~

The skiff glided over the surface of the Ohio under a sultry July sun. Lucy welcomed the breeze that rippled across her face and twisted once again to find a comfortable position in the little craft for her cumbersome body, now swollen awkwardly in the fifth month of pregnancy. Frequently she checked on Gifford, who had sleepily surrendered to the gentle swaying of the boat and the rhythmic sound of the paddles pushing through the water. The Audubons had traveled by coach and flatboat to Louisville where John James had secured a skiff with two black crewmen to take them downriver to Henderson. Away from the jouncing coach and the crowded flatboat, John James and Lucy enjoyed the beauty and peace of the river and renewed their feelings of confidence in each other and their future.[1]

Upon reaching Henderson the Audubons traveled to Meadow Brook where Adam and Elizabeth Rankin extended a warm welcome. The Rankins, noting that the spirits of the young couple were still low because of the failure of the commission business in New Orleans, encouraged Audubon to believe that a mercantile venture could succeed in Henderson. In August, 1812, Tom arrived at Meadow Brook. He, too, was discouraged because the commission house in New Orleans had failed to materialize, but he and John James decided to keep the firm of Audubon & Bakewell in operation. Without much enthusiasm Tom wrote, "Defeated in the brilliant prospects at N Orleans by the war, continued the business

1. Maria R. Audubon (ed.), *Audubon and His Journals*, II, 203–204.

connection with Audubon on the smaller scale of Store Keeping in Henderson."[2]

Unlike the ill-fated Audubon and Rozier enterprise in Henderson, the Audubon-Bakewell store prospered from the beginning. Their success made Lucy's confinement easier to bear. On November 30, 1812, she gave birth to a second son, who was named John Woodhouse Audubon, although Lucy usually called him Woodhouse. Unlike Gifford, Woodhouse was a sickly infant, who required almost constant attention from his mother. The boy remained extremely delicate until he was a year old, "when he suddenly acquired strength and grew to be a lusty child."[3] Now there were four Audubons and Lucy's brother Tom living at Meadow Brook. Well aware that they were imposing upon the Rankins, Lucy had made John James promise that he would purchase a home and establish roots for their growing family as soon as her confinement was over.

Audubon was fortunate to find a house in town. The population of the entire county was but 4,703 and that of the town only 159, and there were few homes. John James purchased a home that had lately belonged to an English doctor. The property was conveniently located adjacent to the store. The main dwelling was a spacious one-and-a-half-story log cabin, far enough removed from the street to provide an atmosphere of country living. Across the front of the cabin stretched a broad porch. There were also several outbuildings, including a stable, a smokehouse, and a stone house. A short distance from the main house there was a prettily laid out orchard.[4]

Early in the fall of 1813 Rankin servants loaded a wagon with the Audubons' and Tom's few belongings. Gifford, not quite understanding the meaning of a home of his own but excited by all the activity, romped about with the Rankin children. Lucy, John

2. Thomas Bakewell, "Autobiography" (in Pears Papers); Thomas Bakewell, "Audubon & Bakewell, Partners," 37.

3. Maria R. Audubon (ed.), *Audubon and His Journals*, I, 32.

4. Workers of the Writers' Program (comps.), *Henderson: A Guide*, 29; *Aggregate Amount of Persons Within the United States in the Year 1810* (Washington, D.C., 1811), 72a; Thomas Towles to J. J. Audubon, 57, Richard Henderson & Co. by Agent to J. J. Audubon, 104, both in Deed Book C, J. J. Audubon to N. Berthoud, 152, in Deed Book D, all in Court of the Chancery, Henderson, Ky.

John Woodhouse Audubon, known to his mother as Woodhouse.

James, and Tom thanked the Rankins for their gracious hospitality and the care they had showered upon Lucy and her infant son. The Rankins promised to visit the Audubons soon. The loading completed, Audubon assisted Lucy into the wagon. She held Woodhouse, who was hidden from view beneath a bundle of blankets that protected him from the cold. After a brief journey into town Lucy arrived at her new house and the task of turning the log cabin into a home began immediately.

The small riverfront hamlet that had so shaken Lucy's confidence in her husband only a short time before could be viewed more objectively now that Lucy had become a property owner with a stake in the fledgling community. Indeed the town had been well planned and it was nicely laid out. One of the founding fathers described the town plan as follows: "The plan of the town contains two hundred and sixty four Lots, of one acre each, lying in squares of four lots; each lot fronting two streets—Twelve acres in the centre of the town are appropriated to public uses. The street fronting on the Ohio is 200 feet in width; and each other street 100. The whole of the town plan is surrounded by a street of one hundred feet in width, adjoining which are thirty-two out lots of 10 acres each."[5] The town's most striking feature was its location atop a bank, seventy-two feet above the low-water mark of the Ohio River. Across the mile-wide expanse of the Ohio lay a broad, level plain of Indiana bottomland some thirty feet lower than Henderson. Ridges and verdant forests of hardwoods characterized the rolling plateau of the surrounding countryside.[6]

In the decade before 1819 the movement of goods and people brought growing populations and prosperity to the West, and Henderson shared in that growth and prosperity. Census figures show that the town's population, which was 205 in 1800, had decreased to 159 by 1810, but by 1820 there were 532 persons living in the town. The Kentucky legislature designated Henderson as one of the state's tobacco inspection points, and the small hamlet became Kentucky's largest market for stemmed dark-leaf tobacco. Ex-

---

5. Advertisement for a sale of lots by Samuel Hopkins, December 15, 1797, reproduced in Workers of the Writers' Program (comps.), *Henderson: A Guide*, 26–27.
6. Workers of the Writers' Program, *Henderson: A Guide*, 17.

pansion of tobacco acreage soon necessitated the construction of
two tobacco warehouses. In 1813 Henderson Academy opened its
doors, and in the following year a courthouse was constructed. During this period there was a significant increase in the sale of town
lots as newcomers moved in and families from the surrounding area
established town residences.[7] Lucy and John James bought their
home in Henderson at the very time that the small village showed
its first signs of growth and prosperity, and they quickly fell into step
with the prevailing boom spirit that characterized Henderson between the years 1813 and 1819.

The demand for merchandise increased and Audubon's profits
multiplied. With the proceeds from the store and the money from
the sale of Mill Grove, John James began to speculate in real estate.
In 1813 he purchased four lots and in 1814 he bought five more
acres in town. As the value of the property increased, Audubon
sold the property at a profit. He quickly learned that he could increase his profit margin by subdividing the lots. Records indicate
that Audubon paid out approximately $4,500 for property that he
later sold for about $27,000. In the period between 1813 and 1819,
Lucy and John James conducted transactions in real and personal
property that reached a value of approximately $50,000.[8]

In the spring and summer of 1813, Audubon and Bakewell discussed another scheme that they thought would enhance the profits
of their partnership. Henderson had neither gristmill nor sawmill,
and it seemed to Tom and John James that a steam-powered mill
combining those functions was needed in the fast-growing town.
The two young men knew that they had neither the ready capital

7. *Return of the Whole Number of Persons Within the Several Districts of the United States,
According to "An Act of Providing for the Second Census or Enumeration of the Inhabitants of the
United States," Passed February 28, 1800* (Washington, 1801); *Aggregate Amount of Persons,*
72a; *Population Schedules of the Fourth Census of the United States, 1820,* Microcopy Collection
33 (142 rolls; Washington, D.C., 1959), vol. 9, roll 24; Workers of the Writer's Program
(comps.), *Henderson: A Guide,* 29, 33; Maralea Arnett, *The Annals and Scandals of Henderson County, Kentucky, 1775–1975* (Croydon, Ky., 1976), 77; Samuel R. Brown, *The Western
Gazetteer* (Rpr.; New York, 1971), 106.

8. Richard Henderson & Co. by agent to J. J. Audubon, 104, David Glenn & Co. to
J. J. Audubon, 132, Audubon to Thomas Asberry, 165, Audubon to T. Bakewell, 240, Au-
dubon to T. Bakewell, 325, Audubon to R. Adkinson, 442, Audubon to J. Boyle, 462, Au-
dubon to William Williams, 464, Audubon to David Nayley, 465, Audubon to Moses Mor-
gan, 467, Audubon to Richard Atkinson, 468, all in Deed Book C; Arthur, *Audubon,* 78.

nor the technical knowledge to undertake such an enterprise alone. They therefore agreed that Tom would travel to Fatland Ford to discuss the venture with William and to secure a loan from him.[9]

Tom's departure was delayed for some time because both Lucy and John James became seriously ill in the summer of 1813.[10] They were sufficiently recovered by the end of August though, and Tom set out for Pennsylvania. He carried a letter from Audubon to Thomas Pears and one from Lucy to Thomas' wife, her cousin Sarah. Tom and Lucy had learned that the Pearses' Pennsylvania farm, Wheat Hill, was not yielding sufficient profit and that the young couple were contemplating a move west to seek a better life. Thinking that the Pearses might be interested in entering a new occupation, the Audubons informed them of the proposed mill venture and expressed a hope that they might be interested in investing.

While Tom was traveling east, John James and Lucy decided that profits from the store were such that the business should be expanded. Tom returned just in time to give his consent to the opening of a branch store in Shawneetown, Illinois, thirty miles downriver from Henderson. David Apperson was selected to manage the new store, which opened for business in January, 1814, and continued in operation at least until 1817 when Apperson renewed his lease for another year. Between 1814 and 1817 Audubon and Bakewell collected the not inconsequential sum of $6,402 as their share of the profits from the branch store.[11]

Lucy and John James were happy to learn that Tom's mission had been successful. William Bakewell had lent his son between three and four thousand dollars for the venture, and Thomas Pears had expressed interest in purchasing a partnership in the mill.[12] However, Tom brought other news that was not as welcome. Lucy learned that her father was not well, that he constantly complained of severe headaches, and that he had lost weight. In addition, Rebecca was making life intolerable for her sisters and her brother

9. Sarah Pears to Thomas Pears, September 22, 1813, in Pears Papers.
10. Nancy Bakewell to Sarah Pears, June 13, 1813, in Pears Papers.
11. Keating, Audubon: The Kentucky Years, 60.
12. Thomas W. Bakewell, "Audubon & Bakewell, Partners," 37.

Will. Although Lucy was saddened by these tidings, she could forget them in the happiness that she experienced in Henderson.

For the first time Lucy could turn her attention to selecting and
ordering furnishings for her own home. She was a tasteful decorator
preferring the dark rich hues of cherry and walnut for the pianoforte, tables, chairs, desks, bedsteads, bureaus, and bookcases. Silver candlesticks adorned the dining room table, and on a small side
table, a silver tea service rested upon a fine linen tablecloth. Lucy
paid particular attention to her kitchen, which she equipped especially well. Always an avid reader, she acquired quite a library. By
1819 she had accumulated 150 volumes. She also procured a considerable collection of musical scores and instruments. Lucy quickly
turned the log cabin into a most impressive home.[13]

The growing affluence of the Audubons brought significant and
welcome changes in Lucy's life. Her days were busy and full. John
James purchased several slaves, who, under Lucy's supervision, attended to the cleaning, washing, cooking, sewing, and a wide variety of other chores. They also arranged merchandise in the store
and tended the property around the Audubon home. Running a
household in town was very similar to country living. Homes in
town were essentially small farms within the city limits. Lucy laid
out a garden near the orchard, and although she was never without
servants, she took pleasure in working the garden herself. A short
distance from the house Audubon had the slaves dig a large pond
which he stocked with turtles, ducks, and wild geese whose wings
had been clipped.[14] The grounds about the Audubon home were a
source of pride to Lucy and John James and were frequently admired
by friends and neighbors.

Prosperity and a sense of permanence came into Lucy's life at an
opportune moment. Her home and the steadily growing business
more than justified the confidence she had displayed in returning to
Henderson in 1812. Her expectations for a stable family life were
fulfilled in this small frontier hamlet. She was mistress of a large and

13. Audubon to N. Berthoud, July 13, 1819, 152, in Deed Book D.
14. Thomas I. Young to Audubon, 338, in Deed Book C; Audubon to N. Berthoud, 151,
in Deed Book D; Scott, *The Southern Lady*, 31; Arthur, *Audubon*, 78; Keating, *Audubon: The
Kentucky Years*, 58.

lively household. There were servants to direct and her family and brother to care for. Tom had purchased property from Audubon, and he had built a home. However, he preferred to live with his sister until such time as he would marry.[15]

John James, too, was delighted with his successful business and the first Audubon home. Tom was an excellent partner, serving behind the counter without complaint while Audubon wandered in the woods. In later years John James confessed that the log cabin held a special place in his memory. "The pleasures which I have felt at Henderson, and under the roof of that log cabin, can never be effaced from my heart until after death."[16]

Secure in the new stability that had come to her life, Lucy had time to become accustomed to, and even contented with, the strange ways of John James, who brought home a number of wild creatures from his excursions into the woods. She helped raise and care for the wild turkey that John James captured when it was only a few days old. The bird rapidly became a great pet to the Audubon children and the entire village. Anxious to protect the turkey from hunters, Lucy tied a red string around his neck so that he would be recognized while wandering about town.[17] Each evening the gobbler could be seen roosting on the roof of the Audubon cabin. Lucy also helped raise a male trumpeter swan that John James caught. "Trumpeter," as he was called, caused a sensation in the Audubon household and throughout the neighborhood. John James recounted the story:

> Its size, weight and strength made carrying it nearly two miles by no means easy. But because it was sure to please my wife and my then very young children I persevered. I cut off the wounded wing-tip and turned the Swan loose in the garden. Extremely shy at first, it gradually became used to the servants, who fed it abundantly. At length it came gently to my wife's call to receive bread from her hand. Indeed it laid its timidity aside to become so bold as to chase my favorite Wild Turkey cock, my dogs, children and servants.[18]

15. Audubon to Thomas W. Bakewell, Deed Book C, 240; Keating, *Audubon: The Kentucky Years*, 59.
16. Maria R. Audubon (ed.), *Audubon and His Journals*, I, 33.
17. Ford, *John James Audubon*, 96.
18. Ford (ed.), *Audubon, by Himself*, 72.

Whenever the gate was left open, Trumpeter made similar assaults upon neighbors or headed for a swim in the Ohio River or a nearby pond. At word of his latest foray the Audubons, their servants, and the neighbors would swarm out to chase the bird home, sometimes themselves being chased in the process. In addition to these unusual pets, on the grounds around the cabin there were numerous cages in which John James kept a variety of other animals captured in the woods. It was, of course, Lucy who made sure that the creatures were properly fed and otherwise cared for.

John James had never considered himself an inept businessman. Now prosperity confirmed his conviction that he was rich enough to be a man of leisure, and his excursions into the forest became more frequent.[19] However, his trips did not seem to irritate Lucy or to make her feel neglected. At times John James took her with him into the woods to see some unusual phenomenon he had witnessed. But usually, Lucy remained home, tending to the children and her household and greeting him when he returned in the evening, often with the carcasses of birds draped over his shoulder.

Yet there were many activities that Lucy and John James enjoyed together. The Audubons maintained a number of fine horses, and weather permitting, Lucy was fond of taking a morning ride. Frequently her husband accompanied her. The Audubons also often swam together in the Ohio River. The evening hours had a special significance for the young couple. Audubon's zest for life filled the cabin. Lucy played the pianoforte that had been sent downriver from Fatland Ford, while John James accompanied her on his fiddle. Gifford and Woodhouse played about the cabin and at times had their chance to plunk on the instruments. On occasion the Rankins, who had recently built a new brick home in town came by to spend a pleasant evening. Others who visited the Audubon home included Senator Talbot, Judge Thomas Towles, the Holloways, and the Alves.[20]

Community social gatherings were frequent diversions in the

19. *Ibid.*, 48–85; Maria R. Audubon (ed.), *Audubon and His Journals*, II, 203–221, 225–46.

20. Edmund L. Starling, *History of Henderson County, Kentucky, Comprising History of County and City, Precincts, Education, Churches, Secret Societies, Leading Enterprises, Sketches*

riverfront village. Horse racing was very popular with the folks in Henderson. National holidays, election days, or an idle boast about the unusual speed of one's mount meant that a race was in the offing. The wide streets of Henderson made an ideal course, and town residents and Kentuckians from the surrounding area lined the streets and jostled their neighbors to secure the best position from which to view the proceedings. For women an afternoon of racing presented the opportunity to show off their finery—the latest styles in dresses, shoes, bonnets, and gaily colored parasols.[21]

While John James joined the other men inspecting the horses and placing bets, Lucy would exchange the latest news about family, relatives, and the goings on in the country with the other women. But conversation stopped when the gun sounded and the horses leaped across the starting line. A fine judge of good horseflesh and horsemanship, Lucy participated enthusiastically in cheering the winner across the finish line. Of course, the winner was frequently John James.

Attending the weddings of friends also provided Lucy with an opportunity to mingle with others. Lucy detailed the account of one such wedding to her sister Eliza, who relayed the information to Sarah Pears. "I received a letter from sister Audubon the other day," Eliza wrote, "giving me a long account of Mr. Fowler and Miss Alves' wedding. It was conducted quite in popular style. They kept open house for two days, and invited, I expect, the whole country."[22] Weddings were indeed festive occasions, and another sojourner in the West described the kind of activities that Lucy witnessed.

> If the wedding was a formal affair it was generally performed in the morning so as to get the necessary legal or religious formalities out of the way in time for dinner. There followed the "hitching," a wedding procession, and, often, a neck and neck horse race for the bottle. The winner was awarded a bottle of fresh spirits which he passed around "to

and Recollections, and Biographies of the Living and Dead (Henderson, 1887), 795; Keating; *Audubon: The Kentucky Years*, 59; Workers of the Writers' Program (comps.), *Henderson: A Guide*, 73; Eliza Berthoud to Sarah Pears, May 12, 1816, in Pears Papers.

   21. Workers of the Writers' Program (comps.), *Henderson: A Guide*, 30.

   22. Eliza Berthoud to Sarah Pears, May 12, 1816, in Pears Papers.

supple up" the party for a gracious repast at the expense of the groom's family. During the wedding dinner, which consisted of enough food to founder the state militia, the bottle was passed freely and frequently from one greasy mouth to another. By the time the last bone had been stripped, and the last of the cake eaten, the fiddler had taken his place. There began a breakdown dance which lasted as long as there were couples to bump into one another upon the pretense of dancing. Fiddlers were worked in relays, but it was only through frequent swiggings at the bottle that they were kept at their business throughout the night.[23]

Periodically John James set out on trading trips that entailed absences of weeks and at times months. He traveled to Ste. Genevieve and Cape Girardeau, Missouri, and Vincennes, Indiana, and he usually turned a profit on his operations. Lucy was probably aware that the business aspects of these trips did not necessitate such lengthy absences. The journeys provided Audubon with an opportunity to see new woods and skies and to trap new birds. Always enticed by any circumstance that promised adventure or danger, John James could not resist the opportunity to hunt with frontiersmen he met in the wilds or to visit with Indians, learning their customs and peculiarities.[24] These trips fulfilled an intrinsic part of Audubon's nature. He would return from a journey exuberant and would recount the latest adventure in detail for the entertainment of his family. Lucy accepted the trips and even approved of her husband's favorite recreation because the woods and the drawings did not yet threaten her primacy in his life.

Lucy even grew accustomed to the odd friends that John James frequently invited into their home to spend a night or even weeks. One such visitor was the naturalist Constantine Rafinesque, whom the Tarascons had given a letter of introduction to Audubon. The naturalist was collecting sketches of the fish of the Ohio, which perhaps accounts for the Tarascons' describing him as an "odd fish."[25] Evidently Rafinesque was a queer looking sort in both dress and physical stature. Audubon described him as an "original."

One night during Rafinesque's stay in the Audubon home, Lucy and John James were suddenly awakened by a great uproar coming

23. Clark, *The Rampaging Frontier*, 262–63.
24. Ford (ed.), *Audubon, by Himself*, 46–75.
25. *Ibid.*, 79; Peattie, *Audubon's America*, 49–57.

from the guest room. Audubon raced to investigate. "To my astonishment, [I] saw him running about naked in pursuit of Bats. He had my favorite violin by the handle and proceeded to bash it against the wall in an attempt to kill the winged animals. . . . I stood amazed while he continued to jump and run round and round until fairly exhausted. Then he begged me to procure a Bat for him—'a new species,' he felt convinced."[26] John James returned to Lucy who was fully awake by then and anxious for an explanation of the noise. No doubt they had a hearty laugh at Rafinesque's antics.

Lucy made even the eccentric Rafinesque welcome in her home. Travelers always brought news of the goings-on outside the insulated world of Henderson, and it was expected that the well-to-do would extend hospitality to strangers. In Henderson the Audubons became recognized members of the upper class. Of course, by virtue of her family and background, Lucy was entitled to consider herself a member of the gentry. John James, with considerably less justification in regard to family and background, was nonetheless unequivocal in his belief that he was well born and able. But it was in Henderson that the Audubons became prosperous. Indeed they were regarded as something of a mercantile aristocracy. Even in this frontier hamlet, social rank depended upon the ownership of land and slaves, and the Audubons had acquired both of these status symbols since moving to Henderson.

Even though civilization was rapidly gaining on the riverfront community, Henderson still had the appearance and the characteristics of a frontier town. The vast majority of its inhabitants displayed a certain roughness and crudity in manners and behavior. As in Louisville, Audubon's fascination with frontier ways helped Lucy to adapt, but her status in the community did even more to make frontier life acceptable. Because she was comfortably secure in the top level of society, she could create a genteel atmosphere reminiscent of her former homes in Derbyshire and Pennsylvania. In addition, the attitude of the townspeople toward her husband was very gratifying to Lucy. It was especially important to the women of the period that their husbands command the respect of the community.

26. Ford (ed.), *Audubon, by Himself*, 81.

Indeed, to a proud woman like Lucy Audubon, it was essential, and John James met her expectations. Not only was he admired as a successful businessman but his physical prowess was heartily applauded by the young men of the Henderson community. Whether the contest involved skill with the gun or the sword, the young men always expected Audubon to compete and to emerge the victor. If a braggart began swaggering about town boasting of his athletic abilities, John James was called upon to uphold the honor of the local talent.[27]

Audubon's sense of humor and love of the coarse practical joke also made him a much sought-after companion. One day John James was traveling back from Louisville with a foreigner to whom he referred in his journal as "D. T." During the course of the journey they came upon a skunk, which D. T. took for a species of squirrel. With a mischievous glint in his eye, Audubon encouraged D. T. in his false assumption and suggested that the animal could easily be caught by hand. John James roared with laughter at the result of the attempted capture. Evidently D. T. accepted his plight good naturedly because he and Audubon continued their travels together. The day after D. T. had acquired his vile smell, snow began to fall and the pair was forced to seek shelter in a nearby cabin. The cabin where they stopped was bustling with activity. They were invited in and asked to participate in the corn shucking that was in progress. During the cold ride the odor of the skunk had become barely perceptible, but as soon as D. T. approached the fire to get warm, the unmistakable fragrance of skunk filled the air. In quick order the cabin emptied, leaving only an embarrassed D. T. and an amused John James, who was once again laughing uncontrollably. No doubt the slave who was left behind to wait upon the pair would have found the situation more humorous had he too been allowed to retreat beyond smelling distance.[28] News of Audubon's exploit spread quickly. Upon his return to Henderson, town wags accorded

27. William Bakewell, Memoirs, cited in Arthur, Audubon, 81–82. See Smith, Daughters of the Promised Land, 90.

28. Audubon, Ornithological Biography, I, 310–11; John James Audubon, Delineations of American Scenery and Character (New York, 1926), 64–67; Ford (ed.), Audubon, by Himself, 41–42.

him something of the conquering hero's welcome. Amid uproarious laughter and thunderous backslapping, John James was the toast of the town for months.

On another occasion Lucy played a part in one of Audubon's playful pranks if only by remaining silent while he perpetrated the hoax. The victim was poor, befuddled, unsuspecting Rafinesque. By day Audubon purposefully guided Rafinesque through the worst possible terrain, frequently leading him in circles. Back at the Audubon cabin in the evening, Rafinesque eagerly collected sketches of the fish of the Ohio River drawn by John James. Audubon assured the naturalist that he had seen each of the fish he drew, but the sketches he gave Rafinesque were of mythical fish. The more comical and otherworldly the products of Audubon's imagination, the more excited Rafinesque became. It must have been difficult for Lucy to contain her amusement as she looked at the sketches of these creatures while trying to avoid Audubon's dancing eyes. Rafinesque later became a professor at Transylvania University and published a book, *Icthyologia Ohiensis*, which described the fish of the Ohio River and its tributaries. Several of Audubon's imaginary fish appeared in Rafinesque's pioneer study.[29]

If Lucy had been a woman of stoic reserve, unsmiling and stern, as was sometimes thought, she could not have long endured a man like John James. But Lucy had a lively sense of humor. She was able to enjoy even the rowdy humor of the frontier. By modern standards it was a rough life, and a rough life encouraged coarse humor.

It was certainly good that Lucy had many light moments to enjoy, for her enterprising husband and brother had numerous serious business decisions to make. In 1814 Thomas Pears sold his farm in Pennsylvania and moved his wife and family to Pittsburgh so that they could be looked after by Benjamin Bakewell, his wife's uncle. After leaving his family in Bakewell's care, Thomas Pears set out for the Audubon home in Henderson where he intended to investigate the advisability of investing in the mill venture that Audubon and Tom had spoken of. The Audubon cabin buzzed with serious negotiations as the three men worked out the financial arrangements

29. Ford (ed.), *Audubon, by Himself*, 82–83; Peattie, *Audubon's America*, 49–57.

that would govern their partnership. Eventually, it was agreed that Pears and Tom were to invest about four thousand dollars apiece, while the firm of Audubon & Bakewell would put up the balance. They initially estimated that the total investment required to build and equip the mill would be about ten thousand dollars.[30]

Before the final agreement was struck, the partners wrote to David Prentice, a mechanic who had once worked for Lucy's father. They asked Prentice to estimate the cost of the necessary machinery for the mill and they offered him the job of constructing the machinery if his fee were reasonable. While the post carried this inquiry northward, Pears stayed on in Henderson enjoying the Audubons' hospitality. He found the profits that John James and Tom had accrued from the stores sufficiently impressive to convince him that the growing Henderson area was an ideal location in which to make money. While awaiting Prentice's answer, he frequently accompanied John James on trips to purchase supplies for the stores.[31]

While her husband, her brother, and Tom Pears were thus engaged Lucy received some disturbing news from Fatland Ford. Her father had had a stroke and was faring poorly. This news proved especially distressing because Lucy's relationship with her father had cooled considerably since her marriage. She knew, too, that her petulant stepmother bore much of the responsibility for the rift.[32]

News from Eliza quickly confirmed Lucy's belief that Rebecca was trying to alienate all the Bakewell children from their father. After William's stroke Rebecca had assumed absolute control of Fatland Ford. Her attempts to make Eliza's life miserable met with rebellion, however. Eliza left home and sought refuge in Pittsburgh with her Uncle Benjamin. Sarah Pears summed up Eliza's situation, "At home she has a father who appears to have entirely lost all affection for her and for all but his wife! A step-mother who has robbed them of their father's love, who will not even suffer him to bestow the

---

30. Sarah Pears to Thomas Pears, June 5, 1814, Sarah Pears to Thomas Pears, June 19, 1814, Thomas Bakewell, "Autobiography," all in Pears Papers.

31. Sarah Pears to Thomas Pears, July 30, 1814, Thomas Pears to Sarah Pears, August 9, 1814, both in Pears Papers.

32. Sarah Pears to Thomas Pears, January 18, 1815, in Pears Papers.

smallest presents upon any of them, who makes their home life wretched, in short anything but a home!"[33]

Lucy decided to share her home with Eliza. She invited her younger sister to come to Henderson and live with her family. Eliza made plans to travel with Sarah and her children as soon as Thomas Pears sent for his family. However, news from Pittsburgh led Lucy to advise Eliza to leave for Henderson with all speed.

Lucy learned that her younger sister had plunged headlong into more difficulties when she took refuge at the Bakewell home. Uncle Benjamin's son, Thomas Bakewell, confessed to the family that he had "loved Eliza ever since he knew what love was, but that he thought it so improbable that she would ever be induced to like him or that she should be unmarried when he should be of a proper age and in circumstances to settle, that he had studiously concealed his affection from every one, even from his own family." But now, living in the same home with Eliza and escorting her to parties and excursions into the countryside, Thomas gave way to his feelings for his cousin and abandoned his shy silence long enough to propose to Eliza. Lucy's aunt, uncle, and cousins were delighted, but they reckoned without Eliza's response. Much to the Bakewell family's distress, Lucy's sister refused her cousin's proposal. Her refusal particularly dismayed Lucy's aunt, who thought that Eliza had led Thomas to believe that she shared his feelings.[34] Eliza was terribly upset because she realized that she was hurting people for whom she had genuine affection. After the proposal she moved out of the Bakewell home and went to stay with Benjamin Page's family, friends of her uncle.

As soon as she could, Eliza followed Lucy's advice and left Pittsburgh. By November she was waiting for John James to meet her in Louisville.[35] Her arrival in Henderson touched off a celebration, and for several days visitors crowded the Audubon home to extend a warm welcome to Lucy's sister. Lucy had everything in readiness. Eliza's room had been specially prepared. An abundance of food and

33. Sarah Pears to Thomas Pears, October 23, 1814, in Pears Papers.
34. *Ibid.*
35. Sarah Pears to Thomas Pears, November 17, 1814, in Pears Papers.

drink of every description awaited guests, and no doubt, Lucy had taken care to invite the most eligible young men in the country.

Once the guests had left, Lucy and Eliza had time to discuss all the events of their lives since they had last met. Lucy asked eagerly for details about each member of the family in Pennsylvania, especially her father. She inquired about friends, news from Derbyshire, and the general state of affairs in the East. She also sympathized with Eliza's feelings toward Thomas Bakewell, and she assured her sister that she had made a correct choice in not entering a loveless marriage.

For her part, Eliza was full of youthful exuberance encouraged by her new environment in the West. The Audubon home, where she was unconfined by Rebecca Bakewell's vigilance, seemed to embody western freedom. Her sister's household throbbed with laughter, music, giggling nephews, enterprising schemes to make money, and constant evidence of life and activity. There was none of the gloom that hung over Fatland Ford. On occasion Eliza even accompanied John James on excursions to purchase supplies for the stores.[36] When she was at home, she attracted even more commotion to the Audubon house. Soon after Eliza's arrival Lucy noticed that an unusual number of young men began to call. She was happy to note that Eliza seemed to take a special interest in one of them, Nicholas Berthoud, who never tired of traveling up and down the river to visit and court Lucy's sister.

Shortly after Eliza settled down in Henderson, Lucy's youngest brother, Will, arrived and moved into his sister's home. Like his sister, Will had been anxious to leave Fatland Ford. His father had made arrangements with the Audubons and Tom that Will would serve an apprenticeship in the Audubon & Bakewell store.[37] Lucy received her young brother warmly and provided him with a comfortable and pleasant home. Will took to life in Henderson readily. He especially enjoyed joining John James in shooting excursions in the woods.

Meanwhile, it became apparent to Lucy that there would soon be

36. Thomas Bakewell to William Bakewell, August 27, 1815, in Pears Papers.
37. Thomas Bakewell to William Bakewell, September 20, 1816, in Pears Papers; Thomas W. Bakewell, "Audubon & Bakewell, Partners," 39.

new arrivals in Henderson who would expect to live with the Audubons. David Prentice had answered the inquiry that Tom and John James had sent. Prentice told them that it had long been his wish to settle in the West, "but being in a pretty decent way here I did not chuse to leave a certainty for an uncertainty. I have held myself ready to embrace the first opportunity that presented of an introduction to business. I think that the erecting of a steam engine for you will bring me into notice, and I am therefore willing to employ myself . . . for very little compensation." Prentice offered to superintend the works "while putting up, for $3 a day and expenses of travelling paid." He told them that he could put up a sixteen-horse engine for $4,000 but that they would have to make provisions for the hauling, the timber, the masonry, and his personal boarding while in Henderson.[38] John James, Tom, and Pears agreed to Prentice's terms. Pears returned East to put his affairs in order and to escort his wife and family back to Henderson. Prentice was instructed to proceed to Henderson with all speed.

In the spring of 1815 Pears, his wife Sarah, and their four children arrived in Henderson and moved into the Audubon home.[39] Prentice and his wife Margaret also came. They moved into Tom's cabin, but they took their meals with the Audubons. Tom, Prentice, Pears, and John James spent many hours studying blueprints and ordering materials. Gifford romped about with three of his Pears cousins while Woodhouse and the Pears infant also demanded their fair share of attention. Lucy had her hands full directing this large household, and her task became more difficult in 1815 when she gave birth to another child, whom John James named Lucy.[40] The second Lucy was an extremely delicate infant, hardly recovering from one illness before she was stricken with another. Having to nurse a sick child and play permanent hostess, Lucy found it difficult to accomplish all the tasks that required her attention.

Had everyone living in the Audubon home at least tried to tolerate the temporarily crowded conditions, the atmosphere in the

38. Sarah Pears copied Prentice's letter and forwarded it to her husband. Sarah Pears to Thomas Pears, July 30, 1814, in Pears Papers.

39. Sarah Pears's correspondence from Pittsburgh ends in March 1815, and resumes May 12, 1816.

40. Maria R. Audubon (ed.), *Audubon and His Journals*, I, 37.

cabin could have been reasonably pleasant. This, however, was not the case. Lucy's cousin Sarah Pears had not wanted to come to Henderson. The letters she wrote to her husband while he was visiting there in 1814 indicate that she opposed the move. In one missive she expressed fears concerning hostile Indians and slave revolts. On another occasion she offered a further objection. "What do you think of the state of public affairs if the war is carried on with the vigour which the English talk of? Do you think that we shall be as safe at H. as elsewhere, and do you suppose that it will affect the business that you propose carrying on there?" She insisted that it was not her intention to suggest difficulties, but it is apparent that she was disappointed when her husband finally decided to move the family to Henderson, although she attributed the disappointment to another. "My dear aunt," she wrote, "is very much disappointed at your determining to settle in Henderson. It will be certainly a severe trial to part with her again." Sarah announced her impending departure from Pittsburgh with obvious dread. "I endeavour to prepare myself for a wilderness and half savages except Mr. Audubon's family and a few others."[41]

Even under the best circumstances, Lucy's cousin evinced a penchant for chronic complaint. In Pittsburgh she had had a comfortable home, servants, and the Bakewells to look after her and the children. Even so Sarah complained that the house was difficult to care for, and that the servants were lazy and took liberties beyond their station. Indeed, her children seemed quite a trial and beyond her capacity to control. On one occasion when she was angered by some bit of childish behavior, Sarah declared that her children were ideally suited for life in Henderson because they, too, were incorrigible savages.[42]

Once in Henderson, Sarah found exactly what she expected to find—an uncivilized town occupied by ill-mannered, ill-bred persons who drank too much, bathed too little, spoke too loud with pronunciations just barely recognizable as English, and carried no-

41. Sarah Pears to Thomas Pears, July 16, August 13, August 20, 1814, all in Pears Papers.
42. Sarah Pears to Thomas Pears, June 19, August 20, October 13, 1814, all in Pears Papers.

tions about equality to unacceptable lengths. Each day she poured her complaints into Lucy's ears. Although Lucy had to listen, she gave a cool reception to Sarah's grumblings, and she was obviously annoyed at them.

Sarah could not understand Lucy's apparent acceptance of the rowdy conditions of frontier life. She felt that this must be affectation in one coming from a genteel background, or it was a capitulation to the way Audubon wanted to live. If John James had succumbed to the influence of the frontier, Sarah feared that her husband might be similarly afflicted. Perhaps her fears were justified, for with at least some folks in Henderson, Pears earned the reputation of being a drunkard. Pears denounced his detractors and insisted that the accusations were blatant lies. Nevertheless, it is curious that Pears seemed to attract character assassins. He himself commented on this phenomenon: "I had plenty of time for reflection—and my thoughts were not of the most agreeable nature, and I could not help blaming myself. There must be something wrong in that conduct which is always misrepresented, and on reviewing my past life I find that that has generally been my lot. In New York I was thought to be a Rake, at Wheat Hill I was represented to your uncle as a Gambler . . . and at Henderson I am a Drunkard."[43]

When Sarah discovered that she was expecting another child, she refused to give birth to the infant at Henderson and demanded that her husband forsake his partnership in the mill. Pears bowed to these wifely pressures, accepted a job with Benjamin Bakewell in Pittsburgh, and demanded that Tom and John James return the money he had invested in the mill. His demands came at a most inopportune time. John James and Tom had secured a lease on two hundred feet of riverfront in March, 1816, and construction of the mill was underway on that site.[44] They, therefore, had little capital to spare. However, Pears did receive his money, and probably all concerned were relieved at the departure of the Pearses. Certainly Lucy was.

Lucy's thoughts were occupied more pleasantly in the spring of

43. Thomas Pears to Sarah Pears, May 24, 27, June 3, 1816, all in Pears Papers.

44. Thomas Bakewell, "Autobiography," in Pears Papers; City of Henderson to Audubon and Bakewell, Lease, 277, in Deed Book C.

1816. The entire Audubon household swirled with activity preparing for Eliza's wedding.[45] Nicholas Berthoud's courtship had always pleased Lucy, and it was to her, John James, and Tom that Nicholas had come seeking approval for his plan to marry Eliza. Eliza's guardians gave him their warmest blessings, and they were delighted to learn that Eliza accepted his proposal. The Berthoud-Bakewell wedding was a splendid affair attended by folks from Shippingport, Louisville, and Henderson. Lucy participated in the wedding, joined the celebration, and was happy to see her younger sister's joy, and to know that she was married to a man of good family, imposing fortune, and large property holdings.

Hardly had Eliza been installed in the beautiful Berthoud home in Shippingport, when Lucy learned that another wedding was in the offing. Tom Bakewell had paid court to many young women, and relatives frequently reported that he was in love and that marriage was imminent. These predictions finally proved true when Tom married Elizabeth Rankin Page in Pittsburgh on July 27, 1816.[46] Elizabeth was the daugher of Benjamin Page, a business associate of Benjamin Bakewell. As soon as the wedding festivities were over, Tom returned to Henderson with his bride.

From the beginning Lucy was disappointed in the lady of Tom's choice, sensing that Elizabeth was going to be as discontented in Henderson as Sarah Pears had been. Her foreboding was soon justified. Elizabeth let it be known that she thought Henderson a dismal and backward place. She regarded Audubon as crude and Lucy as arrogant. By December she had convinced Tom to abandon the partnership and the mill venture. Indeed, Elizabeth was so disenchanted with the frontier that she left Tom in Henderson to put his business affairs in order while she went to Louisville to give birth to their first child and to await Tom's arrival. According to Tom:

> This place never having had any allurements for me, & still less *endearments* since I was married, as Elizabeth dislikes it very much, I have dissolved partnership with Mr. Audubon, he taking all the property and debts due to A & B, & agreeing to pay all their debts, for which I take

45. B. G. Bakewell, *Family Book of Bakewell*, 27.
46. Sarah Pears to Thomas Pears, October 23, 1814, in Pears Papers; B. G. Bakewell, *Family Book of Bakewell*, 27.

loss to about $5000, & he is to pay me $5500, after all the debts owing
by A & B are paid which sum of $5500 is to bear 20 pct per annum until
paid on the above condition. . . . As we are both liable for the debts
due by A & B, I have agreed to remain here & give my assistance to Mr.
A till 1st of July next & to let the business be carried on in the name of
the firm as usual.[47]

Interestingly, Lucy, Sarah, and Elizabeth were very much alike.
All were from socially prominent families. Each married a young
man who was unsuccessful in various business ventures. In search of
economic stability each couple had moved west of the mountains
where the women encountered the rigors of frontier living. Of the
three, only Lucy adjusted and found peace in these surroundings.
She did not abandon her background of culture and sophistication.
Indeed, it was her adherence to elitist decorum in the midst of the
wilderness that so infuriated Sarah and Elizabeth. Surely, they
thought, no one could maintain standards of good breeding while
living in such primitive surroundings. Yet not only did Lucy manage
to import a bit of the English estate into her log cabin but she did it
so well as to make both visitors feel inadequate, even inferior, because they could not make a similar adjustment. Neither Sarah nor
Elizabeth ever forgave the calm and self-assured Lucy Audubon.
    In justice to Sarah and Elizabeth, it should be noted that they
saw a contradiction in Lucy that they were unable to fathom.
To them she had to be one thing or the other—a genteel lady or a
rugged American frontier wife. Lucy was obviously a combination
of the two. She could master the most spirited horse, endure the
physical hardships of an eight-hundred-mile cross-country ride, enjoy slicing through the strong currents of the Ohio, putter about a
garden with muddy hands and frock, and yet she administered a
large household, cared for her children, supervised slaves, and met
the incessant demands of hospitality. It was exasperating to think
that this same woman could conduct herself in such a manner as to
make them feel socially inadequate.
    By 1817 the Audubons' economic situation had deteriorated con-
siderably. Sales at the store began to fall off sharply. When goods

47. Thomas W. Bakewell, "Audubon & Bakewell, Partners," 39.

were sold, it was increasingly difficult to collect money due. All the surplus capital that the Audubons possessed went to construct, equip, and keep the mill in operation. As the months passed, the Audubons' future came to depend upon the success of the mill. But when the mill became operable in 1817, the expected profits did not pour into the Audubons' coffers. Instead the mill continually needed more funds to stay in operation. John James went deeper and deeper into debt to keep the business and his financial future alive.[48]

Several factors contributed to the ultimate failure of the mill. The most obvious one was that the area around Henderson produced little wheat. Moreover, the demand for lumber in the vicinity was not sufficient to justify such a large investment. Years later, with the benefit of hindsight, Audubon wrote, "Well, up went the steam-mill at an enormous expense, in a country then as unfit for such a thing as it would be now for me to attempt to settle in the moon."[49]

The business inexperience of all those involved was yet another reason for the fiasco. Tom explained to his father:

> The Mill . . . has cost $5,000 more than it ought to have done owing to going through so many hands & so many different plans begun, & not finished together with the inexperience of the parties in that business. Mr. Prentice has an excellent head, but no hands—we have a very good Engine put up in a very slovenly imperfect manner which we are remedying by degrees ourselves. He is a capital man to prescribe, but not to administer—his advice & opinion in matters of his profession are invaluable but his execution worthless.[50]

Twice John James took in additional partners, such as Benjamin Page and Nicholas Berthoud, in an attempt to keep the mill operating. For some reason these two level-headed businessmen thought the mill had a chance of succeeding.[51]

During this time of economic stress, a more personal tragedy struck Lucy—she realized that her two-year-old daughter was dy-

48. *Ibid.*; Maria R. Audubon (ed.), *Audubon and His Journals*, I, 34.
49. Maria R. Audubon (ed.), *Audubon and His Journals*, I, 33.
50. Thomas W. Bakewell, "Audubon & Bakewell, Partners," 39–40.
51. Maria R. Audubon (ed.), *Audubon and His Journals*, I, 33–34.

ing. No nursing or care could save the child, who died in 1817. Lucy experienced the overpowering sense of loss and helplessness of a mother who watches a part of herself die. John James, too, felt the death of his infant daughter intensely. Hardly had they absorbed this blow when in 1818 news arrived from France that Jean Audubon was dead.[52]

Mounting debts and declining sales further compounded these personal tragedies in 1818. The "infernal" mill continued to drain Audubon's meager funds, and creditors began to demand the money owing them. Lucy and John James had nowhere to turn for help. They had exhausted their reserve funds and had borrowed or begged all that they could from family and friends. Nor could the Audubons expect any aid from the estate of Captain Audubon. Indeed, since his father's death John James had been bombarded with pleas for financial assistance from his family in France.[53]

To meet their obligations the Audubons began selling the property that they had acquired in Henderson. During the course of the year 1818, Lucy and John James sold twelve pieces of property, for which they received approximately seven thousand dollars.[54] They distributed this money among their creditors, who were little appeased by this token payment of debts long overdue.

The Panic of 1819 dislocated the economy of the whole country, but it had a particularly severe effect in the western states. In Kentucky many banks failed, and credit became exceedingly scarce. Henderson's first bank, which had opened for business in 1818, was one of the first victims of the panic. Like many other banks, it had issued notes without sufficient backing. Friends, like the Berthouds, or other partners could not or would not put any more funds into the mill. Tom was demanding the funds owed to him, while John James was, in turn, requesting Tom's assistance to help discharge the debts owed by Audubon & Bakewell. By the terms of the dissolved partnership, Tom was still liable for these debts, and he man-

52. *Ibid.*, 37–38; Eliza Berthoud to Sarah Pears, May 12, 1816, in Pears Papers: Herrick, *Audubon, the Naturalist*, I, 264; Lucy B. Audubon (ed.), *Life of John James Audubon*, 55.

53. Gabriel du Puigaudeau to John James Audubon, reproduced in Herrick, *Audubon, the Naturalist*, I, 266; Ford, *John James Audubon*, 102.

54. Deeds of Sale, John James Audubon, 462, 464, 465, 467, 468, 471, 516, all in Deed Book C, 4, 18, 20, 21, 84, all in Deed Book D.

aged to get together three thousand dollars toward their payment between 1818 and 1819.[55]

Prentice and Tom Bakewell had entered into a partnership for the purpose of constructing steamboats. Tom tried to help his brother-in-law by giving John James a note for $4,250 signed by Samuel Bowen and Company in Henderson. The note represented the price of the steamboat *Henderson* that Tom and Prentice had sold to Bowen. John James hoped to collect this money from Bowen or, preferably, to get the boat. Steam transport was revolutionizing travel for both goods and passengers on the river, and John James believed that with the vessel he could recoup his fortunes. But before he could take any action, Bowen disappeared down the Ohio in the *Henderson*, bound for New Orleans where he intended to sell the boat. Furious and desperate, John James took a skiff with two slaves as crewmen and chased the *Henderson* to New Orleans.[56]

Audubon arrived in New Orleans one day too late. On the previous day Bowen had surrendered the boat to "prior claimants." Thereupon, Audubon sought legal redress through the civil district court, claiming that he was the legal owner of the boat and that Bowen was guilty of fraud. The court dismissed the case on the grounds that it had no authority to trace the boat out of its jurisdiction. Angry and frustrated with his failure, Audubon publicly denounced Bowen at many of the taverns in the city. After venting his anger, John James sold the slaves and skiff and caught a steamer for Henderson where Bowen had already returned.[57]

During Audubon's absence Lucy had waited anxiously at home. She knew that he had left in a raging temper, and she feared that he might do something rash. However, she hoped that he would return with either the money or the boat. When she heard that Bowen was back in Henderson, Lucy knew that John James had been unsuccessful in his quest. Of greater concern was the news brought to her by Will and James Berthoud, who was visiting at the Audubon home. They informed Lucy that trouble was brewing. Bowen was

55. Workers of the Writers' Program (comps.), *Henderson: A Guide*, 34; Thomas W. Bakewell, "Audubon & Bakewell, Partners," 41.

56. Maria R. Audubon (ed.), *Audubon and His Journals*, I, 34; Arthur, *Audubon*, 84–85.

57. Arthur, *Audubon*, 84–85.

swaggering about town announcing that he would settle accounts with John James when he returned. Lucy had lived on the frontier long enough to know that differences were settled in a personal manner. The law had little to do with such matters.

When John James returned, Lucy, Will, and James Berthoud immediately warned him of Bowen's threats. Lucy said that his life was in danger and insisted that he carry a dagger. The precaution was soon justified when Bowen began walking back and forth before the Audubon house armed with a club.[58]

The encounter came quickly enough. On his way to the mill one morning Audubon was accosted by Bowen. Physically, John James was at a disadvantage. His right arm had been injured at the mill the day before and was supported by a sling. Audubon related the details: "I stood still, and he soon reached me. He complained of my conduct to him in New Orleans, and suddenly raising his bludgeon laid it about me. Though white with wrath, I spoke nor moved not till he had given me twelve severe blows, then, drawing my dagger with my left hand . . . I stabbed him and he instantly fell."[59]

Lucy was naturally thrown into a state of panic when her husband stumbled into the house, bleeding and disheveled from the clubbing, but she quickly regained her composure. She helped Will and Berthoud get John James into bed and set about dressing his wounds. Will and James stayed only long enough to learn what had happened. They then left to check on Bowen. Arriving at the scene of the fight, they found Bowen lying on the ground and bleeding from his wound. Will, Berthoud, and others placed him on a plank and carried him to his house. His wound was serious, and it was thought that Bowen would surely die.

News of the fight and Bowen's condition spread rapidly throughout the town. A crowd quickly converged upon the Audubon cabin, demanding that the knife-fighting Frenchman be horsewhipped. Inside the cabin Lucy, hovering over the figure of her semiconscious husband, heard the angry voices outside. According to Lucy's brother Will, the only thing that saved them from the vio-

---

58. Maria R. Audubon (ed.), *Audubon and His Journals*, I, 34.
59. *Ibid.*, I, 34–35.

lence of the mob was James Berthoud. "Berthoud's appearance and his appeal had such an electric effect on those roughs that they cooled down and looked at the grand old man as a spirit from another world."[60]

It had been a terrifying experience for Lucy. While he lay before her, bruised and battered, a mob was screaming for her husband's blood because he had wounded another man, perhaps mortally. Gifford and Woodhouse huddled together, fearful for their father and confused about the angry shouting outside. Will and the carpenter from the mill prepared guns to use in case Berthoud was unsuccessful in his attempt to calm the mob.

Once the crowd dispersed, the children and Audubon slept. That night Lucy may have sought comfort from James Berthoud, who understood mobs and their hatred of aristocrats. He remembered well the blood lust that descended upon France in the 1790s for all of his class. But more probably Lucy sat beside her husband's sleeping figure, consumed with fear about what the future held for her family. The happiness and security of their life in Henderson was crumbling.

Bowen did recover, and as soon as he was well enough, both parties appeared in court. John James was charged with assault, but the presiding judge, Henry P. Broadnax, ruled that he had acted in self-defense. Evidently, Bowen was known as a troublesome tough because after the trial the judge humorously reproached Audubon. "Mr. Audubon, you committed a serious offense, an exceedingly serious offense, sir—in failing to kill the damned rascal!" Indeed, Audubon was fortunate that Judge Broadnax heard the case. The judge had quite a reputation on the frontier. He was a native of Virginia, an aristocrat who had an exalted sense of the dignity of the court and a great contempt for meanness, rascality, and all low rowdyism.[61]

Another episode demonstrated that the reputation of the Audubons was dwindling in direct proportion to their financial decline

60. Arthur, Audubon, 87–88.
61. Ibid., 88; Harrison Taylor, Ohio County, Kentucky, in the Olden Days: A Series of Old Newspaper Sketches of Fragmentary History (Louisville, 1926), 21, 23, 24; Ann Coleman, The Life of John J. Crittendon with Selections from His Correspondence and Speeches (2 vols.; New York, 1970), I, 18; Keating, Audubon: The Kentucky Years, 76–77.

and that Audubon's efforts to reverse his financial plight were merely bringing his family closer to the bottom of the economic well. In 1819 a young Englishman, George Keats, a brother of the poet John Keats, and his wife Georgiana arrived in America hoping to better their fortune.[62] Coming to Louisville, they became friendly with Tom, who advised them to seek out John James in Henderson. Knowing that Keats had money to invest, Tom may have hoped that the Englishman would invest with his brother-in-law.

Audubon invited the young couple to stay in his home and soon he and Keats entered into a partnership. Surviving accounts differ as to exactly what Audubon and Keats planned to do. It is certain that John James received money from Keats, which he invested in a steamboat, but the facts beyond that are confused. According to Keats, John James swindled him, taking his money for the boat that Audubon knew was at the bottom of the river. But according to other accounts Audubon was unaware that the boat he had bought was submerged.[63] Given Audubon's tendency to plunge into any scheme that sounded promising and his naïveté in regard to business matters, it is likely that he himself was a victim of somebody's chicanery. However, George was convinced that Audubon had been dishonest and complained bitterly about this "Yankee trick" to his brother John.

Keats considered suing Audubon to recover his money but gave up the plan on learning of Audubon's desperate economic situation. From England John Keats expressed what many in Henderson thought, "I cannot help thinking Mr. Audubon a dishonest man. Why did he make you believe that he was a Man of Property?"[64] Lucy came in for her share of unpleasantness with their new guests and partners. Georgiana shared the attitude of Elizabeth Bakewell and Sarah Pears toward Henderson and the Audubons. She thought that Lucy was as dishonest as her husband, representing herself as

---

62. Keating, *Audubon: The Kentucky Years*, 74; Arthur, *Audubon*, 91.

63. Ford, *John James Audubon*, 104; John Gilmer Speed (ed.), *The Letters and Poems of John Keats* (3 vols.; New York, 1883), I, 79, 103; Arthur, *Audubon*, 91–92; Keating, *Audubon: The Kentucky Years*, 75. Keating believes that the boat in question was the one Bowen took to New Orleans.

64. Maurice B. Forman (ed.), *The Letters of John Keats*, 3rd ed. (New York, 1947), 399.

an aristocrat and putting on "airs." With relief, the Audubons watched the indignant couple depart for Louisville.

By the summer of 1819 creditors would no longer wait for payment long overdue. On July 13 Lucy and John James left their home and walked for the last time to the office of their lawyer, one A. Barbour. During the previous year Lucy had come to the same office many times to sign deeds of sale. Nicholas Berthoud met the Audubons when they arrived and the business of reading the deed began. Lucy sat numbly listening as the attorney's voice droned on, saying that Nicholas was purchasing Audubon's share of the mill for $14,000. When he finished reading, Lucy signed her name beneath Audubon's and the attorney began reading the second deed. Nicholas purchased seven mulatto slaves for $4,450. Lucy signed again. For a third time the attorney's dry voice pierced the gloomy silence. Lucy heard the dispassionate legal description of her own home being read. She listened to the list of all the furnishings within the home being ticked off. Every item was going to go, from the smallest kitchen utensil to the goose feather beds and, on the outside, all of the geese, cattle, and hogs. The total cost to Nicholas was $7,000.[65] Lucy's grief was compounded by the realization that the money was not nearly sufficient to satisfy their numerous creditors.

Lucy knew the great heights to which Audubon's optimism could carry him, and now she witnessed the great depths of despair to which he could plunge. She tried to comfort her husband even though her spirits were crippled by the harsh reality of their impoverishment. She was careful to maintain a cheerful and confident face. Yet beneath the outward calm, Audubon knew that Lucy "felt the pangs of our misfortunes perhaps more heavily than I, but never for an hour lost her courage; her brave and cheerful spirit accepted all, and no reproaches from her beloved lips ever wounded my heart." Musing more deeply about his wife during this dismal period, Audubon wrote, "with her was I not always rich?"[66]

His gratitude for Lucy's understanding could not alter the shame of failure that he felt. After disbursing the money received from

65. Deeds of Sale, John James Audubon to Nicholas Berthoud, 92, 145, 151, 152, 328, all in Deed Book D.
66. Maria R. Audubon (ed.), *Audubon and His Journals*, I, 35.

Nicholas Berthoud, Audubon had nothing with which to support his family. Hoping to find a job, he set out for Louisville, carrying his gun and his portfolio, his only remaining possessions. John James described that lonely journey—the first step on the troubled odyssey of the Audubons: "Without a dollar in the world, bereft of all revenues. . . . I left my dear log house, my delightful garden and orchards with the heaviest of burdens, a heavy heart, and turned my face toward Louisville. This was the saddest of all my journeys,— the only time in my life when the Wild Turkeys that so often crossed my path, and the thousands of lesser birds that enlivened the woods and the prairies, all looked like enemies, and I turned my eyes from them, as if I could have wished that they had never existed."[67]

67. *Ibid.*, 47.

CHAPTER V

An Ultimatum

W hile Audubon was absent in Louisville, Lucy remained in Henderson contemplating the sad state of the family's fortunes. She wandered about the house, ran her fingers over the keyboard of the pianoforte, polished dishes that had been in the Bakewell family for generations. These things that had been part of her life now belonged to someone else. At other times she watched her children romping through the garden and orchards, and no doubt her thoughts turned occasionally to the child who grew within her womb. What kind of life would it have in the bleak economic crisis that loomed ahead for the Audubons?

The humiliation and loss of respect within the community was particularly difficult for Lucy to.cope with. She had always been proud and self-confident, secure in her elitist status. Now she had to face the scorn and contempt of the Henderson community, which naturally took delight in the fall of the mighty. She soon learned that impoverishment could impose further indignities upon the family. News arrived from Louisville that John James had been arrested for debt and placed in jail. Without hesitating, although she was soon to deliver another child, Lucy packed the few belongings left to the family and searched for transportation to Louisville. Hearing of her determination to leave, Senator Isham Talbot sent his coach to take Lucy and her children to Audubon.[1]

---

1. Arthur, *Audubon*, 94; Maria R. Audubon (ed.), *Audubon and His Journals*, I, 36; Ford, *John James Audubon*, 106; Corning (ed.), *Letters of Audubon*, II, 15.

As she left Henderson, Lucy had no way of knowing how important her years there had been. During this time, she and John James had shared happiness and prosperity, disappointment and tragedy—experiences that bound them more closely and gave their marriage a firm basis that would stand them in good stead in the future. By the time Lucy arrived in Louisville, John James was out of jail. A friend, Judge Fortunatus Cosby, had advised him to file a petition declaring bankruptcy, and this had effected his release.[2] The Audubons went to Shippingport and the home of Eliza and Nicholas Berthoud. Under the roof of charitable relatives, John James wrestled with the problem of how to make a living for his family.

Audubon asked Nicholas and Tom to find him a clerical post on a river steamer, but they refused to help him. Apparently, Nicholas and Tom believed his request to be a ploy that would allow him to disappear leaving the responsibility of caring for his family to others. When other attempts to secure employment also failed, Audubon decided to rely upon his artistic talents to meet the needs of his family. He advertised for sitters and pupils and received a favorable response. In his journal John James described his initial success and the often morbid chores that were involved in his work. "I at once undertook to take portraits of the human 'head divine,' in black chalk, and . . . succeeded admirably. In the course of a few weeks I had as much work to do as I could possibly wish. . . . I was sent for four miles in the country, to take likenesses of persons on their death-beds, and so high did my reputation suddenly rise, as the best delineator of heads in that vicinity, that a clergyman residing at Louisville . . . had his dead child disinterred, to procure a fac-simile of his face."[3]

Audubon was soon able to rent a small house in Louisville for his family. However, their stay in Shippingport had to be prolonged when Lucy gave birth to a little girl who was named Rosa after Audubon's half sister. Like her sister before her, Rosa was an extremely delicate and sickly child. Shortly after her birth, Lucy and the in-

2. Corning (ed.), *Letters of Audubon*, II, 15; Ford, *John James Audubon*, 106.
3. Maria R. Audubon (ed.), *Audubon and His Journals*, I, 36; Ford, *John James Audubon*, 109.

fant were both stricken with fever that spread in Louisville and the surrounding area.[4]

Lucy soon recovered her health, but she was finding out that the respect she had formerly enjoyed was not so easily regained, even in her own family. On leaving Henderson, she had undoubtedly looked forward to receiving understanding and comfort from her brother Tom and sister Eliza. They and Nicholas Berthoud did welcome her; yet they obviously had the same critical view of her and John James that had prevailed in the Henderson community. Most of their recriminations were directed at Audubon. His cavalier delight in social intercourse and lightness of spirit, which they had once admired, now were seen as serious flaws in his character. Tom, Eliza, and Nicholas came to think of him as shiftless and irresponsible. They believed that his forest wanderings and incessant sketching had caused his financial downfall. Although they did not blame Lucy for what had happened, they made it clear that she and her children were objects of pity. For a woman of fierce pride who denied herself the luxury of self-pity, such sentiments from her own family were infuriating and painful. Perhaps a fellow countrywoman best expressed what Lucy experienced when she noted how difficult it was for a woman to mix with former equals after her fortunes were reversed. "How cutting is the contempt she meets with!—A young mind looks round for love and friendship; but love and friendship fly from poverty: expect them not if you are poor!"[5]

There were at least two people who thought that the Audubons had been dealt their just rewards. Tom's wife Elizabeth and Georgiana Keats, who was staying with the Bakewells awaiting her husband's return from England, hoped that Lucy Audubon would be humbled by financial disaster and that she would recognize her proper social station. They were irritated when Lucy showed no signs of shame. Georgiana complained to her brother-in-law that Lucy was as uppity as ever. John Keats replied:

    4. Ford, *John James Audubon*, 107.
    5. *Ibid.*, 106–107; Thomas W. Bakewell, "Audubon & Bakewell, Partners," 42; Wollstonecraft, *Thoughts on the Education of Daughters*, 73–74; Keating, *Audubon: The Kentucky Years*, 77.

I was surprised to hear of the State of Society at Louisville, [it] seems you are just as ridiculous there as we are here—threepenny parties, half penny Dances—the best thing I have heard of is your shooting. . . . Give my Compliments to Mrs Audubon and tell her I cannot think her either good looking or honest—Tell Mr Audubon he's a fool. . . . If the American Ladies are worse than the English they must be very bad. . . . You know a good number of English Ladies what encomium could you give of half a dozen of them—the greater part seem to me downright American. I have known more than one Mrs Audubon their affectation of fashion and politeness cannot transcend ours.[6]

There seemed to be no end to the bad fortune of the Audubons. John James's fling at making a living as an artist soon came to naught—the number of students dwindled, and the supply of people willing to pay five dollars for a portrait was exhausted. Then personal tragedy struck them again. The seven-month-old infant Rosa died. The death of two daughters was difficult for Lucy to bear. More than a year later she expressed the hope that her girls were with "their grandmother in happier regions."[7]

At this critical juncture John James learned from the Tarascons of Shippingport that the Western Museum of Cincinnati College needed a taxidermist to stuff birds and fish and was offering a salary of $125 a month. John James acquired a number of letters of recommendation and departed for Cincinnati to seek the position, while Lucy and the children remained in Kentucky. Dr. Daniel Drake, the founder of the museum, hired Audubon. As soon as he was able to, John James rented a small, cheaply furnished house and sent for his wife and sons.[8] Lucy had been anxiously awaiting his summons. She was happy to be off, away from the pitying eyes of her well-meaning family. The news that Audubon had a regular job and regular pay revived her hopes for the future.

The Audubons found Cincinnati a pleasant place in which to

6. Forman (ed.), *Letters of Keats*, 451, 453–54.

7. Maria R. Audubon (ed.), *Audubon and His Journals*, I, 37; Lucy Audubon to Miss Gifford, April 1, 1821, in Audubon Collection.

8. Lucy Audubon to Miss Gifford, April 1, 1821, in Audubon Collection; Maria R. Audubon (ed.) *Audubon and His Journals*, I, 37; Ford, *John James Audubon*, 111; Robert Todd to William Lytle, February 12, 1820, in William Lytle Papers, the Cincinnati Historical Society.

live—urban and cosmopolitan, with a population in excess of ten thousand people in 1820. Another sojourner who passed through the town during the same period described Cincinnati:

> Cincinnati is no sooner seen than the importance of the town is perceived. A large steam grist mill, three large steam boats on the stocks, and two more on the Kentucky side of the river, and a large ferry boat, wrought by horses, were the first objects which attracted my attention. The beach is lined with keel boats, large arks for carrying produce, family boats, and rafts of timber. On shore the utmost bustle prevails, with drays carrying imported goods, salt, iron, and timber, up to the town, and in bringing down pork, flour, &C. to be put aboard of boats for New Orleans.

The activity belied the economic crisis that gripped the entire country. The same traveler described the town. "The houses are nearly all of brick and timber: about two hundred new ones have been built in the course of the year. Merchants' shops are numerous, and well frequented. The noise of wheel carriages in the streets, and of the carpenter, the blacksmith, and the cooper, make a busy din. Such an active scene I never expected to see amongst the back woods."[9]

The busy din only served to make the Audubons more conscious of their economic plight. They lived modestly. Lucy learned to shop for bargains, and John James also did his part to keep the expenses down. The low cost of living in Cincinnati helped the Audubons to adjust to pinching pennies. John James wrote, "Our living here . . . is extremely moderate; the markets are well supplied and cheap, beef only two and a half cents a pound, and I am able to provide a good deal myself; Partridges are frequently in the streets, and I can shoot Wild Turkeys within a mile or so; Squirrels and Woodcock are very abundant in the season, and fish always easily caught."[10]

Providing a bountiful table might be easy, but paying the rent and buying other essentials was something else. Lucy and John James quickly realized that the newly established museum was not able to meet Audubon's monthly salary. In fact, Audubon was dis-

9. James Flint, "Letters from America," 238–39, 149, 150.
10. Maria R. Audubon (ed.), *Audubon and His Journals*, I, 49.

missed from the museum in April with a promise that his back wages would soon be paid. In order to augment his income, John James obtained a position as a drawing and painting instructor at two select schools for young ladies.[11] However, he did not long maintain his connection with these schools. Instead, he advertised that he would take students on his own. The tuition brought in from these students, stretched out by Lucy's careful management, allowed the Audubons to survive.

In his memoirs Will Bakewell mentioned that the world owed a debt of gratitude to the "infernal" mill in Henderson. He meant that the Audubon family would have been content to live their lives in the riverfront hamlet had not poverty and disgrace forced them to leave and caused Audubon to turn to painting for a live-lihood. Before coming to Cincinnati, Lucy and John James had viewed his artistic endeavors as a form of recreation. They had certainly not realized the potential value of Audubon's bird portfolio. In Cincinnati the worth of the collection of drawings was brought home to them. Several factors encouraged Lucy and John James to reappraise the drawings. The government-sponsored Rocky Mountain expedition led by Stephen Long stopped in Cincinnati and visited the museum. Thomas Say accompanied Long, and he and Long were shown Audubon's collection, probably by Dr. Drake. In later years John James recalled the importance of having his work praised by these men. "The expedition of Major Long passed through the city . . . and well do I recollect how he, Messrs. T. Peal, Thomas Say, and others stared at my drawings of birds at that time."[12]

At about the same time, Dr. Drake, in a lecture at Cincinnati College, gave Audubon's drawings public recognition. Almost surely both John James and Lucy were in the audience. Even if they were not, they heard that Drake had compared Audubon's work

11. Arthur, *Audubon*, 96–97; Dorothy Gillespie, "John James Audubon: Relations of the Naturalist with the Western Museum at Cincinnati," Cincinnati Society of Natural History, *Ornithology Leaflet*, No. 2 (February 26, 1937), 3.

12. William Bakewell, Memoirs, cited in Arthur, *Audubon*, 81; Lucy Audubon to Miss Gifford, April 1, 1821, in Audubon Collection; Maria R. Audubon (ed.), *Audubon and His Journals*, I, 37.

with that of Alexander Wilson, whom the Audubons had met in Louisville in 1810 and who was now recognized as the leading ornithologist in the country:

> It would be an act of injustice to speak of our ornithology, without connecting with it the name of Alexander Wilson. . . . His labors may have nearly completed the ornithology of the middle Atlantic states, but must necessarily have left that of the western imperfect. . . . As a proof of this supposition it may be stated that Mr. Audubon, one of the artists attached to the museum, who has drawn, from nature, in colored crayons, several hundred species of American birds, has, in his portfolio, a large number that are not figured in Mr. Wilson's work, and which do not seem to have been recognized by any naturalist.[13]

Ten years before, John James had escorted Wilson to his quarters at the Indian Queen to meet Lucy. Wilson had seemed little more than an itinerant salesman seeking subscriptions to his work. Now both John James and Lucy realized that he was a famous man, and moreover, that he had turned drawing birds into a profitable venture. They must have been particularly interested to learn that Wilson's work was regarded as being far from definitive. They recalled, too, that Robert Todd, who had written Audubon a letter of recommendation for the position at the museum, noted a similarity between Audubon's collection and that of Alexander Wilson.[14]

It was at this time that Lucy first assumed the lion's share of responsibility for earning the family living. The climate of opinion was becoming increasingly hostile to working females, but teaching, one of the few areas open to women, was incorporated into the cult of domesticity. In her small home Lucy began privately instructing a group of students in the usual elementary subjects and some of them in music. In the process, she made sure that her own children were educated, clothed, and properly cared for.[15]

John James also gave lessons—in painting—yet once he began to

---

13. Quoted in Adams, *John James Audubon*, 194–95.
14. Robert Todd to William Lytle, February 12, 1820, in Lytle Papers.
15. Arthur, *Audubon*, 96; Harris, *Beyond Her Sphere*, 39, 60; Elisabeth Dexter, *Career Women of America, 1776–1840* (Francestown, N.H., 1950), 219; John Demos, "The American Family in Past Time," *American Scholar*, XLIII (Summer, 1974), 433–34; Aileen S. Kraditor (ed.), *Up from the Pedestal: Selected Writings in the History of American Feminism* (New York, 1968), 39–40.

look upon his drawings and the time spent in the forest as not only enjoyable but the first step on the return journey to economic stability, he became undependable. Unlike Lucy, he could not be trusted to meet class every day or to collect his tuition. When Audubon did meet class, it was with the attitude of a master, impatient and bored with those who had no talent. He did, however, find one student with extraordinary abilities. Joseph Mason, a young lad of thirteen, enrolled under Audubon to study lettering and sign painting.[16] John James discovered that Joseph was interested in botany. They became constant companions and ranged the woods around Cincinnati. Audubon drew, and Joseph embellished his drawings with whatever flower, plant, shrub, or tree best suited the bird represented. Audubon was delighted to have found such a talented youth to improve the beauty of his work.

The Audubons realized that if his work were ever to be published, John James would have to find and paint additional specimens. It would be necessary for him to travel. They therefore decided that Lucy would remain in Cincinnati, teaching to support herself and their sons and trying to collect the money due Audubon from the museum.[17] Meanwhile, Audubon would travel downriver to New Orleans, where he would have open to him a vast expanse of country that had never been exploited by any other naturalist. John James assured Lucy that this course of action would rescue them from their poverty and disgrace.

Audubon persuaded Joseph's father to allow the youngster to accompany him. He left the meager funds that remained in the Audubon coffers for Lucy and made arrangements with Captain Jacob Aumack to travel downriver on his boat without paying a fare. Instead, John James was to serve as hunter for the vessel, providing fresh game for all aboard during the course of the trip. Joseph, for his part, was to perform various cooking and cleaning chores on the boat to pay his passage.[18]

On October 12, 1820, Lucy watched as John James stooped to

16. See Charlie May Simon, *Joseph Mason: Apprentice to Audubon* (New York, 1946).
17. Ford, *John James Audubon*, 113; Lucy Audubon to Miss Gifford, April 1, 1821, in Audubon Collection.
18. Arthur, *John James Audubon*, 99; Ford, *John James Audubon*, 113.

embrace Gifford and Woodhouse. His large frame dwarfed the willowy youngsters. She listened as he told them of his love and of his reliance upon them to care for her. Then he was embracing her, and perhaps to keep her spirits up, she found herself telling him to remember to shave and to make sure that his buckskins were kept clean and properly mended.[19] Then he was gone. She stood flanked by her small sons. Together they waved and watched until the boat was out of sight.

Lucy expected John James to be gone for about seven months; he was gone for fourteen. During his absence events produced a significant change in Lucy. For the first time in her life she had to rely upon her own wits to support herself and her sons. She quickly realized that she had underestimated the task. She had too few students, and at times it was difficult to collect the tuition owed her. Even bare essentials, such as nourishing food for her children, became a problem to provide. At least her husband's skill as a hunter had always meant a bountiful table. Meals for Lucy, Gifford, and Woodhouse were now scanty. Lucy turned her attention to the museum, determined to collect the salary due John James. Her situation became so desperate, her insistence so effective, that she managed at last to collect the back wages owed her husband. With these funds and fees from a few students Lucy paid the rent and fed and clothed her sons. Benjamin Bakewell, who spent two weeks with Lucy in Cincinnati, alleviated some of her economic difficulties.[20]

The process of learning to cope with poverty took a terrible toll on Lucy. She began to sulk and brood over her unfortunate lot. Even though she had agreed to remain behind, Lucy now began to resent being left alone to handle a situation for which she was unprepared. Indeed, she began to blame John James for leaving her with such a weighty responsibility. Because she had agreed to it, she could not complain of the separation, although it was probably the root of her discontent. Instead, she complained of poverty.

One day while traveling downriver, Audubon looked at a pic-

19. Howard Corning (ed.), *Journal of John James Audubon Made During His Trip to New Orleans in 1820–1821* (Boston, 1929), 32; Ford, *John James Audubon*, 114.

20. Ford, *John James Audubon*, 116; Lucy Audubon to Miss Gifford, April 1, 1821, in Audubon Collection; Corning (ed.), *Journal Made During His Trip*, 120.

ture of Lucy and had a premonition that all was not well with his wife and family. After arriving in New Orleans he had a more concrete indication that something was wrong. Audubon and Nicholas Berthoud, whom he met in Natchez and with whom he traveled to New Orleans, went to the post office. There Nicholas picked up a letter from Lucy and a pair of gloves that she had made for him. For John James there was nothing. Shortly afterward Audubon received two letters from Lucy. One made him despondent, while the other "ruffled" his spirits.[21] In both instances Lucy complained about the economic difficulties she was experiencing. A Lucy Audubon who complained was almost a stranger to John James.

By the end of January, John James had accumulated about $300 in fees paid for portraits. He purchased a set of queensware for Lucy and sent her this present along with $270. Throughout his long absence Audubon sent Lucy money and other items whenever possible, but he never earned enough to improve her situation appreciably. In February, when Nicholas Berthoud left New Orleans for Kentucky, he carried with him a number of Audubon's latest bird drawings for Lucy's inspection.[22]

While John James added sketches to the portfolio and drew portraits to earn a living for himself and Joseph, Lucy had decided to leave Cincinnati. The precise date of her departure is unknown, but she arrived in Shippingport at the Berthoud home sometime in late January or early February, 1821. Lucy returned to Kentucky upon Eliza's invitation. Evidently, she had little choice but to swallow her pride and to retreat to the security of her family.[23]

Disheartened with the present and pessimistic about the future, Lucy could only take pleasure in the past. To her cousin she wrote, "It is now a long time since I heard from you though I have written several times without a reply a circumstance which is a source of grief to me; for with my years increases my attachment to old friends and the early scenes of my youth, and now I see the walks and favorite shops I used to frequent in happier times as plainly before me as if no time had elapsed since I last had them." The death

21. Corning (ed.), *Journal Made During His Trip*, 41–42, 112, 114, 120.
22. *Ibid.*, 121, 124.
23. Lucy Audubon to Miss Gifford, April 1, 1821, in Audubon Collection.

of Lucy's father at Fatland Ford gave even sharper focus to Lucy's nostalgic thoughts about the past and better times. In addition, she was still preoccupied with her economic plight. "I am now with my two boys Gifford and Woodhouse at my sister Eliza's," she wrote, "but I expect soon either to go to housekeeping here or return for economy sake to Cincinnati which is a cheaper place. My two children occupy nearly the whole of my time, for I educate them myself." [24]

In this letter Lucy's unhappiness was readily apparent. It is interesting, therefore, that she did not post the letter directly to England, but forwarded it to New Orleans so Audubon could read it and add a postscript. John James saw from it that Lucy's dejection was so great that she did not hesitate to communicate it to others in her family. Even though she had discussed their hope that, once completed, his ornithological study would be published in England, she seemed to refer to it only in passing before harking back to the happy days of her youth. [25]

There was little despondency in her letters to John James. Instead, the missives took on an increasingly sharp and impatient tone. Living with her family and observing the security and success of Nicholas, Will, and even Tom, Lucy grew increasingly bitter over her own situation. The constant condolences of her family merely heightened her resentment. She so resented Tom's patronizing attitude when he condescended to offer her and her sons a home that she refused. [26] It rankled that he had survived financially while the Audubons had not. Even so, the impatience, even hostility, exhibited by some members of her family toward John James seemed to rub off on Lucy. And soon John James himself gave her reason to believe that her family might be correct in assuming that he was shirking his family responsibilities.

On his way to New Orleans, John James learned of plans for an

24. *Ibid.*
25. *Ibid.*
26. John James Audubon Journal, May 23, 1821, in John James Audubon Papers, American Philosophical Society Library, Philadelphia. Journal entries for May 23, 24, 31, and June 1, 1821 are written in letter form and were mailed to Lucy as such.

expedition to explore the Red River. As early as January he began
writing to Lucy about his desire to join the expedition. "After
Breakfast We left the Post of Arkansas with a Wish to see the Country above, and so *Strong* is My Anthusiasm to Enlarge the Ornithological Knowledge of My Country that I felt as if I wish Myself
Rich again and thereby able to Leave My Family for a Couple of
years."[27] Lucy heard more of Audubon's ambitions to accompany
the expedition from Nicholas when the latter returned from New
Orleans. Nicholas probably added that he had refused to assist his
brother-in-law in his efforts to join the expedition.

On March 21, 1821, Audubon read in a New Orleans newspaper
that an expedition was due to leave Natchitoches during the year to
"run the Line of Division" delineating the new territory acquired
from Spain under the terms of the Adams-Onis Treaty. Audubon
immediately set about writing to the president, to congressmen that
he thought might have influence, and to Nicholas in an attempt to
"procure an Appointment as Draftsman for this So Long Wished for
Journey. . . . full of My plans I went home & Wrote to N Berthoud
to request his Imediate Assistance—Walked out in the afternoon
seeing Nothing but hundreds of New Birds, in Imagination and supposed Myself often on the Journey."[28]

As the months passed, it became increasingly evident to Lucy
that she was no longer first with her husband. Expeditions and wanderings, drawings and birds had supplanted her and the boys. This
she could not bear. If John James went on the Pacific expedition,
she would be forced to remain the breadwinner. Lucy warned him
that, if he continued to speak of it, she would not carry on alone
any longer. She asked if he had forgotten that he had an obligation
to help send Gifford to school in Lexington, and she reminded him
that they had a younger son who was difficult to raise without a father's help. Calling his attention to the ill effects of the whole ordeal of separation, Lucy told him that she had grown thin and felt
too run-down even to seek comfort in the music she so dearly
loved. Although Lucy said that she could not carry on alone, she

27. Corning (ed.), *Journal Made During His Trip*, 71.
28. *Ibid.*, 137–39.

steadfastly maintained that she preferred Audubon to go anywhere rather than return to Kentucky defeated. She would not have him return to her in need, nor would she go to New Orleans to join him until he could promise her financial security.[29]

Lucy's ultimatum indicates how deeply her pride had been wounded by economic adversity. As much as she needed her husband, she refused to endure the further humiliation of having John James return to her clothed in failure. In Kentucky, Lucy had at least the security of a roof over her head. If she went to New Orleans, she thought, it was quite likely that Audubon would leave her alone in a strange city to fend for herself and the boys while he went off on some expedition. She preferred to depend upon her family despite their pitying attitude.

John James was staggered by Lucy's angry letter, and then, before he could respond to the first, another message came downriver. Lucy again demanded that he not return to her in need and, further, that he send her money, which she needed badly. She also upbraided him for the recent attacks he had made upon her family, reminding him that the Berthouds and Uncle Benjamin had been especially good friends.[30]

Audubon's response was a curious blend of anger, love, and unrealistic philosophy. He demonstrated an uncanny ability to turn the entire situation around. In his view, Lucy had forsaken him, was disloyal, and lacked courage. Giving her a lecture on courage, he wrote:

> When I arrived I knew not how long I might remain, and had no Models, and from Week to Week expected to go Else where—certainly I have lost a great deal Not to have one.
>
>   Thou art not it seems daring as I am about Leaving one place to go to another without the *Means*, I am sorry for that, I never now will fear *Want* as long as I am Well, and God will Grant me that as I have received from Nature My Little talents—I would dare go to England Without *one Cent*, one single Letter of Introduction to any one, and on Landing would Make Shillings or Pence if I could not Make More but no doubt I Would Make *enough*.

29. Audubon Journal, May 31, 1821.
30. *Ibid.*

On the subject of education and the children Audubon made it clear that his career came first and that formal schooling was not essential:

> If I do not go to England in the Course of Twelve Month We will send *Victor* (do call him) to Lexington College—hope My Dearest friend that our sweet Woodhouse will lose the habits that makes thee at present fear he has not the Natural gifts about him. . . . but he is yet a boy and has not had the opportunities of Victor to Improve, The Latter Was thy only attention for some years before John required any—I will agree with thee that the educating of children is perplexing, but how sweet the recompense, to the Parents when brought up by themselves only, it is rendered Two fold.

In the course of his lengthy discourse, John James also loosed his considerable romantic charm. "Dear girl how much I wish to press thee to My Bosom." Thanking her for a pair of suspenders, John James revealed that his Gallic blood still ran warm with desire for Lucy: "I have received a good pair of Suspenders, but thou does not say that they are from thy hands, I hope they are; I am so much of a Lover *yet* that every time I will touch them I think & bless the Maker-thank thee Sweet Girl for them." Of Lucy's attachment to her family, especially Eliza and Nicholas, Audubon asked, "Why Lucy Do you Not *Cling* to your better friend your husband—Not to boast of my *Intentions* any More toward thy happiness I will Merely say that I am afraid *for thee*, We Would be better Much better, happier: If you have not wrote to Your Uncle *do not*. I want No ones help but those who are not *quite* so engaged about their Business." In another letter he was particularly vigorous in his denunciation of Nicholas. "Mr. B. according to thy way of thinking has *done Wonders* for us, and according to My way of thinking he has acted *indeed* Wonderfully—but . . . his silence on the serious aid I have been fool enough to ask of him since I have *fooled* what I had—Gaggs me." Finally, John James responded to Lucy's warning that he not return to Kentucky in need with a threat of his own: "Your great desire that I Should Stay away is I must acknowledge very unexpected—If you Can bear to have me go [on] a Voyage of at Least Three Years without Wishing to see me before—I cannot help thinking that Lucy probably would be better pleased should I *Never* return—And so it May be." But his anger and hurt feelings eased enough for him to apologize before closing the letter. "My Dearest Girl I am sorry of the Last part I wrote yesterday. . . . I love thee so dearly, I feel it so powerfully, that I cannot bear any thing from thee that as the appearance of Coolness."[31]

Although Lucy never hinted at it, there was another reason for the acid reminder to John James, that he was both husband and father. Lucy Audubon was too feminine not to have been irritated by reports that John James was paying court to the Creole beauties of New Orleans. Her only consolation, small as it must have been, was that John James sent her a "word for word" account of his involvement with an "extra-ordinary Femelle."[32] Audubon's discourse ran on for eight pages—each page a prick to Lucy's feminine vanity, a spark to ignite jealousy, and a tribute to Audubon's naïveté.

The saga of the "Fair Incognito" began one day when he was approached by a graceful young woman, her Creole mystique accentuated by the flowing veils that concealed what promised to be a beautiful face. After quizzing him about his credentials as an artist the young woman whispered an address and told him to meet her there in thirty minutes. Audubon fumbled for a pencil and scribbled down the street and number. The young woman cautioned him not to follow her immediately.

After she disappeared John James glanced at the address, and while still rather befuddled by the bold approach and the mysterious deep-throated whispers, he walked toward the rendezvous. Arriving at the house sooner than instructed, he retreated to a nearby bookstore where he dallied for a time. At the appointed hour he returned to the house and ascended the stairs. Greatly affected, Audubon told Lucy of the meeting, "I walked upstairs I saw her apparently waiting 'I am glad you have come, walk in quickly.' My feelings became so agitated, that I trembled like a Leaf—this she perceived, [and] Shut the door with a double lock and throwing her veil back showed me one of the most beautiful faces, I ever saw." In addition to exceptional beauty, he wrote, the woman had the

31. Audubon Journal, May 23, 31, June 1, 1821.
32. Audubon Journal, May 23, 1821.

"smile of an angel" and a voice soft, low, and beguiling. However, John James, by his own description, embodied complete innocence, often blushing and fluctuating between a mumble and a chronic loss of breath.[33]

After inquiring as to his marital status, ascertaining that his wife was not in New Orleans, quizzing him about the fees he charged for drawing likenesses, she demanded that he forever maintain the confidence of her name (if he should learn it), and her residence. Audubon assured her that he would keep this information secret. It was then that the young woman made a request that shocked Audubon. Her dark eyes steadily fixed on the Frenchman, she inquired, "have you ever Drawn a full figure?" Nervously, Audubon replied yes. Her steady gaze held as she shot back, "Naked?" Audubon froze. "Had I been shot with a 48 pounder through the Heart my articulating Powers could not have been more suddenly stopped." His momentary incoherence fled when the soft voice persisted, "Well why do you not answer[?]" John James mumbled a simple yes. Then the beautiful young woman rose and paced across the room several times. Before Audubon could recover, she sat down and continued calmly, "I want you to draw my Likeness and the whole of my form Naked but as I think you cannot work now, leave your Port Folio and return in one hour be silent."[34]

According to Audubon, the woman had judged his feelings perfectly. He hurried from the apartment looking for all the world like a thief, half running, half walking, and looking over his shoulder. An hour later he returned and began to sketch his disrobed subject. When Lucy came to his description of these sessions she must have been stunned, but Audubon's ego spared her no detail.

> When drawing hirelings in company with 20 more I never cared but for a good outline, but Shut up with a beautifull young Woman as much a Stranger to me as I was to her, I could not well reconcile all the feelings that were necessary to draw well, without mingling with them some of a very different Nature—
> Yet I drew the curtains and saw this Beauty.
> For ten days at the exception of One Sunday, that She went out of

33. *Ibid.*
34. *Ibid.*

the City, I had the pleasure of this beautiful woman's Company about one hour Naked, and Two talking on diferent subjects, She admired My work more every day at least was pleased to Say so, and on the 5th sitting she worked herself in a style much superior to Mine."[35]

As the narrative drew to a close, Lucy must have been especially vexed by her husband's evident regret that his relationship with the "fair incognito" ended with only the recompenses of a "delightful kiss" and a gun worth $125. John James lamented, "She never ask me to go see her when we parted, I have tried several times in vain, the Servants allways saying 'Madame is absent.' I have felt a great desire to see the Drawing since to Judge of it as I allways can do best after some time."[36]

Audubon's profuse praise of another woman's beauty evoked both pain and anger in Lucy. Yet it would be far too simplistic to attribute Lucy's reaction to simple jealousy. When she was angry, Lucy usually expressed her grievances clearly, but never once did she reproach Audubon about the Creole beauty. Lucy knew that John James was flirtatious, that he had a keen eye for feminine charms, and that women found him very attractive. It was not Audubon's interest in pretty women that Lucy feared, but his obvious preoccupation with exploring expeditions, new birds, and new drawings. These were the lures that were drawing Audubon's attention away from his wife and family.

However, in justice to Audubon, it must be noted that he himself was experiencing great difficulties while he was in New Orleans that made it impossible for him to better provide for Lucy. Competition among artists in the city was intense. He was frequently without work. Even when he was commissioned to do a portrait, he could not always collect his fee. His economic plight was clearly reflected in his tattered clothing and shaggy hair. Indeed, Lucy's humiliations were mild by comparison to the crushing blows that John James suffered. Old friends snubbed him. "Many Men formerly *My Friend* passed Me without uttering a Word to me and I *as Willing* to Shun those *Rascalls*."[37]

35. *Ibid.*
36. *Ibid.*
37. Corning (ed.), *Journal Made During His Trip,* 199.

Like Lucy, Audubon became noticeably bitter. He sought to lose himself in his drawing and became increasingly sensitive when his work was criticized or underestimated. He gave vent to his feelings by chiding those who annoyed him in the slightest way. Once he denounced a man who had shot several snipes and sold one to him as a "Stupid Ass" who knew nothing about the birds, "Not even where *he* had Killed them." [38]

During the summer of 1821, Lucy was pleased to learn that John James had found a position at a fixed monthly salary. On June 16 Audubon described in his journal how he came to secure the post:

> I had attended a Miss Perrie [sic] to Enhance her Natural tallen for Drawing, for some days When her Mother Whom I intend Noticing in due time, asked Me to Think about My Spending the summer and fall at their farm Near Bayou Sarah; I Was glad of such an overture, but would have greatly prefered her Living in the Floridas—We Concluded the Bargain promising Me 60 Dollars per Month for One half of My time to teach Miss Eliza all I could in Drawing Music Dancing . . . so that after the . . . Diferent Plans I had formd as Opposite as Could be to this, I found Myself bound for several Months on a Farm in Louisiana. [39]

Thus, it was somewhat casually that John James came to Feliciana. When he arrived at Bayou Sara, he wished that he were instead with Lucy and "My Dear Boys." Yet on the short walk from Bayou Sara to the Pirrie home, Oakley plantation, Audubon's indifference gave way to enchantment with the beautiful country. He had stumbled into a paradise for naturalists. For three months Audubon's journal entries seethed with excitement about the beautiful birds his sketches brought to life. The portfolio grew ever larger with the best drawings Audubon had yet created. [40]

While Audubon divided his time between instructing Eliza Pirrie and drawing, Lucy remained in Kentucky, occupying herself with her two sons and her sister's three children. Eliza became seriously ill during the summer. It was, of course, Lucy who nursed her and assumed the management of the Berthoud household.

38. *Ibid.*, 123.
39. *Ibid.*, 159.
40. *Ibid.*, 159–60.

As October drew to a close, Lucy began to receive a flood of messages from John James. She learned that he had returned to New Orleans after being dismissed from his post at Oakley because of a disagreement with Mrs. Pirrie. However, he demanded that she leave Kentucky and join him in New Orleans where he had rented a small house on Dauphine Street for the family.[41]

Lucy did not immediately respond, and Audubon became very uneasy about her silence, fearing that she would refuse to come. It is evident from his journal entries that, throughout November and early December, John James expected her arrival any day. When he was told by John Gwathway on November 11 that Lucy expected to leave Louisville on the first steamer, Audubon wrote, "This News Kept me Nearly Wild all day. Yet No Boat arrived No wife No Friend yet near."[42] Hardly a day passed that Audubon did not meet the steamers coming downriver. Indeed, in anticipation of Lucy's arrival he spent forty dollars on new clothes and a much-needed haircut.

Perhaps it took Lucy some time to decide whether or not she would risk joining Audubon in New Orleans. He had not yet met her requirement that he first establish economic security for the family. It should also be noted that the money John James sent to Lucy for steamer fare never reached her and was eventually returned to Audubon. Finally, on December 18, Lucy, Gifford, and Woodhouse arrived at New Orleans on board the *Rocket*.[43]

Lucy had spent untold hours traveling up and down the river and east and west across her adopted country during the fourteen years that she had been married to John James. She had spent much time saying hello and good-bye, yet this meeting after fourteen months of separation must have been the most tender that they had ever had. Both she and John James had suffered from poverty, from other people, and for the first time, from each other. Indeed, both emerged from their experience deeply scarred.

The Audubons walked slowly along the levee, Gifford, Woodhouse, and John James chatting and laughing. John James took

41. *Ibid.*, 209–211.
42. *Ibid.*, 210.
43. *Ibid.*, 223.

them to dine with the Pamars, a New Orleans family that had be-friended him.[44] After dinner they walked to the little house on Dauphine Street and Lucy unpacked and settled in her first Louisiana home. Once Lucy was with Audubon she clutched again at that strand of hope that his book would soon be published. Most important, she was once again with him, a part of his work and a part of his life.

44. *Ibid.*, 224.

CHAPTER VI

Poverty Without
Prospects

O n the day after Lucy arrived in New Orleans, she and John
James spent many hours evaluating the total collection of bird
drawings.[1] She saw that the drawings he had completed in Feliciana
during the summer and fall of 1821 were superior to his earlier
works. They agreed that further specimens had to be found and
drawn and that the drawings already completed had to be improved
upon before a publisher was approached.

Pleased with Lucy's approval, happy at being reunited with his
family, and confident of his maturing artistic talent, Audubon was
impatient to finish his work. With his characteristic penchant for
overstatement, he announced that he would draw ninety-nine new
birds in as many days.[2] After years of wandering and working, he
was still a poor man, shunned by his fellow artists in New Orleans
and considered something of an oddity and a failure by friends and
family. Yet he was certain that leaving the business world had been
the right course to pursue. Enthusiastically, he assured Lucy that
wealth and fame would be theirs as soon as his drawings were
completed.

Lucy listened while John James described their future in glowing
terms, but his resonant voice, still heavily marked by a rhythmic
French accent, was no longer able to awaken her confidence in the
future. She noted the difference between John James's economic
position and that of his former, now wealthy partner Rozier, who

1. Adams, *John James Audubon*, 251.
2. Corning (ed.), *Journal Made During His Trip*, 226.

visited them on Christmas Eve. After more than three years of poverty and humiliation, her mind was full of doubts and misgivings.
As the new year wore on, Lucy quickly learned that her apprehension was well founded.

To meet the family's expenses Lucy had to depend upon the fees
that John James received from a few students to whom he gave art
and music lessons. This money was hardly sufficient to provide for
the lodging, food, and clothing of the four Audubons and Joseph
Mason, who was still with John James. Nevertheless, Lucy insisted
that her children's education was just as essential as food and shelter. Gifford and Woodhouse were enrolled at Professor Branard's
academy where the boys "received notions of geography, arithmetic, grammar, and writing, for six dollars per month each."[3]

Additional funds had to be squeezed from the Audubon coffers so
that John James could continue working on his collection. Because
he was faced with the necessity of providing for his family, he was
not free to hunt for new specimens, and he had to contract with
hunters, agreeing to pay them one dollar for every new specimen
brought him. Impatient with the number of bird carcasses procured
in this manner, early each morning John James and Joseph would
walk to the French Market and search through the stalls for likely
specimens to purchase.[4]

Lucy never knew when her husband would take in a house guest
for an extended stay, making it necessary to stretch their scanty
funds to feed yet another person. However, the visit of one such
guest demonstrates that Lucy had not lost the capacity to enjoy
gaiety and lightness of spirit. One day John James encountered an
old friend, a Mr. Matabon, who was wandering about the French
Market penniless and hungry. According to John James, Matabon
was a famous flute player. Audubon took him home and invited him
to share their meager fare and cramped quarters. While the musician stayed, each evening music and singing drifted lightly from the
little house on Dauphine Street. Lucy, John James, and Matabon
made an excellent musical trio. After the talented musician left,

3. Arthur, *Audubon*, 241; Maria R. Audubon (ed.), *Audubon and His Journals*, I, 51.
4. Corning (ed.), *Journal Made During His Trip*, 226, 204.

Audubon wrote, "Mr. Matabon's departure is regretted by us all, and we shall sorely miss his beautiful music on the flute."[5]

Still, song and music could not distract Lucy for long from the grim poverty of her household. Her husband was unable to secure additional students, and he had difficulty collecting fees owed him by some of the students he had. Every day Lucy had to worry about simply feeding her family, and every week she returned more and more frequently from the market with only bread and cheese to place upon the table.

From John James there were no more comforting words. The optimism that he had expressed in December was evaporating. By January he was in a deep state of depression, gloomy, ill humored, and ashamed of his economic plight. The first entry in his 1822 journal read, "Two months and five days have elapsed before I could venture to dispose of one hundred and twenty-five cents to pay for this book, that probably, like other things in the world, is ashamed to find me so poor."[6] Audubon's spirits sank so low that he began to doubt the quality of his drawings, and he spoke of doing them over.

The dismal months of early 1822 strained the relationship between Lucy and John James. Both of them were despondent. Socially ostracized because of their poverty, they were almost constantly together, but neither was capable of giving cheer to the other. By Audubon's account, Lucy was understanding. "I have few acquaintances; my wife and sons are more congenial to me than all others in the world, and we have no desire to force ourselves into a society where every day I receive fewer bows."[7] But his testimony must be doubted, for it is evident that Lucy was in part responsible for her husband's gloom. His work on the birds was very important to her, but the practical-minded Lucy insisted that the collection was secondary to the welfare of her family. She badgered John James continually: he must meet his students for lessons, he must procure additional students, and he must collect all the funds owing him. The sharp missives Lucy had written from Kentucky might have "ruffled" his spirits, but they were as nothing compared to the ver-

5. Arthur, *Audubon*, 241; Maria R. Audubon (ed.), *Audubon and His Journals*, I, 52.
6. Maria R. Audubon (ed.), *Audubon and His Journals*, I, 50–51.
7. *Ibid.*, I, 51.

bal attacks she now launched in person. Her message was always the same: John James had first to be a husband and father. After this he could have his birds.

John James had frequently thought of leaving New Orleans. He had endured great hardship and humiliation in the city, and competition among artists was so intense that he could not acquire enough students to provide for his family. He suffered a bad blow when Mrs. William Brand, his best-paying and most faithful student, announced that because she was expecting a child she would have to discontinue her drawing lessons. John James began to speak of leaving New Orleans for Natchez where he hoped that he would find less competition among artists.[8]

The Brands had become very fond of John James and Lucy. William Brand, a wealthy New Orleans builder, wanted to help the talented Frenchman and his forlorn family. Brand also realized that his wife was in great need of an education. And when John James suggested that Lucy be employed as a tutor and companion to Mrs. Brand, the builder was quick to employ her.[9] Lucy welcomed the opportunities that this post would bring. There would be a steady income, and the work would distract her thoughts from the constant consideration of poverty. The money she brought home from her new job soon became the only source of income for the family.

Once Lucy was employed, John James was once again free to wander in the woods and work on his drawings. The number of his students dwindled, and by March he was determined to leave for Natchez. Audubon did not ask Lucy to accompany him at this time probably because he knew that his wife would reject the invitation. She had employment, and her sons were in school. Arrangements were made for Lucy to move into the Brand home while John James was absent.[10] Only Joseph accompanied Audubon.

Audubon took passage upstream on the steamer *Eclat* after only four months with his family. Lucy and the two boys went to the landing to bid him adieu. Walking back to the Brand home, she must have wondered if there would ever be any stability in her life

---

8. Herrick, *Audubon, the Naturalist*, I, 320; Adams, *John James Audubon*, 252.
9. Arthur, *Audubon*, 246.
10. *Ibid.*, 247; Adams, *John James Audubon*, 252.

with Audubon, or if there would ever be another time when she could walk to her own home.

John James left New Orleans just as he had arrived—penniless. But he visited the captain of the vessel and drew portraits of him and his wife in return for free passage to Natchez for himself and Joseph. While traveling upriver, he did several portraits of passengers in black chalk. When he and Joseph stepped off the boat in Natchez, John James had at least a few dollars jingling in the pockets of his tattered pantaloons.[11]

At the Brand home in New Orleans Lucy plunged into the task of instructing Anne Brand. Pregnancy had had an adverse effect upon the young woman's health, and Lucy spent a great deal of time with her. As usual, she spent her free time with Gifford and Woodhouse, who were growing up rapidly.

Gifford was thirteen years old in 1822 and Woodhouse was ten—difficult ages for boys to be without a father's authoritative guidance. Lucy worried not only about providing the boys with the essentials of life but also about the image that the boys had of their father. They had heard unkind appraisals of him while living in Shippingport for over a year. They were aware of the tension that had existed between their parents while they lived on Dauphine Street, and they were hard put to understand why their father had to leave them only a few short months after they had come from Kentucky to be with him. To Lucy fell the task of maintaining in her children a confidence in the man whom she herself doubted. It was painful for her to realize that she was unable to provide the security and sense of roots for her sons that her parents had given her.[12]

Soon after John James arrived in Natchez, he wrote a letter informing Lucy that he was traveling to the Arkansas Post to find out if an expedition to the Pacific was being formed. Lucy was not pleased that her husband was still dreaming of an enterprise that would do little to improve their economic standing. He spoke only fleetingly of a student he had acquired in Natchez, one Melanie Quegles, to whom he was giving lessons in music, drawing, and

11. Arthur, *Audubon*, 247–48; Herrick, *Audubon, the Naturalist*, I, 320.
12. Audubon Journal, May 23, May 31, 1821; Adams, *John James Audubon*, 252.

French. Instead of appraising his new student in terms of fees to be earned, Lucy's artistic and sensitive husband seemed mainly interested in analyzing the student's disagreeable father, "His small grey eyes, and corrugated brows, did not afford me an opportunity of passing favourable judgment."[13]

Soon a second letter from Audubon relieved Lucy's anxiety. He told her that no Pacific expedition was being planned, that he had found some excellent bird subjects, and that he had made several sympathetic and helpful friends. Prominent among the latter was the Wailes family who owned a plantation in Louisiana across the river from Natchez. Audubon was a frequent guest at the plantation, hunting with the Wailes brothers and later drawing specimens yielded by the hunt. A Natchez physician, Dr. William Provan, also became fond of John James and frequently opened his pocketbook to help the struggling artist. Audubon's new friends also helped him in other ways. Provan procured several students for him in Natchez, and through the influence of the Wailes family, John James was hired to teach drawing to the young ladies at Elizabeth Academy in Washington, a small hamlet seven miles from Natchez.[14]

After securing this new position, Audubon wrote Lucy asking that she and the boys join him in Natchez. Lucy refused, but she did send Gifford and Woodhouse to join their father after John James assured her that they would be enrolled in a school and that he was once again steadily employed. Evidently, Lucy refused to go at this time because she felt that she had an obligation to fulfill with the Brands. Mrs. Brand's baby was due soon, and this was the young woman's first pregnancy. She had been ill almost constantly, and she would probably have been terrified had Lucy left her before the child was born. Lucy would not abandon her young charge who was in such dire need of strength and reassurance.[15]

When Gifford and Woodhouse arrived in Natchez, Audubon enrolled them at Brevost Academy. He had rented a small house on South Union Street and here the family lived. The boys were most

13. Arthur, *Audubon*, 248; Audubon Journal, March 24, 1822, quoted in Buchanan, *Life of Audubon*, 71.

14. Arthur, *Audubon*, 250–52.

15. Adams, *John James Audubon*, 252; Ford, *John James Audubon*, 135.

frequently on their own or with Joseph, because their father's work schedule was rigorous. Each day John James walked the seven miles to and from Washington, and when he returned in the evening, he had other students to meet in Natchez.[16]

Audubon became depressed because he was obliged to confine himself to the classroom and "his work interfered with his ornithological pursuits." In late June he was stricken with a fever and became so seriously ill that he had to resign his post at the academy in Washington. During his illness, Dr. Provan came to the rescue, caring for John James, paying tuition for Gifford and Woodhouse, and putting food on the table at the Audubon home.[17]

Once he had recovered, John James secured a position at Brevost Academy in Natchez. But his spirits remained low because he could not find time to work on his bird drawings. Indeed, he began to surrender hope that his dreams of fame and fortune would ever be realized. He confided these bleak thoughts to his journal, "But while work flowed upon me, the hope of completing my book upon the birds of America became less clear; and full of despair, I feared my hopes of becoming known to Europe as a naturalist were destined to be blasted." Evidently Joseph Mason also came to believe that Audubon's work would never be published. In July the lad decided to return to Cincinnati without having achieved the rewards that John James had promised him two years earlier.[18]

In August, Lucy wrote to John James to tell him that at last she was free to join the family in Natchez. Anne Brand had given birth to her baby, a sickly infant who had lived for only a short time.[19] Lucy, knowing from experience the sorrow of losing a child, had offered the despondent mother all of the consolation she could.

When Lucy arrived in Natchez in early September, John James met the boat and escorted her through the hurly-burly atmosphere of Natchez-Under-the-Hill.[20] They passed gamblers, thieves, rivermen, and prostitutes. Many of the buildings were dilapidated, and

16. John James Audubon, Journal Entries, March 24, July 8, 1822, quoted in Buchanan, *Life of Audubon*, 71–72.
17. Audubon Journal, July 8, 23, 1822, quoted *ibid.*, 71–72.
18. Audubon Journal, July 8, 23, 1822, quoted *ibid.*, 72.
19. Audubon Journal, September 1, 1822, quoted *ibid.*, 72.
20. *Ibid.*

the odor of cheap whiskey drifted from the numerous grog shops that dotted the street. The following account provides an excellent description of this colorful riverfront haunt.

> Drifting around the wide sweep of river. . . . they saw . . . Natchez-under-the-Hill. Danger, at least from the river, was behind the rivermen, and here they found a market for their produce, and fun which ran the whole category from drinking freely of raw liquor to alluring and painted Delilahs who had "entertained" and fleeced a whole generation of Kentuckians. . . . "Natchez-under-the-Hill" in its heyday would surely have put to shame those hellholes of antiquity, Sodom and Gomorrah. . . . There was one main street which ran from the road ascending the "hill" to the water's edge. . . . Lining either side of this muddy thoroughfare were rows of wooden shanties which were alternately gambling houses, brothels and barrooms. The sunken sidewalks were blocked day and night with fashionably dressed dandies from the plantations back of the hill, rough, crudely dressed river bullies who smelled of a hundred days' perspiration, sailors and foreign merchants, and tawdrily arrayed, highly rouged and scented females who could not recall the day of their virginity. Life in the underworld was cheap, gamblers cheated at cards and shot protesting victims without mercy, boatmen, blear-eyed with bad whisky or green with jealousy over deceptive whores, bit, kicked and gouged one another. The town under the hill knew no God, no law, no morals.[21]

As Lucy and John James ascended the bluff to the top, the scenery took on a more pleasant appearance. Carriages, horses, and pedestrians thronged the streets. Numerous graceful homes stood under huge oak trees whose entwined branches seemed to provide a canopy of soothing shade over the town. One traveler described Natchez as "a considerable place, with a town-house, and several good streets and well-furnished shops." Another visitor compared Natchez with the small towns in the West Indies, noting the many houses with balconies and piazzas, the small shops kept by free mulattoes and French and Spanish creoles, and the great mixture of color of the people in the streets.[22]

21. Clark, *The Rampaging Frontier*, 89–90; See also, Timothy Flint, *Recollections of the Last Ten Years*, 213.
22. W. Bullock, "Sketch of a Journey Through the Western States of North America, from New Orleans, by the Mississippi, Ohio, City of Cincinnati, and Falls of Niagara, to New York, in 1827," in Reuben G. Thwaites (ed.), *Early Western Travels, 1748–1846* (32 vols.; Cleveland, 1904–1907), XIX, 131; Cuming, "Sketches of a Tour," 320.

Lucy's new home, a pleasant-looking small frame cottage, needed only a woman's touch to transform it into a cozy place to live. However, Lucy had little time to devote to household duties. When John James had heard that she was coming to Natchez, he secured a position for her as governess for the children of a clergyman, one Parson Davis. Each morning Lucy and John James awoke at dawn, Lucy prepared breakfast for the family, and frequently, William Provan stopped in for toast and coffee. Soon the boys went off to school, Lucy left to teach the Davis children, and John James plunged into the woods seeking new birds. Apparently, Audubon no longer had his teaching post at the academy, and so he spent his time hunting, drawing, and tutoring a few students. For a time the Audubons enjoyed a steady income, but this happy and unusual situation did not last. Lucy found the minister to be extremely slow in paying her salary, and so she quit her post. John James was once again hard pressed to provide for his wife and children.[23]

Dr. Provan again came to the rescue, frequently paying for the Audubons' food and clothing and buying drawing materials for John James, who had recently become interested in painting in oils. Indeed, he was taking lessons from John Stein, an itinerant painter whom he met in Natchez.[24] Provan, apparently, was wise enough to realize that the best way to help the Audubons was to secure a teaching position for Lucy and thus to leave John James free to pursue his work on the birds.

On a trip into Louisiana in early 1823, Provan visited Beech Woods plantation in what is now West Feliciana Parish, and there he spoke about Lucy to Jane Middlemist Percy, the widow of Robert Percy and the owner of the extensive estate. Provan knew that Jane Percy was looking for a teacher to instruct her daughters and those of the neighboring planters. The doctor convinced Mrs. Percy that Lucy was a woman of refinement and intelligence, a well-qualified and experienced teacher.[25] Dr. Provan told Mrs. Percy of the eco-

23. John James Audubon, Journal Entries, September 1, November 3, 1822, quoted in Buchanan, *Life of Audubon*, 72–73; Alice Ford (ed.), *The 1826 Journal of John James Audubon* (Norman, 1967), 81.

24. Maria R. Audubon (ed.), *Audubon and His Journals*, I, 52.

25. Arthur, *Audubon*, 258–59.

nomic difficulties that plagued the Audubon family, and he assured her that Lucy would be willing to come to Beech Woods as a teacher. Mrs. Percy gave the doctor permission to hire Lucy pending her approval.

Provan returned to Natchez and repeated Mrs. Percy's offer of employment to Lucy. He told her what would be expected of her and what she in turn would receive. She was to have her own residence, a small cottage and school combined, and she was to receive one thousand dollars a year or perhaps more—considerably higher wages than most women could expect to earn. In turn, Lucy was expected to provide instruction in reading, writing, arithmetic, music, and proper social behavior to the Percy girls and the daughters of the well-to-do planters in the surrounding area.[26]

Provan explained to Lucy that her employer was not an easy woman to get along with, that she was, in fact, a formidable female who ran the large plantation with precise efficiency, and that she made every decision, from the purchase of another slave to who was desirable company. Lucy showed little interest in William's appraisal of Jane Percy's personality. She was concerned only that her employer be able to meet her salary. Once William assured her that Jane Percy was both reliable and solvent, Lucy did not hesitate to accept the position.

Audubon was, of course, delighted with the arrangement. Lucy's salary would provide the family with an assured income, leaving him free to wander and draw. This time he would say farewell to Lucy and the boys. He was going to remain in Natchez dabbling in oils for the time being. Then he and Stein intended to travel about the country in a wagon offering to paint the portraits of wealthy families. John James hoped to have Gifford accompany him on this venture, and he promised that he would go to Beech Woods to pick up his son as soon as he and Stein were ready to begin.[27]

As Lucy prepared for her journey into Louisiana, she probably

---

26. *Ibid.*, 259. See Flexner, *Century of Struggle*, 54; Kraditor (ed.), *Up From the Pedestal*, 72–73.

27. Arthur, *Audubon*, 259–60; Ford, *John James Audubon*, 136. Stein's name is at times spelled Steen.

wondered what kind of life awaited her on the Feliciana plantation. She was pleased with the prospect of having her own private dwelling at Beech Woods. She had seen the beautiful Feliciana birds that Audubon's drawings had brought to life, and she had heard Anne Brand, a Feliciana native, speak of the lovely countryside. Lucy must have experienced a rush of hope—hope that this new country and her new position would provide peace and security.

The area known as West Feliciana had had a colorful and significant history.[28] It is situated just east of the Mississippi River and south of the thirty-first parallel in the northeast corner of the Florida parishes. Originally, it was a part of the vast expanse of territory claimed by France in the seventeenth century and called Louisiana. Under French control, settlement lagged, and West Feliciana remained largely undeveloped and sparsely populated. At the end of the French and Indian War, that part of Louisiana east of the Mississippi River, excluding the Isle of Orleans, came under English control. The British government, anxious to encourage settlement, offered land grants to any persons who would move there. Soon settlers from the Carolinas and Virginia entered the area, giving the population a strong Anglo-American character.

During the war for American independence, Spain declared war on Great Britain, and under the leadership of Bernardo de Galvez, the Spanish in Louisiana launched successful military campaigns against the English in East and West Florida. As a result, Feliciana as part of West Florida came under Spanish control. Spain continued the British policy of encouraging settlement by offering land grants to Americans. Many persons who accepted grants came from

28. For further details on the history and development of West Feliciana, see Milton Rickels, "Thomas Bangs Thorpe in the Felicianas, 1836–42," *Louisiana Historical Quarterly*, XXXIX (April, 1956), 169–97; Sidney Joseph Aucoin, "The Political Career of Isaac Johnson, Governor of Louisiana, 1846–1850," *Louisiana Historical Quarterly*, XXVIII (July, 1945), 941–89; Louise Butler, "West Feliciana: A Glimpse of Its History," *Louisiana Historical Quarterly*, VII (January, 1924), 90–120; James A. Padgett (ed.), "The West Florida Revolution of 1810, as Told in the Letters of John Rhea, Fulwar Skipwith, Reuben Kemper, and Others," *Louisiana Historical Quarterly*, XXI (January, 1938), 76–202; Miriam Reeves, *The Felicianas of Louisiana* (Baton Rouge, 1967); Edwin Davis (ed.), *Plantation Life in the Florida Parishes of Louisiana, 1836–1846, as Reflected in the Diary of Bennet H. Barrow* (New York, 1943).

the Mississippi Territory, and Anglo-Saxon influence continued to be preponderant in the area.[29]

Feliciana rapidly became the richest and most populous area in the district of West Florida. Observing the growing power and expanding wealth of their American neighbors, the people of Feliciana grew restless under the domination of a decaying Spanish empire. Planters in West Feliciana took the lead in declaring the independence of West Florida in 1810.[30] The rebels called a convention, drafted a constitution, established a government, and elected a president for the West Florida Republic, which stood for seventy-four days before being annexed by the United States.

The topography of Feliciana is quite different from that of the rest of south Louisiana. Unlike the low flatlands and marshes to the south and the prairies to the west, Feliciana is a land of rolling hills and gently sloping valleys. Instead of the murky bayous that crisscross the landscape in other southern parishes, in Feliciana numerous spring-fed creeks, their water swift moving and crystal clear, interlace the countryside. The soil is loess, and capable of supporting staple-crop production.[31]

In 1820 Feliciana still had many of the characteristics of a turbulent frontier area. If the testimony of some of the young women in the area is to be believed, crude manners and rowdy behavior characterized the young men of the parish.[32] Indeed, maintaining law and order was still regarded by many as the province of the individual. Justice or injustice came swiftly and often violently as each man acted as the guardian of his own rights. The law had little to do with arbitrating individual differences or preventing crime or determining punishment.

29. See, Reeves, *The Felicianas of Louisiana*; Jack Holmes, *Gayoso: The Life of a Spanish Governor in the Mississippi Valley, 1789–1799* (Baton Rouge, 1965); John Walton Caughey, *Bernardo De Galvez in Louisiana, 1776–1783* (Gretna, La., 1972).

30. For an account of the revolution, see James A. Padgett (ed.), "Official Records of the West Florida Revolution and Republic," *Louisiana Historical Quarterly*, XXI (July, 1938), 685–805; Isaac Cox, *The West Florida Controversy, 1798–1813: A Study in American Diplomacy* (Gloucester, Mass., 1967).

31. Rickels, "Thomas Bangs Thorpe," 173–74.

32. Charlotte Swayze to Mary C. Weeks, August 3, 1824, in David Weeks and Family Papers, Weeks-Hall Memorial Collection, 1782–1894, Department of Archives and Manuscripts, Louisiana State University, Baton Rouge.

In 1820 there were only 12,732 inhabitants in old Feliciana, of whom 7,164 were slaves. Even though the blacks outnumbered the whites, there were few large plantations and most landowners were yeoman farmers who worked their own land assisted by a few slaves. Yet the rich soil, the easy access to river transport, and the steady westward march of cotton cultivation foretold the coming of greater landed interests. In 1820 Feliciana farmers produced 9,000 bales of cotton, and there were 115 cotton gins and 12 sawmills in operation throughout the parish.[33]

The major population center of the parish, St. Francisville, was only a crude village in 1820. The population of the small hamlet was probably less than two hundred persons. St. Francisville did, however, have an ideally located landing on the Mississippi. This landing was known as Bayou Sara, although as late as 1830 it had no separate identity as a village apart from St. Francisville. The port, which served as the major outlet for the agricultural produce of the interior, consisted of several crudely constructed warehouses, wharves, and a tavern or two. A few commission merchants and the keel and flatboaters who plied the river lived at Bayou Sara landing. The main section of the village, St. Francisville, perched on top of a ridge above Bayou Sara, served as a supply center to the residents of the interior. It boasted a number of merchants, who advertised a wide variety of goods, and also several lawyers and doctors.[34] When Feliciana was split into East and West Feliciana parishes in 1824, St. Francisville became the parish seat of West Feliciana.

By the mid-1820s it was evident that the rough edges of the frontier were fast being smoothed by civilization. A review of scattered issues of the *Louisianian*, the *Louisiana Journal*, and the *Asylum and Feliciana Advertiser* reveals that the number of merchants in St. Francisville increased during the 1820s. These men offered a wide variety of goods at competitive prices. Advertisements also indicate

---

33. *Census For 1820*. Book I (Washington, 1821); *Population Schedules of the Fourth Census*, Microcopy 33, Vol. 2, roll 31.

34. See scattered issues of *Time Piece, Louisianian, Louisiana Journal, Asylum and Feliciana Advertiser, Crisis*, and *Florida Gazette*, spanning the period May, 1811, to June, 1829, in office of the *Democrat*, St. Francisville, La.; Timothy Flint, *Recollections of the Last Ten Years*, 215.

that the number of skilled artisans offering necessary services to the farmers of the interior increased. In 1825 St. Francisville enjoyed a thriving commerce, but for some reason the population did not keep pace with the bustling activity. This concerned the editor of the *Louisiana Journal*, who complained, "Between three and four thousand teams traverse our streets annually, bringing to our landing the produce of the finest cotton growing country upon earth, and carrying therefrom the products of the states of Virginia, Pennsylvania, Ohio, Kentucky, Tennessee, Indiana, Illinois, and Missouri. We ourselves are lost in wonder that the growth of our village does not keep pace with our commerce."[35]

By the 1820s residents of the interior were coming to town on occasion to enjoy social events. They gathered at places such as Stephenson's Hotel for cotillion parties and fireworks displays.[36] A visit to St. Francisville was a welcome relief from the isolation of small farm or large plantation.

Policy jury proceedings and the correspondence of residents reveal that increasing attention was being given to developing roads, establishing ferries across the Mississippi River, and building bridges across major streams.[37] A stage route connecting the parish with Natchez was already in operation. Police jurors were also becoming concerned about education, and plans were laid for the establishment of public schools.

A number of families in the area could boast of fine libraries. The practice of exchanging books with neighbors and friends was widespread and at times costly when the books were not returned and owners could not remember to whom they had lent these printed treasures so important on the frontier.[38] A public library had been established in St. Francisville as early as 1815.

The editor of the St. Francisville *Time Piece* had for some years

35. *Louisiana Journal*, October 22, 1825; St. Francisville *Asylum*, January 29, 1825.

36. *Asylum and Feliciana Advertiser*, November 15, 1821; *Louisiana Journal*, February 5, March 24, 1825.

37. East Feliciana Parish Police Jury Minutes, vol. 2, July 22, 1818–July 25, 1822 (in Department of Archives and Manuscripts, Louisiana State University, Baton Rouge), 1–164; *Louisiana Journal*, July 28, 1827; Charlotte Swayze to Mrs. David Weeks, July 14, 1824, in Weeks Papers.

38. *Louisiana Journal*, May 27, 1824, February 5, 1825.

been advocating the need for education in the area. As early as 1811 he wrote, "Let any man of ordinary mind, cast his eyes around him, and view the fate of education, in this country, and if his heart is not chilled at the contemplation, it is because he has neither taste for science, or love of knowledge. How many fine youths do you see in this vicinity, who are lost to the world for the want of an education?"[39] The editor best expressed the feelings of the well-to-do, those who had found prosperity in Feliciana and were anxious to provide their children with educational and cultural advantages that were better than or at least equal to those that they had enjoyed. This ardent concern about education served to lure many fine tutors, and even a few exceptional scholars to the parish. Anne, Theodosia, and Lavinia Colder, who came to the parish from New England and set up Society Hill Seminary and, later, Lyceum, were obviously scholars of the classics. The Colder sisters offered a more soundly based academic program than Lucy did.[40]

In many respects St. Francisville resembled Henderson, Kentucky, when Lucy and John James first settled there. The trappings of the frontier were still very much in evidence, yet the residents were eagerly importing civilization. And Lucy Audubon, like the Colders, was a part of that importation. She was expected to bring with her knowledge, polish, and the *savoir-faire* that the nouveaux riches on this agrarian frontier wanted their children to possess.

39. *Time Piece*, May 23, 1811.
40. *Louisianian*, May 15, 22, 29, June 5, 12, 26, July 10, 17, 1819; *Louisiana Journal*, March 4, May 27, 1824, March 31, May 19, October 15, November 5, 1825; succession records in the St. Francisville courthouse indicate that considerable sums of money were spent on education. Concern about education was not the norm in frontier areas. See, Everett Dick, *The Dixie Frontier: A Social History of the Southern Frontier from the First Transmontane Beginnings to the Civil War* (New York, 1964), 170–80; Thomas Clark, *Frontier America: The Story of the Westward Movement* (New York, 1959), 389–91.

CHAPTER VII

A Particular House
in Louisiana

On her initial trip to Beech Woods Lucy and her sons were escorted by Dr. Provan, and the party certainly made the journey by carriage. As the vehicle rumbled along the narrow roadbed, Lucy could observe that the Feliciana countryside resembled the Henderson area more closely than it did the flat lowlands around New Orleans. The road wandered along ridges running like so many fingers toward the Mississippi River. It was surrounded by lofty timber, high rolling hills, and gently sloping valleys. Only small flecks of sunlight were able to penetrate the thick forest canopy that shaded the road. On each side of the road, undergrowth of multicolored shrubs and vines stretched upward entwining and mingling with the branches of the trees and climbing to the very pinnacles of the tallest hardwoods so that frequently the roadbed seemed to be embraced by a solid wall of dense foliage.

From the road Lucy saw only a small portion of the twenty-two hundred acres that comprised the Percy plantation. Like many visitors before her, she was impressed with the atmosphere of tranquility that seemed to envelop this autonomous little world. Turning from the road, the carriage rolled up the drive and stopped before the Percy home, the center of plantation activity and authority.

The "big house" of Beech Woods was not overly impressive. It lacked the splendor and stately design that characterized many Feliciana plantations even in the frontier setting of the 1820s. Writing to a friend in England, Robert Percy described his home as a comfortable place where, without inconvenience, he could "lodge a

Lucy Audubon

dozen of friends when they pass a day with us."[1] The home that Lucy saw was built around two roomy cabins of rough-hewn timber connected by a dogtrot.

Even though the Percys were far from being the wealthiest planters in the parish, they were nonetheless well-to-do. In 1819 the main dwelling, slave quarters, other outbuildings, and one thousand arpents of land were valued at $20,000. The household furnishings and utensils were evaluated at $1,100. At that time, the Percys owned fifty slaves appraised at a total worth of $14,580. Horses, pigs, cattle and other livestock were appraised at $2,300, while an additional two thousand arpents of land were valued at $40,000.[2]

Lucy Audubon and Jane Percy should have felt a kind of kinship. As her crisp brogue testified, Jane was a native of Scotland. She had spent much of her youth in England where she met and married Robert Percy, an officer in the British Royal Navy. After resigning his commission, Percy settled at Beech Woods with his family in 1804. The Percys found prosperity in the planting business and gained the respect and admiration of the community. Robert Percy had served the settlement as alcalde, as associate judge of the superior court under the West Florida Republic, as a member of the parish police jury, and as justice of the peace.[3] After his death in 1819 his widow capably managed the plantation.

No accounts of the first meeting between Lucy and Jane Percy survive, but it is likely that these two highly intelligent women quickly sized each other up. Jane Percy was a domineering woman, preoccupied with her own importance as mistress of Beech Woods. She would probably have intimidated a less confident woman than Lucy Audubon. Lucy's excellent qualifications made her quite a valuable acquisition. If, as is likely, Jane Percy realized that Dr. Provan's praise was entirely warranted, she would have eagerly con-

1. Robert Percy to J. Swift, 1810, cited in John Hereford Percy, *The Percy Family of Mississippi and Louisiana, 1776–1943* (Baton Rouge, 1943), 59–60.

2. Succession Records of Robert Percy, Box 82, 1819, in St. Francisville Courthouse, St. Francisville, La. The year 1819 was a depression year, so appraisals are low.

3. Percy, *The Percy Family*, 6, 9, 48, 58–60; East Feliciana Police Jury Minutes, vol. 2, July 1819; Cuming, "Sketches of a Tour," 333; Stanley Clisby Arthur and George de Kernion, *Old Families of Louisiana* (Baton Rouge, 1971), 185.

firmed the terms of Lucy's employment. Such a teacher would be an unexpected boon in this backwoods area.[4]

Lucy was assured that she would be paid one thousand dollars annually and that she would be provided with private lodgings. In addition, she would be allowed to collect tuition from the neighboring planters who chose to board their daughters at Beech Woods to be educated. Pleased with the understanding reached, Lucy and her sons moved into the little cottage a short distance from the main house. She wasted no time getting her school into operation. Jane Percy's three daughters, Margaret, Sarah, and Christine, were her first students, but it was not long before neighboring planters received the news that Lucy Audubon was established at Beech Woods. They came to appraise the new teacher, to discuss tuition and boarding fees, and to hear about the academic program she would be offering.[5]

While Lucy was involved in organizing the school, ordering materials, and speaking to prospective students and parents, John James and Stein arrived at Beech Woods to pick up Gifford, who had been anxiously awaiting his father. Evidently Audubon stayed only long enough to add Gifford's baggage to the back of the wagon before father, son, and itinerant artist set out to find wealthy patrons to paint.[6]

During his brief visit, John James noted that Lucy was content with and even enthusiastic about her new position. Visitors had frequently commented upon the charm of the Percy plantation.[7] Life on the plantation reminded Lucy of the Derbyshire estate of her youth and of Fatland Ford. Indeed at Beech Woods she found a small measure of the security she had enjoyed in her youth and first years of marriage. Five years before, Lucy could not have understood insecurity. By 1823 she knew that being well-to-do was an accident of birth, that lady luck was fickle, and that misfortune could visit even those to the manor born.

4. Captain Walsh to Zephyr P. Ogon, September 20, 1822, in Antonio Patrick Walsh Papers, Department of Archives and Manuscripts, Louisiana State University, Baton Rouge; Ford (ed.), *The 1826 Journal*, 333–34; Ford, *John James Audubon*, 136.
5. Ford, *John James Audubon*, 136; Arthur, *Audubon*, 259.
6. Ford, *John James Audubon*, 136–37.
7. Cuming, "Sketches of a Tour," 334.

Once John James and Gifford departed, Lucy had a difficult time comforting her younger son. Woodhouse had never before been separated from his older brother, and Lucy was hard pressed to explain that he was not old enough to accompany Gifford. She was concerned that Woodhouse did not match Gifford in wit or maturity at a similar age. Woodhouse had perhaps suffered more than Gifford from the lack of stability that haunted the family. Whatever the case, Woodhouse was not lonely for long. The artists had not traveled very far before John James and Stein began to disagree. The partnership was dissolved, and Audubon and Gifford returned to Beech Woods.[8]

When her husband appeared unexpectedly, Lucy introduced him to Jane Percy and asked that he be allowed to stay and help with the students. She gambled that Mrs. Percy was pleased enough with her performance at Beech Woods to overcome any preconceived notions she may have had about Lucy's husband and to allow John James to stay. It is a tribute to Lucy that a woman such as Jane Percy ignored her better judgment out of deference to Lucy's wishes, for Mrs. Percy was not a woman to give in easily or readily to abandon her preconceptions.

Unfortunately for John James, his reputation had preceded him to Beech Woods. Jane Percy had heard about the quarrel between Audubon and Lucretia Alston Pirrie of Oakley plantation. Indeed, by the time the story had reached her, it had probably been blown all out of proportion, making John James seem quite the libertine. Audubon had come to Oakley during the summer of 1821 at the invitation of Mrs. Pirrie to teach her only child, Eliza, drawing, music, and dancing. In the course of the four months that Audubon spent at Oakley, Mrs. Pirrie came to believe that he was far too attentive to her daughter. Mrs. Pirrie was further encouraged in this notion when Eliza became ill, and Dr. Ira Smith, the attending physician and an ardent suitor of Eliza's, questioned the advisability of continuing the lessons. Referring to this period, John James wrote, "I saw her during this Illness at appointed hours as if I was an

8. Ford, *John James Audubon,* 137; Arthur, *Audubon,* 260–61; Herrick, *Audubon, the Naturalist,* I, 324; George B. Grinnell (ed.), "Some Audubon Letters," *Auk,* XXXIII (1916), 119.

Extraordinary ambassador to some Distant Court—had to Keep the utmost Decorum of Manners and I believe Never Laughed Once With Her the Whole 4 Months I was there." John James described his departure from Oakley in bitter terms, alleging that Mrs. Pirrie had ridiculed and abused him.

After meeting the volatile Frenchman, the middle-aged Presbyterian widow probably gave even more credence to the stories she had heard. Even though Jane Percy must have had difficulty understanding what a woman like Lucy Audubon saw in a man who was unable to support her, she softened her opinion of John James because of Lucy. She was also influenced by William Provan, who was courting her daughter Sarah and who spoke well of the artist. Even so, the Pirrie story must have stayed at the back of her mind.[9]

In any case, Jane Percy's hospitality, even to invited guests, was limited. Once, Jane sent a message to one Captain Antonio P. Walsh informing him that his friend Monsieur Housset was dangerously ill at Beech Woods and inviting him to visit his sick friend. Somewhat grudgingly, Mrs. Percy also informed Captain Walsh "that She hopes She will always be able to Sacrifice her own Feelings in the cause of Humanity, when She thinks it would Conduce to the gratification & happiness of an individual, who is a Stranger, to See any of his Friends or Countrymen." No sooner had Captain Walsh arrived at Beech Woods than he determined not to return. He explained to a friend, "My dear Sir—Not wishing to have Mrs. Percy to make a Second Sacrifice of her Feelings in the Cause of Humanity, and I not wishing to Expose also a Second time mines, I am with great regret obliged to decline of having the satisfaction of paying another visit to poor Monsieur Housset, persuaded that I would have to encounter the same treatment I have Experienced this day. . . . P. S. If you think that my respects are admissable to Mrs. Percy I hope that you Will present them."[10]

Both Lucy and John James realized that he was an unwelcome

9. Arthur, *Audubon*, 221–24. For a detailed account of Audubon's doings at Oakley, see Corning (ed.), *Journal Made During His Trip*, 159–97, 193; Mrs. Percy may have met Audubon at a funeral in 1821. Ruthven Deane (ed.), "Extracts from an Unpublished Journal of John James Audubon," *Auk*, XXI (1904), 337.

10. Message to Captain Walsh, September 19, 1822, Captain Walsh to Zephyr P. Ogon, September 20, 1822, both in Walsh Papers.

guest. Audubon's pride smarted at the realization that he was acceptable only because of his wife, and that he was regarded as something of a curiosity. Lucy realized that Audubon's presence at Beech
Woods was potentially dangerous to the security they had so recently found. She cautioned her husband to give Jane Percy a wide
berth. His sensitive nature and short temper in combination with
Jane Percy's tendency to criticize and dictate were ideal ingredients
for an explosion. The blowup was not long in coming. While Lucy
was teaching, John James spent his time practicing in the use of oils
by painting his own likeness with the aid of a mirror. Seeing the
results of his work, Jane Percy asked him to paint portraits of Sarah
and another of her daughters. The project went on well enough at
first, but when John James began laying on the colors, he gave the
girls rather yellow complexions. When Jane Percy saw the sickly
looking figures in the portrait, she demanded that Audubon change
the coloring. He refused, Jane insisted, and John James flew into a
rage. Audubon's anger was quickly matched by Jane Percy's. She
was not accustomed to refusals, much less being shouted at, and she
ordered Audubon off the plantation.[11] Evidently Lucy had over-
heard the argument. She told her husband that his conduct had
been rash, childish, and indefensible. She surely would not con-
done or defend conduct that jeopardized the only security they had
known for years. John James packed his few belongings and stomped
down the drive of Beech Woods.

Lucy returned to her teaching duties and may even have apologized to Jane Percy for her husband's behavior. Meantime, John
James sought refuge in Bayou Sara and the lively solitude of the Feliciana woods.[12] After three days of sulking, he was willing to brave
the Percy wrath to apologize to Lucy. Waiting in the woods for the
cover of darkness, John James stole into the little cottage. He asked
Lucy's forgiveness. Her anger had cooled, and she readily accepted
his profuse apology.

Lost in their affection for one another, neither of them heard the
cottage door open. It was not until the door of their bedroom was

11. Arthur, *Audubon*, 262, 263.
12. *Ibid.*, 263.

thrown open that the Audubons realized that their privacy had been invaded. Standing in the doorway was Jane Percy, and behind her stood a slave holding a lantern. It was he who had seen John James creeping into the cabin and had informed his mistress.[13] Mrs. Percy was appalled that John James had been so bold as to return to Beech Woods. However, her chief objection was finding her children's teacher in bed with a man—even her husband. She demanded that John James leave Beech Woods immediately.

Audubon had been insulted, embarrassed, and humiliated many times in his life, but the experience of being ordered from his wife's bed had no equal. Walking the fifteen miles back to Bayou Sara in the dead of night, John James vented his rage upon the wind that rustled through the woods. He had been degraded before his wife, treated like a vagabond—and this had been done by a woman. Audubon would never forget that walk, nor the "Scotch stiffness, so well exhibited *toward me at a particular house in Louisiana.*"[14]

For Lucy, Jane Percy's behavior was an unspeakable breach of propriety and privacy. She, too, had been humiliated. Because the cottage was so small, her sons would have been awakened by the loud, angry voices, and they must have heard their father being ordered from the house. It must have galled her to realize that she could do nothing but swallow the insult. If she left her employment, what would become of them? John James would never finish the collection, and she would be hard pressed to find another position that paid as well. She would not quit, but neither would she forget or forgive Jane Percy for making it clear that poverty had conquered pride.

Lucy considered her husband's feelings. She knew that his anger was merely a façade hiding the gloom and depression that the incident produced.[15] In this incident Lucy showed herself to be of independent mind, rejecting her husband's advice in a serious crisis that meant separation for the family. Lucy, while greatly humiliated and provoked, remained calm and able to think in terms of the future.

13. *Ibid.*
14. Ford (ed.), *The 1826 Journal*, 67.
15. John James Audubon to Lucy Audubon, May 15, 1827, in Audubon Collection.

Audubon, however, allowed his emotions to control his reason and permitted his injured pride to jeopardize his own and his family's very subsistence.

It was not long before an abrupt, even curt, message arrived from John James, demanding that Gifford pack his clothes immediately and meet him in Bayou Sara. He informed Lucy that as soon as his son arrived they would leave for Natchez. Audubon could neither understand nor accept the fact that his wife had remained at the scene of his humiliation, and his message was a cutting reminder that in his opinion Lucy and the boys should have left Beech Woods with him.[16]

Lucy knew that John James needed the solace that Gifford could provide, yet it was with sorrow that she watched her son hurry down the road. She wondered if her family would be ripped asunder in their struggle to survive. She turned her attention to Woodhouse who was disconsolate over his brother's departure and sorely confused about the events of the night before. There were classes to prepare for and students to meet, and Lucy must have consoled herself with the thought that the days came only one at a time.

Several weeks went by, and the natural reserve that Jane Percy had so much admired in Lucy cooled to a rather icy withdrawal. Yet the mistress of Beech Woods could find no fault with Lucy's work. Indeed, Lucy found solace among her students. She spent her days in the classroom and her evenings with Woodhouse, all the while worrying about Gifford and John James in Natchez.

Lucy was teaching when a message arrived from William Provan advising her that John James and Gifford were dangerously ill with yellow fever.[17] She dismissed her class, packed a small bag, and informing Jane Percy of the emergency, asked for the loan of a horse so that she could go to her husband and son. A horse and gig were immediately made ready. Lucy had no hesitation in taking the journey alone. A faint-hearted person would have been left gasping by the way that she guided horse and gig over the narrow rutted road. She demanded maximum speed of the horses because, after twenty-

16. Arthur, *Audubon*, 263; Corning (ed.), *Letters of Audubon*, I, 27.
17. Arthur, *Audubon*, 265–66; Maria R. Audubon (ed.), *Audubon and His Journals*, I, 53.

one years in her adopted country, she knew only too well the dangers of yellow fever. Equally impelling, William Provan's message had said that John James was calling for her.[18] Once in the vicinity of Natchez, Lucy found her way to the plantation of George T. Duncan, whose hospitality John James and Gifford had been enjoying when they were stricken.

Lucy found her husband and son in serious condition. Both of them were delirious and bathed in sweat. For a time their survival was in doubt, but finally both patients rallied under her care. However, their recovery was slow. August turned into September, and back at Beech Woods, Jane Percy was becoming impatient at the absence of her teacher. She probably knew that Lucy would not abandon John James and Gifford until they were fully recovered, and perhaps Jane felt a twinge of remorse for her midnight raid upon the Audubon boudoir. Whatever the case, she sent Lucy word to return to Beech Woods and to bring John James and Gifford with her. Father and son could convalesce while Lucy returned to her classroom.[19]

Lucy probably had to coax John James into returning to the place that he had been twice ordered to leave. Yet he had no place else to go, so he swallowed his pride and accepted the Percy offer. At Beech Woods, Lucy resumed her teaching duties, and John James regained his strength, although he again became despondent about the future. He began to speak of returning east to try his luck once again in the mercantile world. Lucy flatly rejected this idea. They had both worked too hard and had sacrificed too much for her husband to resume a career that was so contrary to his liking. Lucy was determined that his drawings would be published. She suggested that John James travel to Philadelphia, the center of learning and science in the early nineteenth century, and present his bird collection for publication.[20] Immediately Audubon's gloom evaporated, and his quick smile and ready wit returned. It was impossible for Lucy not to be pleasantly affected by Audubon's jubilance.

The proposed trip to Philadelphia fitted in nicely with the plans

18. Ford, *John James Audubon*, 138.
19. *Ibid.*
20. Arthur, *Audubon*, 266.

that Lucy and John James had made for Gifford. He was only fourteen years old, but he had some understanding of the adversity that
had affected his family. The boy had been willing enough to become
an apprentice artist and travel about the country with his father and
Stein, but this enterprise had failed. Gifford had received all the
education that Lucy could provide. He was becoming restless in the
world of children, and it was obviously time to place him in a more
mature environment. Although Lucy believed in the genius of her
husband, she knew that few people appreciated artistic talent.
Therefore, she had determined to encourage Gifford to become a
businessman. She wrote to Nicholas and Eliza asking if a position as
an apprentice in the Berthoud business could be arranged for him.
Anxious to help, Nicholas offered to start his nephew as a clerk in
his countinghouse.[21]

Hence, one day in October the four Audubons walked down the
drive of Beech Woods, and after all the good-byes were said, Lucy
and Woodhouse watched and waved until Gifford and John James
were out of sight. Lucy would miss them both, but she was most
apprehensive about Gifford. Although Louisville seemed far away,
she was consoled knowing that Eliza and Nicholas would look after
the welfare of her first born.

With her husband gone, Lucy turned her attention to her students. In addition to the Percy daughters, she was teaching a number of other young girls. They included Isabel Kendrick, Miss Mar-
shall, Ann Mathews, Ann Eliza Ratliff, the Swayze girls, Julia Ann,
Sallie Ann, and Augusta Randolph, Caroline Hamilton, and Virginia Chisholm. Mrs. Audubon's school was quite an attraction
both for parents and students. Life on the isolated plantation was
very lonely, particularly for the young girls of the planter families.
Attending Lucy's school was an opportunity for the young ladies to
associate with other girls their own age and was as much a social as
an educational experience. Lucy's young charges were from the
most affluent families in Feliciana.[22]

21. *Ibid.*
22. Sarah Turnbull Stirling, "Audubon in West Feliciana," *Americana*, VII (July, 1912),
634–35; Succession Records of Stephen Swayze, Box 92, 1828, Succession Records of John
Hamilton, Box 41, 1829, both in St. Francisville Courthouse, St. Francisville, La.

The students found the tall, slender Englishwoman rather fright-ening. She was very serious both in bearing and speech, and an icy stare from her gray eyes made even the contemplation of mischief inadvisable. The girls quickly learned that Mrs. Audubon's for-midable appearance was no mere surface impression. Lucy was not an easy task mistress. She gave the students a great deal more than the basic elements of reading, writing, and arithmetic. She begged, borrowed, and purchased books so that she could familiarize the girls with good literature. She had few musical scores, but made do with what she had, and continually tried to procure more. In return for the time and energy she put forth in the classroom, Lucy ex-pected results. She had little patience with students who did not apply themselves. Yet those girls who put forth maximum effort quickly learned that Mrs. Audubon was not to be feared. She greeted good work with quick wit and a ready smile and occasion-ally with the gift of a book.[23] Honest mistakes were met with pa-tience and understanding.

Outside of the classroom Lucy served as a surrogate mother to all of her students who were boarding with the Percys. It was Lucy who untangled incorrect stitches in the clothing they made. It was to Lucy they brought their adolescent problems and dreams. She was also there to listen and to temper the gossip sessions when each tried to outdo the other in publicizing the latest rumors in the parish. When a trip to St. Francisville was in the offing, the girls came to Lucy for money to buy new shoes or material or their favorite vari-ety of sweets.[24]

Lucy never lost her fondness for the freedom of the outdoors and for physical activity. She went for walks in the scenic woods sur-rounding Beech Woods and swam frequently in the springhouse, even giving swimming lessons to the students. On occasion she went to St. Francisville to procure supplies for her students or merely to browse through the stalls of the market place. She met and opened

23. Muschamp, *Audacious Audubon*, 144–45; Lucy Audubon to Charlotte Swayze, July 22, 1826, in James Kilbourne Collection, privately owned by Mrs. Stephen Dart, St. Fran-cisville, La.
24. Charlotte Swazye to Mary C. Weeks, August 3, 1824, in Weeks Papers; Succession of Stephen Swayze.

accounts with the merchants of St. Francisville and Bayou Sara, and she grew fond of the community that gave her the respect she had hungered after for years. Most important, after only one year at Beech Woods Lucy had saved about one thousand dollars.[25] It had been many years since she had known such economic security.

During the fourteen months that Audubon was absent, Lucy heard from her husband frequently. The missives he wrote from Shippingport contained no surprises. He had met with an expectedly cool reception from her family. In the view of Nicholas and Eliza, he was again chasing a rainbow while Lucy remained in some forlorn outpost working and earning the money he squandered. Lucy could no doubt picture them. Yet, because his letters revealed an acute awareness of being snubbed and disregarded by family and one-time friends, Lucy was surprised that John James chose to remain in Kentucky until the spring before starting to Philadelphia.[26]

In January, Lucy received a letter that revealed the depth of his torment. He had written to her on the day that Nicholas' mother had died. The old Frenchwoman had been one of the few people who had retained a genuine affection for her fellow countryman after his financial disaster in Henderson, and her death accentuated his feeling that he had lost much in his life. "I was silent; many tears fell from my eyes, accustomed to sorrow. It was impossible for me to work; my heart, restless, moved from point to point all round the compass of my life. Ah, Lucy! what have I felt to-day! how can I bear the loss of our truest friend? This has been a sad day, most truly; I have spent it thinking, thinking, learning, weighing my thoughts, and quite sick of life. I wished I had been as quiet as my venerable friend, as she lay for the last time in her room."[27]

After John James had arrived in Philadelphia in April, 1824, Lucy received news that was as disappointing to her as it was to her husband. John James wrote that he had found no one interested in publishing his collection. His work was rejected and criticized by

25. Turnipseed and Babcock Ledger, 1827–28, July 7, 1827, p. 9, John Swift Account Books, January 1, 1830, p. 5, both in Department of Archives and Manuscripts, Louisiana State University, Baton Rouge; Ford, *John James Audubon*, 154.

26. Arthur, *Audubon*, 266, 267.

27. Maria R. Audubon (ed.), *Audubon and His Journals*, I, 54.

fellow artists, often severely. Even though he conveyed the full weight of his disappointment to Lucy, Audubon, nevertheless, left a good margin for hope. Quite a few talented artists had praised his work. One engraver, a Mr. Fairman, had valued the drawings highly, but he had advised John James to take the collection to England where the opportunities for publication would be greater. Audubon also let Lucy know that he had exhibited his work in Philadelphia for the general public. The exhibition had not paid well, but the reception famous artists had given his work encouraged him greatly. John James wrote to Lucy, "I am now determined to go to Europe with my 'treasures' since I am assured nothing so fine in the way of ornithological representations exist."[28]

Leaving Philadelphia, Audubon traveled to New York. Lucy learned that he was no more successful there than he had been in Philadelphia in finding a publisher for the collection. Yet for the first time in many years, she had news that must have rekindled the pride she had once had in her husband. John James wrote that his collection had been examined and praised by the members of the Lyceum of Natural History and that he had been unanimously elected to membership. Indeed, after being in the city for only eleven days, he had read a paper before the lyceum membership, and it had been well received.[29]

From New York, John James traveled up the Hudson River, visiting Niagara Falls, and then he went on to Buffalo and Lake Erie. Finding himself short of funds, he set out on foot for Pittsburgh, arriving there in September, 1824. Evidently Lucy's Uncle Benjamin gave Audubon a better reception than he had expected. According to John James, the cordial greeting was prompted by the news that his drawings had been praised by many important people in Philadelphia, but this is not likely. Benjamin Bakewell had experienced financial disaster himself. He felt a natural sympathy for Lucy and John James, and he had always tried to help the Audubons whenever he could. After John James had earned a few dollars draw-

28. Herrick, *Audubon, the Naturalist*, I, 327–36; Arthur, *Audubon*, 271–75; Maria R. Audubon (ed.), *Audubon and His Journals*, I, 55–58; Ford, *John James Audubon*, 141–47.
29. Herrick, *Audubon, the Naturalist*, I, 338; Arthur, *Audubon*, 278; Ford, *John James Audubon*, 148–49.

ing portraits in black chalk, he made his way to Cincinnati. There he was able to borrow fifteen dollars with which to purchase passage to Louisville.[30]

In Louisville he saw Gifford and learned that the boy was well satisfied with his new job. Nicholas was profuse in his praise of the boy's industry and serious mind. But Nicholas seemed unimpressed with Audubon, his collection, and his dreams of Europe and fame. John James stayed only a short time because, as he noted, "too much notice was taken of my rough appearance. I decided to move on quickly to Bayou Sara."[31]

When John James arrived in Bayou Sara, he learned that yellow fever was epidemic in the area. The captain of the steamer would not chance docking, so his bedraggled passenger was brought to shore in a dinghy. He walked up the hill to St. Francisville and found the village deserted. Audubon wrote: "All had withdrawn to the pine woods. On rousing the postmaster I learned to my joy that my wife and son John were well. In the calm, heavy, suffocating atmosphere it seemed to me as if I were breathing death." Not until after midnight did John James secure the loan of a horse and begin the journey to Beech Woods. In the darkness he lost his way and did not arrive at Lucy's cabin until early morning.[32]

In spite of the early hour, Lucy was busy giving a piano lesson to one of her students when John James appeared in the door. Surprised and delighted, Lucy forgot her pupil. She kissed and embraced John James, who noted that in that instant all of his toils and trials were forgotten, and he was once again happy. The Audubons had a great deal to talk about after such a lengthy separation. Yet Lucy's first concern must have been Audubon's appearance. His tattered clothing, uncut hair, and shaggy beard told her of the suffering he had endured. Indeed, John James himself thought that he looked like a "Wandering Jew."[33]

30. Arthur, *Audubon*, 282–83; Herrick, *Audubon, the Naturalist*, I, 344–45; Ford, *John James Audubon*, 150–53.
31. Ford (ed.), *Audubon, by Himself*, 133–34.
32. *Ibid.*, 134.
33. *Ibid.*; Peattie, *Singing in the Wilderness*, 222.

John James spent several days resting and sharing with Lucy the happenings of his trip. Of course, the collection of birds dominated the conversation. Although he had found no one willing to publish his work, Audubon told Lucy of the approbation his work had received from such scholars and artists as Thomas Sully, Charles Lucien Bonaparte, Charles LeSueur, Dr. Richard Harlan, and Rembrandt Peale.[34] He spoke with determination when he talked of going to England and of finding an engraver.

Lucy had long believed that in the country of her birth her husband's talent would be recognized. Three years earlier, an English visitor to Natchez, a Mr. Leacock, had told John James that it would take him several years to be noticed in England, but Lucy had disagreed vigorously and predicted quick recognition.[35] Now in the winter of 1825, she agreed with John James that the European venture would be a success. The problem was to earn sufficient funds to get John James across the Atlantic, and to provide him with money to maintain himself in a respectable manner while he pursued his objective. Lucy had already saved a fair sum. To secure more, they decided that whenever John James was not working on the collection he would offer lessons in art and dancing to any of Lucy's students who were willing to pay the extra tuition.[36] From time to time Audubon would also offer fencing lessons to the young men in the area. However, they agreed that he would devote most of his time to collecting and drawing new specimens, and to improving upon the drawings he already had.

For a year and a half Lucy and John James lived and worked together at Beech Woods in harmony with each other and their surroundings. They found here a measure of peace, and they recaptured a sense of mutual understanding that they had not experienced in many years. They were no longer faced with abject poverty and the bleak struggle merely to survive. Lucy could allow herself the luxury of concentrating upon the elusive dream that she and John James had been chasing since they had decided in Cincin-

34. Herrick, *Audubon, the Naturalist*, I, 327–44.
35. Buchanan, *Life of Audubon*, 73; Arthur, *Audubon*, 257.
36. Ford (ed.), *Audubon, by Himself*, 134.

Thos. Edwards ·825

This silhouette of Lucy was evidently made on a trip to New Orleans with John James the year before he left her to seek his fortune in England.

When Audubon, already styling himself naturalist, sat for this silhouette with Lucy, he was on the verge of winning his long
struggle.

nati to work toward the publication of Audubon's work. She had been unable to do that as long as food, shelter, and clothing for her family had been in doubt.

Although Lucy had improved their economic condition at Beech Woods, neither she nor John James could forget that they lived in someone else's home and were dependent upon the whims of an employer. They shared the dream, or rather the ambition, of regaining the economic and social status that they had lost. Even though Lucy supported the family, she never confused the roles that society assigned to men and women.

By the early nineteenth century, beliefs about the intrinsic inferiority of women culminated in the cult of domesticity, which sharply circumscribed the spheres in which the female could respectably exist. A sharp dichotomy was drawn between the home and the economic world outside of the home. Nature and the moral superiority of women designated the home as their proper sphere. The idealization of motherhood was an important corollary to the notion of separate spheres. The world outside of the home was the man's domain because nature endowed him with the superior intellectual, emotional, and physical capacities to deal with all the activities of the world. Most important the man dealt with economic struggles. His home was a refuge from a hostile world where his wife insured a tranquil environment and provided him with physical and spiritual refreshment. Indeed the economic dependence of the female upon the male had long been a cardinal tenet of the prevailing belief in male superiority.[37]

Of course, Lucy had never heard of the cult of domesticity or the doctrine of two spheres, but she was innately a product of place and time. In both Kentucky and Louisiana, Lucy lived in a frontier community where the interdependence of men and women was traditionally greater than that in the urban and newly industrialized

37. Smith, *Daughters of the Promised Land*, 54, 66, 275; Anne F. Scott and Andrew M. Scott, *One Half the People: The Fight for Woman Suffrage* (Philadelphia, 1975), 8; Walter E. Houghton, *The Victorian Frame of Mind, 1830–1870* (New Haven, 1957), 343; Kraditor, *Up From the Pedestal*, 9–12, 63, 81; Benson, *Women in Eighteenth Century America*, 157–58, 211; Andrew Sinclair, *The Emancipation of the American Woman* (New York, 1966), 116–17; Scott, *The Southern Lady*, 15; Harris, *Beyond Her Sphere*, 3, 22, 33; Dexter, *Career*, 219–27; Demos, "The American Family," 433–35.

communities of the East. From an early age she understood and embraced the conventions that assigned her to the province of the home. When she married Lucy wanted and fully expected her husband to be the dominant figure in her family, just as her father had been in his. In her view John James had fully satisfied her expectations until misfortunes beyond his control shattered their prospects for a comfortable and secure life. In Henderson, Lucy had unquestionably taken great delight in her position as mistress of her own large and lively household, in bearing, raising, caring for and educating her children, in serving as surrogate mother for her brothers and her sister, and in hosting visits by neighbors and friends. Once deprived of her home and left to her own devices in Cincinnati, Lucy proved unable to cope with what she considered a hostile world, and she quickly retreated to the security of her sister's home. Indeed, Lucy had resented being left on her own to provide for herself and her sons, and in bitter terms she had reminded Audubon that he was failing to fulfill his role as a man, a husband, and a father. It was necessary, at the very least, that he provide financial security for the family.[38]

Lucy, however, was also a child of the Enlightenment, nurtured and schooled by a liberal and dominant father, possessed of an exceptional education, and accustomed to having her opinions, as well as her womanhood, respected. Lucy, therefore, regarded her marriage as a partnership in the fullest sense, and John James unquestionably held the same view. He frequently commented upon her penchant for independent thinking, and he actively sought and respected her opinion in all matters. Indeed, the deal struck between the Audubons regarding their future was remarkable for the period. It was by mutual consent that Lucy became family provider and guardian of the Audubon coffers. Once she found occupation and an environment that would allow her to successfully meet her end of the bargain, Lucy proved far more forceful and determined than John James. Neither her husband's periodic moments of despair nor

38. Lucy Bakewell to Miss Gifford, October 16, 1803, September 5, 1805, William Bakewell to Miss Gifford, October 12, 1804, Lucy Audubon to Miss Gifford, April 1, 1821, all in Audubon Collection; Corning (ed.), *Journal Made During His Trip*, 120; Audubon Journal, May 23, 31, 1821.

Jane Percy's humiliations nor the fact that she lived amid a society that regarded artists and artistic endeavors as something of an oddity deterred Lucy from the single aim that Audubon go to England and his work be published.[39]

In the pursuit of her goal Lucy appears quite the liberated woman. However, such a description is misleading if not inaccurate. Clearly, Lucy was reacting to an emergency situation. She assumed the role of family breadwinner reluctantly and was embarrassed for both herself and her husband. Only through Audubon's success would she find contentment. Lucy knew that her "partner of destiny" would never be at peace, never truly content, unless he attained fame and economic security through his own labors—through his drawings. Only then could he make up for the humiliations visited upon himself, his wife, and his sons. She knew that it was essential for John James one day to ride through Louisville in a "coach and six," and it was just as essential that she should ride beside him. Her role as family provider was only a temporary expedient that would allow the Audubons to return to affluence. John James would again be a respected figure and Lucy, returned to a home of her own, would again derive status and respect from her husband's position in society.[40]

Lucy's students contributed a good deal to the Audubons' happiness in West Feliciana. Lucy was delighted to see her students' wholehearted acceptance of her husband. She knew that the girls were a bit infatuated with the handsome, long-haired Frenchman. She must have smiled inwardly when the students giggled and chattered and vied with each other to procure a lock of Audubon's hair.[41] Their homage was medicine to John James's bruised and battered pride. Not only did the students feed Audubon's undernourished ego, their youthful zest for the lighter side of life encouraged Lucy and John James to resume many activities that they had formerly enjoyed. They swam together in the springhouse while

39. Ford (ed.), *The 1826 Journal*, 333; Arthur, *Audubon*, 257; John James Audubon to Lucy Audubon, June 20, 1827, in Audubon Collection. See also, Scott, *The Southern Lady*.

40. Gerda Lerner (ed.), *The Female Experience: An American Documentary* (Indianapolis, 1977), xxx, xxxi; Ford, *John James Audubon*, 156; Lucy Audubon to Mrs. Gifford, November 27, 1834, in Audubon Collection.

41. Arthur, *Audubon*, 296–97; Ford, *John James Audubon*, 156.

giving lessons to the students. They danced together in the cotton gin house, demonstrating to the students the graceful steps of the cotillion. And surrounded by their young and carefree charges, they often laughed together.[42]

Yet it must have been evident to Lucy that the years of being sneered at had taken their toll on John James. He had little patience with practical jokes aimed at him. One of the Randolph girls, obviously trying her best to make a favorable impression on John James, asked one of her friends, probably Ann Mathews, to teach her something in French that she could repeat to Mr. Audubon. Evidently, Ann could not pass up this opportunity to play mischief. She carefully instructed her to say "Bon soir, chat." Miss Randolph proudly repeated this greeting to John James who promptly flew into a rage. The girl was appalled to learn that she had said "Good night, cat."[43] When Lucy learned of the incident, she soothed Audubon's ruffled feathers and had more than a few reproving words to say to the imaginative Miss Mathews. She knew that none of her students would have dared to play such a prank on her. She made certain that the girls extended her husband the same respect that they gave her.

The Audubons quickly realized that the planter families in West Feliciana were virtually starved for a taste of social life and for cultural entertainment. They decided that dancing lessons offered on the weekends with all the pupils gathered at the same time would be a profitable undertaking. It was arranged that on Friday and Saturday nights for a period of three months John James would give lessons in the hotel ballroom at Woodville, Mississippi, a village several miles distant from Beech Woods. A class of sixty pupils, ranging in age from eight to eighty, was organized.[44]

These weekend soirees rapidly became the favorite entertainment of the well-to-do for miles around. It was an opportunity for boy to meet girl. For wives, mothers, and grandmothers, it was a chance to leave the lonely plantation with their men and to see and

42. Ford, *John James Audubon*, 156; Arthur, *Audubon*, 292, 296–97; Stirling, "Audubon in West Feliciana," 639.

43. Arthur, *Audubon*, 296; Stirling, "Audubon in West Feliciana," 639.

44. Arthur, *Audubon*, 293.

talk with each other. For the men, too, these outings provided an opportunity to speak to other planters about crops, slaves, and hunting. After the first gathering Audubon's reputation as an entertaining performer spread, and many came merely to watch the antics of the flamboyant Frenchman.

John James described opening night of the dancing classes:

> One day I went over to begin my duties. I dressed at the hotel, then with my fiddle under my arm entered the ballroom. My music was highly appreciated at the start. I placed the gentlemen in line, thinking to let the young ladies compose themselves a little. How I toiled before I could get one graceful step or motion! I broke my bow and, nearly, my violin in my excitement and impatience! Next I had the ladies, alone, take the same order and try the same steps. Then I tried both together—pushed one here, another there—all the while singing to myself to assist their efforts. The many parents who were looking on seemed to be delighted. At the close of this first lesson I was asked to *dance to my own music.* This I did—until the whole room came down in thunderous applause, in the clapping of hands and shouting. Thus ended my first lesson and an amusing comedy. Lessons in fencing, for the young gentlemen, came next.[45]

Lucy did not accompany John James to Woodville, but she awaited his return at night and laughed heartily while Audubon gave her a demonstration of the lumbering grace of many of the older men who found it impossible to point a toe or bend their stiff legs. Lucy had a calming effect upon her exasperated husband and reminded him that he could endure stiff legs to earn money to publish the collection. He was, after all, receiving a handsome fee for his instruction, which he turned over to Lucy to add to their growing savings.[46]

Lucy welcomed Audubon's contributions to the family savings, but she was just as happy when John James was off wandering and drawing. Usually she saw him off in the morning, a gun in his hand and a pack on his back. She seldom knew when she would see him again, at dusk, at dawn, or several days hence. After a productive hunt, he would remain at Beech Woods drawing the new specimens

---

45. Ford (ed.), *Audubon, by Himself,* 134–35.
46. *Ibid.,* 135; Ford (ed.), *The 1826 Journal,* 261; Arthur, *Audubon,* 296. Audubon may have spent most of his earnings on art supplies.

or improving the representation of a drawing already finished. Lucy was there to appraise his work. She listened as John James told her of the habits and behavior of this or that specimen, and she spent many hours taking notes as he talked. In Feliciana the collection ceased to be Audubon's alone. It became partly Lucy's, and she could speak of "our work." [47]

Lucy was pleased to note that Audubon's work improved daily, and that he was more interested than ever before in finding out everything possible about the habits of each specimen. He corresponded regularly with the most prominent figures in the field of natural history—the men whom he had met in Philadelphia and New York. He shipped them lizards, snakes, alligators, insects, shrubs, and fruits. Of course, to Lucy the most important fact was that she was involved in all of his doings. [48]

Just as in Henderson, the area surrounding Lucy's cottage rapidly began to resemble a zoo. Baby alligators, vultures, turkey buzzards, snakes, and a variety of other animals were in residence. Evidently, Lucy was not too familiar with alligators, for sometime later Audubon wrote, imitating his wife, "Alligators!!!!! Who in the known world ever heard of such things?" Perhaps Lucy's exclamation was prompted by the knowledge that Audubon had once lost a baby alligator in a friend's cabin. On another occasion, John James captured a black snake, two moccasins, and a rattlesnake and was preparing to send them to Dr. DeKay in New York. He placed the live rattlesnake in a tub of whiskey "where it laid a few moments motionless, then feeling the spirit," the reptile sprang from the tub striking at everything within reach before it was recaptured. Lucy cautioned John James to use greater care since her students were in the vicinity. [49]

Inside the cottage Lucy prepared a small room, which John James called his little "laboratoire." [50] There he kept his collection, which he was eager to show any visitor. At night he worked there, while

---

47. Arthur, *Audubon*, 301; Ford (ed.), *The 1826 Journal*, 126, 261.
48. Ford, *John James Audubon*, 155–59; Ford (ed.), *Audubon, by Himself*, 115; Herrick, *Audubon, the Naturalist*, I, 344; Arthur, *Audubon*, 304–307.
49. Ford (ed.), *The 1826 Journal*, 87; Ford (ed.), *Audubon, by Himself*, 112–20, 115; Arthur, *Audubon*, 303.
50. Ford (ed.), *The 1826 Journal*, 126.

Lucy, seated nearby, sewed, read, or took notes for him. She was hard pressed to maintain order in the laboratoire, and she was always on the alert for any creatures that John James had brought in and forgotten to remove.

During the day, Lucy was frequently reminded of her husband's work. The unpleasant odor of a carcass that John James had left wired on the wall outside too long might drift in through the open windows of her classroom, driving Lucy and her students outdoors in search of sweeter-smelling air. Robert Dow Percy, Jane Percy's son, recalled the stench of a big gobbler that eventually became one of Audubon's most celebrated plates. "It weighed twenty-eight pounds. Audubon pinned it up beside the wall to sketch and he spent several days lazily sketching it. The damned fellow kept it pinned up there till it rotted and stunk—I hated to lose so much good eating."[51]

It is strange that Jane Percy allowed Beech Woods to become a sort of laboratory for the Frenchman. The most credible explanation is that she valued Lucy too highly to chance losing her. By 1825 Lucy had gained a certain measure of economic independence. She had money saved, and in two years her reputation had spread throughout West Feliciana. Mrs. Percy must have realized that Lucy could practically choose her employer if she ever left Beech Woods. Indeed, having Lucy on her plantation carried with it a certain distinction and prestige that did not escape Jane Percy. Another possible explanation for Mrs. Percy's silence concerning Audubon could have been her certainty that the Frenchman would soon be off on a mission to Europe, leaving Lucy poorer and more dependent on her. Whatever the case, Jane and Audubon did exchange a few civil words. At least Mrs. Percy asked Audubon how to prevent a certain species of insect from killing her beech trees.[52] John James did not record his reply on this occasion.

The Audubons enjoyed many quiet moments in the Feliciana countryside. They would walk through the woods in the evening, drinking in the lively sights and sounds. Lucy's favorite haunt was the sandy shore of Bayou Sara Creek, a short distance from Beech

51. Arthur, *Audubon*, 300.
52. Ford (ed.), *The 1826 Journal*, 150.

Woods. John James remembered one evening stroll: "I thought of an evening when we were walking, gently arm-in-arm together, towards the waters of the Bayou Sarah, and I watched thee bathe thy gentle form in its currents."[53] It had been years since Lucy and John James enjoyed the happiness of the outdoors.

The Audubons had a number of friends in West Feliciana with whom they visited and with whom both were comfortable. Among them was Nathaniel Wells Pope, the young man who had clerked in the Audubon and Rozier store in Louisville and who had received many severe tongue-lashings from Rozier for neglecting his duties to wander in the woods with John James. Pope had become a doctor. He moved to St. Francisville in 1823, and there he met and married Martha Johnson, the daughter of a prominent Feliciana family. Nathaniel was well thought of in the community. In 1824 he was elected selectman for the town of St. Francisville, and he was spoken of as a likely candidate for the police jury. Another person who befriended the Audubons was Augustin Bourgeat, the owner of Bush Hill plantation. Bourgeat was a French creole and a skilled hunter who had married a Feliciana native, Jane Browder. Ann Mathews' father, Judge Mathews, was also a good friend. Lucy, especially, respected and admired him.[54]

Audubon, Nathaniel, and Augustin were almost constantly in the woods. They hunted together and discussed and, at times, disagreed about the habits of this or that creature. As each of them tried to prove his opinion correct, they all learned a good deal. Their favorite gathering place was the Pope cabin, evidently a very humble dwelling. Here John James never tired of spreading his drawings on the floor for his friends' inspection, and from these people he no doubt accepted criticism. Nathaniel and Augustin helped Audubon to capture alligators and various other creatures. Augustin always seemed to know the special haunts of whatever specimen John James was pursuing. On occasion Lucy accompanied John James to the Pope home. She was always comfortable in the easy and congenial atmosphere of the small cabin, and she and

53. *Ibid.*, 74.
54. Ford, *John James Audubon*, 70; Arthur, *Audubon*, 291, 297–99; Corning (ed.), *Letters of Audubon*, I, 10; *Louisiana Journal*, March 4, 1824.

Martha quickly became friends. It was evident that Lucy made an impression on the younger woman. Mrs. Pope remembered Lucy as a woman with "fine dark gray eyes shaded by long dark lashes. Expression was her chief attraction. She was very gentle and intelligent. Her whole appearance impressed me with respect and admiration."[55]

Lucy and John James had yet another reason to be pleased with their life in Feliciana. Woodhouse had the opportunity to live with his parents without the tensions of poverty, probably for the first time he could remember. He hunted with his father and collected insects, which he preserved in whiskey for his father's friends. He watched as his father spent hours sketching the smallest detail on whatever specimen he was drawing. When he was reluctant to spend time seated next to Lucy at the piano, John James was there to see that he did whatever his mother bid. In imitation of his father, Woodhouse drew and followed John James about at every opportunity.[56]

By the spring of 1826 Lucy and John James decided that the time had come for Audubon to begin his journey. The collection was ready. Lucy had saved sufficient funds to provide John James with enough money for passage to England and to maintain him for a time once he arrived. She made certain that he carried with him letters of introduction from such personages as Henry Clay, Rufus King, and other men of note. On April 26 Lucy watched John James hurry down the drive of Beech Woods. It is likely that she felt both hope and fear, for if Audubon failed in his quest of a publisher in Europe, they would have exhausted all their opportunities for future security.

Early one morning several weeks later, Lucy was awakened by John James gently shaking her shoulder. After quieting her fear that something had gone amiss with their plans, John James explained that he had gone to New Orleans where he had booked passage on the *Delos* for Liverpool, but that the vessel would not be ready to sail for several days. Lucy was surely pleased that her husband chose

55. Arthur, *Audubon*, 298–99, 304.
56. Ford (ed.), *Audubon, by Himself*, 116–17; Stirling, "Audubon in West Feliciana," 639; Corning (ed.), *Letters of Audubon*, I, 6.

to ascend the Mississippi, and ride through the dark magnolia woods of Feliciana to spend a few days with her rather than remain in New Orleans until the *Delos* was ready to depart. Perhaps they both felt that their separation this time would be exceptionally long. Certainly, John James had no wish to spend several days in a city that had received him so poorly. He confided to his journal that "New Orleans, to a man who does not trade in dollars or any other such stuff, is a miserable spot." Lucy and John James made the most of the few days they had together. They joined in the wedding festivities of Lucy's student Virginia Chisholm, and Dietrich Holl.[57] They spoke to each other confidently about the ultimate success of the work to which they had both given so much.

On the morning of May 27, Lucy and John James were up before dawn, moving about the cabin silently so as not to wake Woodhouse. They traveled to Bush Hill where they enjoyed breakfast with Augustin and Jane. After breakfast Lucy walked arm in arm with John James to the end of Bourgeat's road, and they embraced and said good-bye. Audubon mounted the horse Bourgeat had lent him and cantered off toward Bayou Sara.[58] Lucy watched until Audubon turned in the saddle and waved a final time. It would be three years and eight months before she would see him again.

57. Ford (ed.), *The 1826 Journal*, 3, 4.
58. *Ibid.*, 4.

CHAPTER VIII

A Pyrrhic Victory

Once John James was gone, Lucy had little time to dwell on being lonely. Having given Audubon most of the money she had saved, Lucy had to find funds to support herself and Woodhouse. A number of people owed her and John James tuition for lessons given their children, and Lucy counted upon being able to collect this money. Apparently, her need was immediate and the sum owed her was considerable, for there was a certain urgency in her requests for payment. To Charlotte Swayze she wrote: "I take the liberty of writing to let you Know that three weeks have elapsed since the period when my account became due, and as I make my arrangements to discharge my own expenses at this time, depending upon the punctuality of those who owe me, I shall be obliged by your remitting to me the amount of Miss Clarissa's tuition both to me and Mr. Audubon as *soon as you can*." Before closing the letter Lucy added, "I am in great haste."[1]

It is understandable that Lucy was concerned about meeting her financial obligations. She remembered well when the name Audubon on an account ledger meant a loss for whoever had extended credit. Since Lucy had been in West Feliciana, that condition had changed. The ledger books of two local merchants, John Swift and Turnipseed and Babcock, indicate that Lucy was given credit at their stores and that she met her obligations promptly.[2]

When her requests for payment went unheeded, Lucy won-

---

1. Lucy Audubon to Charlotte Swayze, July 22, 1826, in Kilbourne Collection.
2. Turnipseed and Babcock Ledger, 1827–1828, Swift Account Books.

dered how much longer she would be able to meet her obligations promptly. Evidently, she had miscalculated the amount of money that she and Woodhouse would need immediately when she gave Audubon the family savings. Excited and optimistic about Audubon's journey, Lucy overlooked the fact that tuition had never been paid promptly. Ready cash was always scarce in a frontier area, and when cash was available, planters rarely considered school teachers important enough to be paid first.

Even though Lucy experienced difficulties in procuring the money due her, she remained a conscientious teacher. A friend and admirer described her in the classroom: "In the school room she was tireless, passing from one child to another, seeing that each was properly at work, helping, explaining, encouraging. During the hours of school each child received a personal supervision that was practically continuous. She was tall, slender, erect, always clad in black, and always wore her white cap. I never saw her without her spectacles." However, it would be a mistake to suppose that Lucy restricted herself to the classroom or spent her mornings and evenings in the cloister of her cottage. Indeed, just as she had done in Henderson, Lucy presented the community with something of a paradox. Some persons saw "Madame Audubon" as a "most kindly, gentle, benignant woman," who, according to one observer, "was loved and admired by everyone and—by most people—I think a little feared, for she had the repose and dignity of a great lady, and was not given to jokes and laughter."[3]

Yet there was another Lucy that only a few persons saw. Early in the morning on a nice day she would stride down the path that led to the stables.[4] Her spectacles would have been left behind. Instead of a black dress, she would wear a simple riding habit that she had fashioned and made herself. Her long fingers would move lightly over the leather crop that swung to and fro in rhythm with her steps. At the barn she would be greeted by a slave leading a horse that danced and snorted at the prospect of a dash through the

3. Muschamps, *Audacious Audubon*, 144–45.
4. Corning (ed.), *Letters of Audubon*, I, 13. Since Lucy's correspondence is not available, her doings must be discovered from Audubon's replies to her letters. Ford (ed.), *The 1826 Journal*, 352.

woods and the bucket of oats that would come afterwards. The slave would head the horse and weight the saddle while Lucy gathered the reins and mounted the impatient animal. Guiding the animal down the drive of Beech Woods at a brisk canter, she would soon be surrounded by lofty hardwoods and the vibrant silence of the wooded hills.

Even today, a ride alone through the dense woods that still exist around the site of the old Percy plantation would be a formidable undertaking, yet Lucy did not hesitate to ride alone. She enjoyed the exhilaration of commanding a spirited mount and the refreshing silence of the serene countryside. Surrounded by these natural beauties, perhaps Lucy felt closer to John James. On occasion she rode with Woodhouse, instructing the boy to be gentle but firm with his mount. She rode, too, with the Percy girls, directing them in the arts of proper horsemanship for young ladies. The fact that their reserved school mistress could handle the most restless animal on the Percy plantation made Lucy an even more esteemed figure in the eyes of her charges.

There were times when Lucy grew weary of the endless prattle of youngsters and sought the conversation and companionship of adults. She visited the Bourgeats, the Popes, Judge Mathews, and the Holls. Always a welcome guest, Lucy spent many agreeable hours on a Saturday and Sunday with the women in these families. She was particularly fond of visiting Virginia Holl.[5] The women sewed, spoke of the success of their gardens, and chatted about the latest local news. Their conversations ranged over a wide variety of topics. They discussed who was getting married; who had died and of what cause; the increasing number of runaway slaves and the number apprehended; the latest senseless murder in Bayou Sara or St. Francisville and who was suspected; the most recent scandals and the roguish behavior of the parish dandies; persons who had left the parish and for what reason; persons who had returned and why; which merchants were offering the best prices; the latest slave punishments, births and deaths; and the slovenly behavior of house servants. Finally, the women spoke of their own families—the tem-

5. Corning (ed.), *Letters of Audubon*, I, 10, 15, 19, 34.

perament, peculiarities, likes and dislikes of husbands and children. The conversation moved on in a steady rhythm with the circular movement of needles and thread. These gossip sessions produced more than quilts, tablecloths, and clothing. Speaking to other women was one of the few social outlets for females in any frontier area.

Lucy's friends were always delighted when she visited and participated in the conversations because her quick wit and terse comments always stimulated discussion. Indeed, Lucy seemed quite remarkable to some of the more provincial females of West Feliciana. She was educated, dignified, and poised, and lacking property or meaningful assistance from her husband, she used her own talents to support her family and finance her husband's ambitions. This put Lucy in a different category from the many women like Jane Percy who had taken over the management of plantations at the death of their husbands.

Of course, Lucy chose her friends from the small group of people who respected John James or, at least, appreciated his talent and hoped for his ultimate success. She would not have been comfortable with those who mixed admiration for her with pity for her choice of a husband. Yet, it is evident that Lucy was largely responsible for the respect given her husband. Judge Mathews, Dietrich Holl, and others could never have respected John James had they not recognized that Lucy was capable of supporting and caring for herself and her family. Audubon would have earned only their contempt had he gone off and left behind a helpless wife.

Although Lucy enjoyed these occasional visits with her friends, she spent most of her time at Beech Woods. Teaching filled her days. After classes in the evenings she most frequently strolled down to the clear waters of Bayou Sara.[6] On occasion Woodhouse accompanied her, and mother and son were frequently seen wading about in the rippling waters.

At night Lucy devoted her time to the education of her son—a task not without difficulties.[7] Beech Woods was a fierce competitor

6. Ford (ed.), *The 1826 Journal*, 74, 261.
7. *Ibid.*, 334, 353; Corning (ed.), *Letters of Audubon*, I, 6, 19.

for Woodhouse's attention. Academic pursuits seemed dull to a boy who had experienced the excitement of a hunt and the exhilaration of making a perfect shot. When Lucy called his attention to more serious matters, she had to combat the excuse that his father would have approved of his preoccupation with hunting, roaming the woods, swimming, and riding. Yet, whatever the excuse, Woodhouse knew that protest was useless. Whether it were arithmetic or piano lessons, Lucy demanded and would settle for nothing less than his best effort. When the lessons were ended, Lucy would write to Gifford and John James or read or sew before retiring. Bedtime came early on the plantation, for each morning Lucy had to be up at dawn.

Life at Beech Woods was not always smooth for Lucy. Apparently, only a short time after Audubon had gone to New Orleans to board the *Delos*, Lucy and Jane Percy quarreled. The cause of the dispute was John James. Exactly what ruffled Mrs. Percy after Audubon's departure is difficult to determine. Of course, Jane Percy was as changeable as the wind and seemed to enjoy disagreements for their own sake. Yet, before his departure, she and Audubon seemed to be on tolerably good terms. At least, she had given Audubon letters to deliver to her relatives in England, and her brother, Charles Middlemist, who was visiting Beech Woods, had entrusted John James with a sum of money to give his wife who lived in London.[8]

There is a possibility that Jane Percy's sudden annoyance stemmed from Lucy rather than John James. Lucy may have brought the problem of overdue tuition to Mrs. Percy, asking that she write to the neighbors requesting payment.[9] If Lucy did ask for such help, it is very likely that Jane would have told her that she would have no need of assistance had she not given her husband the money that she had worked so long and hard to save.

Jane Percy did, in fact, come to disapprove of Lucy once she realized that Lucy loved John James. Having witnessed for a year and a

8. Ford (ed.), *The 1826 Journal*, 333–34, 327; Corning (ed.), *Letters of Audubon*, I, 15, 26, 28; John James Audubon to Lucy Audubon, May 15, 1827, in Audubon Collection.

9. Corning (ed.), *Letters of Audubon*, I, 26, 28; Lucy Audubon to Charlotte Swayze, July 22, 1826, in Kilbourne Collection. Evidently Charles Middlemist was also in debt to Lucy.

half the strong bond that existed between the Audubons, she had no choice but to conclude that their marriage was based upon genuine affection and not, as she had initially believed, upon Lucy's ability to do her duty as a wife and endure a shiftless husband. In Mrs. Percy's narrow view, Lucy should have found Audubon insufferable, and instead of giving him affection and money, she should have dismissed him from her life. Mrs. Percy had advised the younger woman many times to send John James away. Indeed, she had shown Lucy exactly how to proceed when she twice ordered John James off the plantation. She could not understand why Lucy had refused to follow her advice, and she heartily disapproved what she did not understand.[10]

One might wonder, further, if the mistress of Beech Woods were not a bit jealous of Lucy. The respect that her daughters and the other students extended to Lucy would not have escaped Jane Percy. She would not have appreciated the fact that Lucy Audubon's word on a subject carried more weight than her own. Nor would the unbending Jane Percy have approved the deference and respect extended to Lucy by many of Feliciana's most prominent families. To Mrs. Percy such an attitude was unthinkable. Lucy Audubon was merely an employee and not to be accepted as a social equal. It is more than likely that Jane Percy experienced feelings similar to those felt by Georgiana Keats and Elizabeth Page Bakewell many years before. Lucy never lost the knack of making people, particularly other females, feel somehow inferior and always at a disadvantage.[11] Jane Percy would not have easily accepted being made to feel inadequate.

Although Mrs. Percy avoided engaging the sharp-tongued Lucy Audubon directly, she felt no inhibition in speaking disparagingly of Lucy's eccentric husband. She knew that an attack upon John James was a double-edged sword, for Lucy was vulnerable to criticism aimed at her husband.

10. Corning (ed.), *Letters of Audubon*, I, 27; Ford (ed.), *The 1826 Journal*, 333–34; Arthur, *Audubon*, 263; John James Audubon to Lucy Audubon, May 15, June 20, 1827, both in Audubon Collection.

11. This feeling was best expressed by Georgiana Keats. See Forman (ed.), *Letters of Keats*, 451, 453–54.

After her confrontation with Jane Percy, Lucy wrote to John James warning him that he was again unwelcome at Beech Woods. She also began to consider leaving the Percy plantation. She thought of returning to Shippingport, but she had no intention of rushing off while so much money was still owed her. She decided, instead, to bide her time, and to look for a neighboring family who needed a teacher for their children. She even allowed herself to hope that Audubon would find a publisher quickly and send for her. Lucy decided that, if all went well with Audubon and if she could collect the funds owed her, she and Woodhouse would join him in England during the summer of 1827.[12] This would give her a year in which to collect the money due her and to find a new position that would be more agreeable than that at Beech Woods. Lucy informed John James of her plans, but to keep from worrying him, she was very vague about leaving Beech Woods.

Not until late October did Lucy learn anything of Audubon's progress in England. The letter spoke of the good beginnings that John James had made, and even though she knew her husband's tendency to exaggerate, she must have felt that, at last, the Audubons were on the road to economic recovery.

John James began by telling her how much he missed her and that he had high hopes for success. "Absence from thee, my Lucy, is painful, believe me," he wrote, "and was I not living in hope to be approaching the long wished for moment of being at last well received in the learned world, and of being also likely to be remunerated for my labours, I could not stand it much longer. No really, Lucy, I could not. I am fonder of thee than ever in my life. The reason is simply this, that I hope shortly to gain the full cup of thy esteem and affection." Lucy then read that the drawings had been well received. Audubon's collection had been exhibited at the Royal Institute, "and 413 persons rushed in [in] two hours. My fame reached distant places so quickly that [on] the third day persons of wealth arrived from Manchester to view them. I have been presented to one of the noblest and oldest peers of England, *Lord Stanley*. He, Lucy, knelt down on the rich carpet to examine my

12. Ford (ed.), *The 1826 Journal*, 352; Corning (ed.), *Letters of Audubon*, I, 26.

style closely. This renowned scientific man received me . . . with the warmth of friendship, . . . and said, 'Mr. Audubon, I assure you this work of yours is unique, and deserves the patronage of the crown.'" Lucy also learned that Audubon planned to travel to Derbyshire, Oxford, London, Edinburgh, and Paris where he would be presented to important personages and exhibit his work.[13]

Lucy was pleased to note that her husband was personally accepted and that he moved freely among Liverpool's elite. She read, "I have many comfortable nights at gentlemen's [country] seats in the neighbourhood, and the style of living is beyond all description. Coaches call for me and waiters in livery are obedient to me as if I myself was a lord of England. I hope this may continue, and that the end of all this may be plenty of the needful." Lucy was surely encouraged that Audubon seemed to realize that personal acclaim was secondary to acquiring "plenty of the needful"—financial security. Yet, her husband's ego was boundless. She read, "If I was not dreading to become proud, I would say that I am, in Liverpool, a shadow of Lafayette and his welcome in America."[14]

Lucy shared the good tidings with her friends in West Feliciana, and she told them of her plans to join Audubon soon. By November, Lucy received confirmation of all that John James had written. He sent her newspapers from Liverpool that carried favorable accounts of the drawings he had exhibited.[15] These, too, she shared with her friends.

In the same month, Lucy received an answer to her first letters. John James assured her that he would heed her advice about not returning to Beech Woods. "Yes, should I return to America and to Louisiana, I would go to my good friend Bourgeat's with great pleasure, without trespassing one foot north of his line." He also told her that, if she should leave Beech Woods, he would prefer her going to Nicholas in Kentucky or, better still, to New York. "The latter I would greatly prefer, viewing the quickness of communication with this country. Or the thing still more preferable [would be] for thee to come over with John only, and travel with me, or remain

13. Ford (ed.), The 1826 Journal, 324, 325.
14. Ibid., 326–27.
15. Corning (ed.), Letters of Audubon, I, 6.

with me either in London or Paris where I think I may reside a long time." After presenting these options, John James realized that Lucy was quite capable of making the most practical decision. "I have always afforded thee the following of thy wishes in all things, and I again entreat thee to do nought but thy pleasure respecting the offers now adverted to."[16]

Lucy was indeed practical, and she was becoming increasingly annoyed because she was unable to collect the tuition owed her. To make matters worse, the smouldering animosity that existed between Lucy and Jane Percy now erupted into open conflict. The tension became intolerable when Charles Middlemist informed his sister that Audubon had not yet delivered the money he was entrusted with to Mrs. Middlemist in London. Mrs. Percy complained to Lucy. Lucy wrote to John James asking him to discharge this obligation as soon as possible, and she determined to leave Beech Woods at the first opportunity.[17]

Apparently, Nathaniel Pope helped Lucy to procure another position. It was arranged that at the end of the fall school term, Lucy would move to Beech Grove, the plantation of William Garrett Johnson, a prominent cotton planter in West Feliciana.[18] Lucy was pleased with the financial arrangements that she made with the Johnsons. She was to receive one thousand dollars per year in addition to board and lodging, and William Johnson agreed to collect tuition from the neighboring planters who chose to send their daughters to the school.[19] It was insurance that Lucy would receive payment for her services instead of promises that did nothing to fill her pocketbook.

In the fall of 1827 Lucy and Woodhouse prepared to leave the small cottage that had been their home for four years. Lucy had known many moments of happiness at Beech Woods, and she had found there a measure of peace and security. Yet she refused to go on working while her pay lagged, and she would not tolerate Jane

16. Ford (ed.), *The 1826 Journal*, 333–34.
17. *Ibid.*, 334.
18. For further information on the Johnson family, see Aucoin, "The Political Career of Isaac Johnson," 941–89; Arthur and de Kernion, *Old Families of Louisiana*, 166–75.
19. Herrick, *Audubon, the Naturalist*, I, 434; Stirling, "Audubon in West Feliciana," 634–35; Arthur, *Audubon*, 387.

Percy's unpleasantness for any reason other than to support her family. When William Johnson's carriage arrived to transport her and Woodhouse to Beech Grove, it is unlikely that Lucy entertained any sorrow at leaving, but she must surely have wished that she were, instead, on her way to England and John James.

Beech Grove was not as large as the Percy plantation, although it comprised about six hundred arpents of rich land. On it were slave quarters, a barn, various outbuildings and the main dwelling, all of which were crudely constructed. The large main house had a broad porch stretching across the front. There were four large bedrooms, one of which was upstairs, a spacious parlor, and a handsomely furnished dining room. Either the large front bedroom or the study was probably converted into a classroom for Lucy.[20]

Classes began in February. Lucy was pleased with her students and anxious to establish the same rapport with these girls that she had enjoyed with her class at Beech Woods. Among her students at Beech Grove were the two Johnson girls, Susan and Malvina; Jane and Susan Montgomery; Jane and Mary Harbour; Mary, Anne, and Louisa Carpenter; Margaret Butler; Caroline Hamilton; and Mary Rucker. Ellen Johnson, the youngest of the Johnson children, was too young to attend classes. She wanted to be with her sisters and the other girls, though, and every time she could escape the watchful eye of her mother or the servants, Ellen stole into the classroom.[21] There must have been times when Ellen made Lucy think about her own little girls who had not lived long enough to romp about and tug upon her skirts.

Lucy found that the atmosphere at Beech Grove was much more pleasant and familylike than that at Beech Woods. William Johnson and his wife were kind, generous, and understanding, and they welcomed Lucy into their home and into their family.[22] Indeed, they considered themselves fortunate to have found such a capable teacher for their children. Mrs. Johnson was delighted to have a

20. Succession Records of William Garrett and Judith Johnson, Box 143, 1869, in St. Francisville Courthouse, St. Francisville, La.
21. Stirling, "Audubon in West Feliciana," 634–35, 637.
22. Herrick, Audubon, the Naturalist, I, 434; Corning, (ed.), Letters of Audubon, I, 21; John James Audubon to Lucy Audubon, May 15, 1827, in Audubon Collection.

female companion, and she hoped that Lucy would not leave for England anytime in the near future.

In March, Lucy received additional news from John James. The letter had been posted in Edinburgh. She learned that his reception in Scotland had been even more cordial than that he had received in Liverpool. She read, "My situation in Edinburgh borders almost on the miraculous; without education, [and with] scarce one of those qualities necessary to render a man able to pass through the throng of the learned here, I am positively looked on by all the professors and many of the principal persons as a very extraordinary man."[23]

Although Lucy was pleased at the news of accolades bestowed upon John James, she was overjoyed to learn that the goal that they had both worked for had been reached. Her eyes raced over the lines of tiny, scrawling script that spelled out their triumph.

> It is now a month since my work has been begun by Mr. W. H. Lizars of this city. It is to come out in Numbers of five prints [each,] all the size of life and in the same size paper [as] my largest drawings that is called double elephant. They will be brought up and finished in such superb style as to eclipse all of the kind in existence. The price of each Number is two guineas, and all individuals have the privilege of subscribing for the whole or any portion of it. Two of the plates were finished last week. . . . I think that the middle of January the first Number will be completed and under way to each subscriber. I shall send thee the very first, and I think it will please thee. . . . I cannot yet say that I will ultimately succeed but at present all bears a better prospect than I ever expected to see.[24]

Lucy was impressed and surprised with the businesslike attitude that John James seemed to take toward his work.

> It is not the naturalist that I wish to please altogether, I assure thee. It is the wealthy part of the community. The first can only speak well or ill of me but the latter will fill my pockets. The University of Edinburgh having subscribed, I look to the rest of them, eleven in number to follow. . . . As soon as it is finished I will travel with it over all England, Ireland, and Scotland, and then over the European Continent, taking

23. Ford (ed.), *The 1826 Journal*, 345.
24. Ibid., 346.

my collection with me to exhibit it in all principal cities to raise the
means of supporting myself well; and [I] would like most dearly to add
thyself and my sons also.[25]

Plowing through the long missive, Lucy realized that John James
· had not yet received her letter informing him that she intended to
meet him during the summer, for he said that he was doubtful that
she would risk coming. Lucy surely appreciated the logic and sin-
cerity of her husband's desire that the family join him:

> I am now better aware of the advantages of a family in unison that ever,
> and I am quite satisfied that by acting conjointly and by my advice we
> can realize a handsome fortune for each of us. It needs but industry and
> perseverance. . . . It is now about time to know from thee what thy
> future intentions are. I wish thee to act according to thy dictates, but
> wish to know what those dictates are. Think that we are far divided,
> and that either sickness or need may throw one into a most shocking
> situation without either friend or help, for as thou sayest thyself, "The
> world is not indulgent." Cannot we move together and feel and enjoy
> the natural need of each other? Lucy, my friend, think of all this very
> seriously. Not a portion of the earth exists but will support us amply,
> and we may feel happiness anywhere if careful. When you receive this,
> sit and consider well. Consult N. Berthoud, thy son Victor, or such a
> person as Judge Matthews [sic]. Then consult thyself and in a long,
> plain, explanatory letter give me thy own heart entire. In this country
> John can receive an education that America does not yet afford, and his
> propensities are such that, attached to me, he would be left at my death
> possessor of a talent that would be the means of his support for life.[26]

It is evident from the letter that Audubon doubted that Lucy
would join him. By advising her to consult Nicholas, Gifford, and
others, John James was revealing the terrible battering that his pride
had taken within the family circle. He was, in fact, telling Lucy
that he thought she no longer trusted his judgment as head of the
Audubon family. But John James was creating doubts for Lucy that
she did not, in fact, have. She had determined to meet Audubon
before she had any news of his success. Lucy's desire to join him

---

25. Ibid., 346–47; John James Audubon to Lucy Audubon, December 10, 1826, in Audubon Collection.
26. Ford (ed.), The 1826 Journal, 348; John James Audubon to Lucy Audubon, December 10, 1826, in Audubon Collection.

only deepened once she learned that he had found a publisher, that he wanted to provide Woodhouse with the best possible education, and that he missed her and wanted her with him to share his success.[27] Indeed, had she been able to collect the money owed her, she might well have left for England rather than moving to Beech Grove. Instead, she had agreed to remain at Beech Grove for a year, and therefore, she would not be able to leave for England during the summer of 1827 as she had initially planned. Lucy saw this as only a temporary delay. Still, she no doubt let the Johnsons know that if John James sent for her she would leave her employment to meet her husband without a backward look.

Even though she was unable to join Audubon immediately, Lucy was able to enjoy his success at once. She shared the news of his triumph with the Johnsons and her other friends and wrote to Gifford and other members of her family to tell them the encouraging news. She must have spent long hours talking to Woodhouse about living abroad and discussing with him the opportunities that a European education would afford. It was ironic that her future now seemed to rest in the land of her birth.

Sometime in April Lucy received another letter from John James boasting of his continued success. He sent her copies of the numerous invitations he had received to give her "an idea of the circles" in which he moved. He told her that he had been elected by acclamation to the Society of Arts and Sciences and that he expected to be elected in the same manner to the Wernerian Society. Most important, the number of subscriptions allotted to Scotland had been filled. Her husband's ravenous ego was devouring praise from every quarter. Enclosed within the letter was a report of George Combe, a phrenologist, who had conducted a test upon Audubon's skull, which, Combe reported, closely resembled Raphael's.[28] No doubt Lucy greeted this information with a slight shake of her head and a wry smile.

One portion of the letter was disquieting. Even though Lucy knew that she could not join John James during the summer, she

27. Ford (ed.), *The 1826 Journal*, 352.
28. *Ibid.*, 353, 354.

was nonetheless upset with the manner in which he had received the news that she would join him. He told her that although he was pleased that she wanted to come, she should not be in too great a hurry to join him. Indeed, it seemed that he was telling her that she should not think about leaving for Europe anytime soon. Lucy was impatient with his lack of clarity and the carelessness with which he dismissed the news that she would come. She could see no reason for his sudden caution. He had found a publisher, he moved in the most elite circles, and his economic situation had improved considerably. How else could he afford to dress as he described to her: "I have come to fine dressing again—silk stockings and pumps; shave every morning; and sometimes dress twice a day. My hairs are now as beautifully long and curly as ever, and, I assure thee, do as much for me as my talent for painting."[29] Lucy chafed at the slowness of communication. She wanted to know why John James had changed his mind about sending for her and Woodhouse as soon as possible.

At the same time Lucy was growing more concerned about communications from Gifford that were very clear. He found his father's letters to him incredible and patronizing, and those to Nicholas positively embarrassing. The following excerpt from a letter to Nicholas shows that the young man had ample cause for protest:

> Think of Lords sending their carriages to Mr. A. with best compliments, &c., &c., to go to spend days and nights at their hall, to see the wonderful locks that hang about his shoulders in full abundance. . . . Think of the same personage selling a Wild Turkey painted in oil for fifty guineas, and you will have a very moderate idea of my success in Edinburgh.
>
> I have wrote to you often, for I am no more lazy now than I was at Shippingport. I regularly do with four hours sleep, and I hope yet to see my family derive the benefit of my labours. . . . Make Victor draw, at all leisure hours, anything from Nature, and keep all his work, no matter how indifferent in his eyes or yours.[30]

Gifford received instructions to draw in the Audubon "style" so that one day he too might be received as a "miniature" Lafayette with

---

29. Ibid., 352, 354.
30. Ibid., 351.

"Lords of England" looking in "wonder" at his work. Perhaps in imitation of Nicholas, Gifford's response to his father was silence and indifference. His mother received both his complaints and those of Audubon who was constantly irritated by his son's silence.[31]

Lucy was forced to steer a difficult middle course between her husband and her son. She could appreciate Gifford's embarrassment but she also understood her husband's need to proclaim his success, particularly to those who had looked down upon him and judged him lazy and shiftless. Yet Nicholas had assisted them during their darkest hour in Henderson; the Audubons still owed him money; and it was Nicholas who was providing Gifford with a job and with business training in his countinghouse. John James seemed unaware that his son was no longer a child. Lucy knew that Gifford admired Nicholas, enjoyed working in the countinghouse, and was proud of his fledgling success in the business world. She understood, too, that her son resented directives from his father encouraging him to follow a career that had brought nothing but disgrace to the family. Lucy pleaded her son's cause to John James, much to her husband's chagrin.[32]

As the spring of 1827 wore on, Lucy waited for a letter from John James advising her when she could expect to join him. That message never came. She began to wonder that Audubon could tout his success on one hand and tell her that there was no need for her to hurry to meet him on the other. Obviously depressed, Lucy wrote to Gifford telling him that his father had stopped speaking about when she and Woodhouse might leave for Europe.[33] She began to think that John James was so taken with the trappings of success that he had forgotten his wife and sons. Bitterness mixed with Lucy's despondency. She believed that she had given as much to the collection as had John James and that now, with success in view, she was being passed over. While John James went to the theater, rode in sedan chairs, visited country estates, met famous

31. Corning (ed.), *Letters of Audubon*, I, 3, 4, 27, 67, 60; John James Audubon to Lucy Audubon, May 15, June 20, November 25, 1827, November 2, 1828, all in Audubon Collection.

32. Corning (ed.), *Letters of Audubon*, I, 70; John James Audubon to Lucy Audubon, May 15, June 20, November 25, 1827, November 2, 1828, all in Audubon Collection.

33. Ford, *John James Audubon*, 211.

people, and took bows, she remained at work in the backwoods of Louisiana.

The fact that John James did not seem to care a jot for her financial situation did not escape Lucy either. He merely advised her to sue those who owed her, and the only comment he made about her move to Beech Grove was one referring to past wounds inflicted by Jane Percy: "I am uncommonly pleased that Mr. Johnsons family is agreable to thee and that if I wanted to go to bed to thee there I would not be sent back 15 miles on foot to Bayou Sarah instead!!!" He did ask for an explanation of her reasons for leaving Beech Woods, but he did not ask if his wife was in need of funds.[34] John James also expressed surprise that Lucy had decided to leave Beech Woods. He said that he had thought her too attached to Jane Percy ever to leave. Lucy must have fumed on reading this remark. John James was reminding her that she had sided with Jane Percy on the two occasions that he had been ordered off the plantation. Audubon ought to have realized that, had she left her employment, there would have been no money to support the family, no time for him to draw, and no money for him to go to Europe in search of a publisher.

Once Lucy began to feel neglected, she seized on large and small issues alike with which to rebuke John James. She complained about the expense and time involved in reproducing his work in life size. It seemed to her that all the monies received from subscribers would continually be reinvested to keep the publication going. At forty years of age, Lucy was hardly enthusiastic about Audubon's estimate that it would take about sixteen years to complete publication of the entire collection. She informed John James that she was not doing well financially because she was unable to collect the debts owed her. She complained further that she had never received the watch he supposedly bought for her in Liverpool, and that if he had sent her the money she would have preferred purchasing her own watch.[35] These complaints masked a deeper anxiety. Lucy had always been remarkably tolerant of her eccentric husband, but she

34. Corning (ed.), *Letters of Audubon*, I, 21, 26, 27.

35. *Ibid.*, 27, 59; John James Audubon to Lucy Audubon, May 15, 1827, in Audubon Collection.

was stringently inflexible in her determination to be first in Audubon's life. As in the past, when she began to doubt Audubon's love for her, Lucy seized upon the most familiar complaint with which to chide her husband—their lack of money.

It is evident that Lucy would reject wealth and fame if it meant that she would have to be second in her husband's affections. Nor did she have the slightest intention of allowing John James to dictate the future of their sons by making them subservient to his birds and his ambitions. Consequently, she wrote to John James telling him that she did not agree with his plans for Gifford. She cautioned him that if Gifford were to take charge of traveling about Europe procuring subscribers as Audubon intended, he would soon be regarded as shiftless and somewhat of a "rambler."[36] In speaking so, Lucy was flinging at John James a cruel reminder. She did not want her son to get the same reputation that her husband had. To make the situation more unbearable to her, Audubon's coolness was quickly becoming public knowledge. As word of his success spread among family and friends, the fact that Lucy remained in West Feliciana was difficult for her to explain, especially since she had been speaking of leaving for so long. There were times when Lucy probably regretted spreading the news of Audubon's success.

However, Lucy was not always peevish over real or imagined grievances. Even though she was becoming increasingly alarmed by Audubon's indifference to her, she was proud of his success. She fretted about his health, worried that he might not procure subscribers for his work, and wondered if he was in need of money. Nor did Lucy neglect the numerous little tasks that John James asked her to perform. She gathered and shipped seeds, tree segments, and acorns to Rathbone Brothers & Company in Liverpool. The Rathbone family had been particularly helpful to John James, and in return he had asked Lucy "*to be at some trouble and expense to bring this to a good conclusion. . . . Recollect that those are troubles that I give thee so as to repay troubles that I have given in exchange to others.*"[37] Lucy encouraged Woodhouse to draw and skin as many

36. John James Audubon to Lucy Audubon, May 15, June 20, 1827, in Audubon Collection.
37. Corning (ed.), *Letters of Audubon*, 66, 59; Ford (ed.) *The 1826 Journal*, 337.

creatures as possible, just as his father had directed. She even packed and sent the rattlesnake skins that John James had requested. Lucy asked Augustin, Nathaniel, and Woodhouse to help her with these chores. She enjoyed doing these things, and she hoped to meet those people who had been so helpful to John James.

CHAPTER IX

A Choice

As the spring of 1827 drew to a close, Lucy had good reason to be pleased with her new position at Beech Grove. Even though tuition was not due until January when planters sold their crops, William Johnson advanced her a portion of her salary after the spring term. Although she had not yet collected the debts owed by some of her former students, her financial situation was once again stable.[1]

Lucy enjoyed a leisurely summer of strolling through the woods, reading old and new books, and visiting with friends. She attended the biggest social event in the parish, the wedding of Ann Mathews, one of Lucy's most mischievous charges of Beech Woods, and William Chase.[2] Lucy had been in West Feliciana long enough to see a number of her students change from frivolous and giggling girls into mature young women, and she took pride in the part she had played in the transformation. However, the music and gaiety of Ann's party were likely to make her miss her husband. Many of the guests had been Audubon's students at the weekend dance sessions that he had conducted in Woodville, and they plied Lucy with polite questions about her husband and when she would be joining him. These questions could only have made Lucy more conscious of the fact that she had no answer to give. She had written to Audubon several times during the summer, asking him to say clearly

1. John James Audubon to Lucy Audubon, May 15, 1827, in Audubon Collection; Arthur, *Audubon*, 387; Corning (ed.), *Letters of Audubon*, I, 28.
2. Corning (ed.), *Letters of Audubon*, I, 35.

and definitely when he would send for her and Woodhouse, but no reply had come.

Later in the summer, Lucy received the first number of *The Birds of America*. As she held the tangible evidence of Audubon's success in her hands, she fully understood his pride in the accomplishment, and her own enthusiasm was rekindled. She saw to it that the St. Francisville *Louisiana Journal* carried the following story:

> We have had a glance at the proofs of Mr. Lizar's coloured engravings of Mr. Audubon's drawings, and if we can trust first impressions, they are the finest specimens of the kind that have ever been laid before the British public. The colours are so exquisitely laid in—so highly brought up—that it requires close examination or the eye of a connoisseur, to discover that they are not paintings. Besides their value in natural history, each print is a picture of itself. The action of the birds is admirably given; and it is action made subservient to scientific purposes. These prints will be published in sets—a set comprising five engravings—but we trust that the publishers will also sell each print separately. This will greatly increase the means of gratifying both taste and fancy, and consequently the sale. But we must reserve our further remarks to another occasion.[3]

Lucy also paid particular attention to the instructions that John James sent along with his work. He wanted her "to see if the Library of New Orleans and the College Library there also would subscribe." He suggested that Lucy allow Judge Mathews to take care of this matter, and he cautioned her not to enlist "Subscribers *that will not pay well*."[4] Evidently, Lucy traveled to New Orleans to carry out this task herself rather than entrusting it to Judge Mathews as her husband had advised. There is no evidence to indicate whether or not Lucy procured the subscriptions that she sought, but her success is not as important as the fact that she chose to travel to New Orleans and to work as a solicitor to advance the publication. It was a chance to feel that she was once again a part of her husband's work.

While she was in New Orleans, Lucy enjoyed the hospitality of Anne and William Brand, who had never forgotten her friendship and assistance during the illness of their infant. Lucy spent her days

3. *Louisiana Journal*, July 28, 1827.
4. Corning (ed.), *Letters of Audubon*, I, 18.

soliciting subscribers and visiting the city's numerous shops. It was customary for friends to advise each other whenever they planned a trip to New Orleans. Invariably, the traveler was deluged with requests to purchase things that were more readily available in the city than in St. Francisville, and Lucy had a lengthy shopping list. The trip was a welcome break in the routine of plantation life, but after several days, Lucy gladly left the bustling city and returned to the peaceful surroundings of Beech Grove and her classroom.

At Beech Grove, Lucy's peace was soon shattered by a number of letters she received from Audubon. John James had responded to the complaints that she had sent across the Atlantic several months before with rebukes and stinging remonstrances of his own. She had hoped that her husband's response would reassure her that he had not forgotten his family. Instead, he had chosen to cast himself in the role of a martyr—a husband and father abandoned by his wife and children. He reasserted the rights that society ascribed to the male, to make decisions for his wife and children and to expect obedience.

> I am married, every one Knows it—and yet I have no Wife nor I am likely to possess one—I have come to a highly Civilized Country where Talents are appreciated and where any one with Industry and Care can live . . . without my Wife and my Children, nay I am denied the privilege of every Father in the World, that of Judging what is best for them to do—and I have perhaps lost sight of Them for ever—Such is the Situation of Thy husband that after Years of Labours, in the midst of encouragement. . . . Sorrows fret my poor mind constantly.[5]

His jumbled phrases provoked anger and frustration in Lucy. She could not understand how Audubon had arrived at the conclusion that she did not want to join him and that she was encouraging Gifford and Woodhouse to disregard their father's advice. It was of small comfort to her that Audubon seemed to think she was not solely responsible for his sorrows. He implied that her family was also involved in her effort to make him miserable. The reference to her relatives was unmistakable. "It is probable that many blame me much in America for this *appearance* of carelessness and absence

5. John James Audubon to Lucy Audubon, May 15, 1827, in Audubon Collection; Scott, *The Southern Lady,* 17.

from my family, and the same doubtless think and say that I am pleasuring whilst thou are Slaving thy life away; but can they Know my Situation, my Intention. . . . I am sure they cannot for they do not Know me a Jot: yet I have to bear the blame and hear of those things by various channels much to the loss of my peace."[6]

In response to demands that Lucy had made several months before, Audubon supplied an account of his earnings for the year. He said that he had received $3,902, which was enough "to maintain" them all even in "this Country in a style of Elègance and Comfort that I hope to see thee enjoy." But he did not urge her to join him. He advised, instead, that she wait a little longer. "Thou art quite comfortable I know in Louisiana therefore wait there with a little patience. I hope the end of this year will see me under headway sufficient to have thee with me with comfort here and thou I need not tell thee that I long every hour of the time I am absent for thee. I conceive it best to be prudent."[7] A John James who spoke of patience and prudence was a stranger to Lucy.

Lucy soon learned that she had made a mistake by masking her complaints to Audubon in economic terms. Had she told him the truth, that she simply missed him and felt neglected, she might have fared better. Instead, she had given Audubon a weapon with which to cause her great pain.

> I may be induced to remain in England the rest of my Life, or accidents may Send me to America once more; but what ever takes place, and whatever my Situation may be hereafter, I have, and will always have the consolation to think that I have done all I can, or could Since my Misfortunes in Kentucky, to restore thee to comfort—the diference of habits between us are very diferent, so much so indeed, that what I conceive real comfort is misery to thee. Those are misfortunes indeed, but it is too late to take such things in consideration and I am Still anxiously inclined to meet thy Wishes and procure all I can for thy Sake.

His typical circumlocutions were clear enough. John James was absolving himself of the responsibility of determining when she should come and was placing that decision upon her. "I have no

6. John James Audubon to Lucy Audubon, June 20, 1827, in Audubon Collection.
7. Corning (ed.), *Letters of Audubon*, 24, 25.

wish to have thee unless thou art convinced of being *comfortable in thy own Way*," he declared.[8]

Audubon roused Lucy's anger to new heights by forbidding her to mention money matters in her letters because he did not want his newly found wealthy friends the Rathbones to know that he was not a man of means. He had let Mrs. Rathbone and her beautiful daughter Hanna read Lucy's letters, and her references to being short of funds because she could not collect the debts owed her had embarrassed him. He explained, "Recollect that they know nothing of our Pecuniary standing or situation and that I do not think it fit to disclose this portion of our present situation—Indeed I believe that every one who knows me thinks that we are well off, at least independent of the World—I think it will be soon the case but untill then *Mum*."[9]

The reference to the beautiful Hanna possibly gave Lucy a pang of jealousy. She had no intention of remaining "mum" to avoid offending her husband's young admirer. Any jealousy she felt for the girl was fleeting, however, for her real adversary was *The Birds of America*. Audubon was only using people like the Rathbones to introduce him into the right social circles where he could promote the book. He wanted Lucy to write letters that portrayed him as a man of talent and affluence and herself as a lady in comfortable circumstances.[10] Lucy must have realized that Audubon was also using her, but she soon grew weary of bickering by mail.

At Beech Grove the Christmas season had arrived, and she had more pleasant things to think about. For the first time in several years she was going to see Gifford. He was coming down from Louisville to visit for several weeks. In high spirits, Lucy hurried about the plantation making preparations. A special bond existed between Lucy and her eldest son. At eighteen, the young man's temperament closely resembled his mother's.[11] The two corresponded frequently, and it was to Gifford that Lucy confided her doubts and fears about Audubon and his activities in Great Britain.

8. John James Audubon to Lucy Audubon, June 20, 1827, in Audubon Collection.
9. Corning (ed.), *Letters of Audubon*, I, 53, 53–54.
10. *Ibid.*, 12, 26, 50, 53.
11. *Ibid.*, 62, 76.

Lucy and Woodhouse awaited Gifford's arrival with joyous anticipation. It took Lucy some time to become accustomed to her son's
changed appearance. In three years he had grown tall and become
quite handsome, but he was far too slender for his mother's liking.[12]
Of course, Lucy assumed that he had not been eating properly, and
she made a special effort to see that his favorite meals were prepared. Lucy noted with pride that her son's physical growth was
matched by a personal maturity.

Woodhouse was not especially concerned with the changes in his
brother's looks. He was merely delighted that Gifford was at Beech
Grove, and he looked forward to hunting and roaming the woods
with him. The younger boy took every opportunity to question his
brother about his life in Louisville.

Lucy spent many hours talking to Gifford about John James and
The Birds of America. She could speak candidly to her son, and she
allowed Gifford to read some of the letters from his father that had
caused her so much pain. Gifford tried to comfort his mother, but
he was unable to reassure her that all would be well when he himself doubted that it would be. Gifford had already come to the conclusion that his father's alleged success was a fairy tale. Impressed
with his own business acumen and influenced by Nicholas' opinion
of his father, Gifford believed that *The Birds of America* would turn
out to be little more than a monument to his father's ego.[13] An enterprise that would take so many years to complete and would
require the reinvestment of almost all the money earned from
subscribers hardly seemed good business procedure to the young
eighteen-year-old who was certain that he knew more about such
matters than his father.

After seeing some of the letters that his father had written to
Lucy, Gifford was certain that his judgment about his father's work
was correct. He sympathized with his mother and thought that his
father's attitude toward her was intolerable.[14] With the brutal simplicity that frequently characterizes young men, Gifford concluded
that there was only one answer: his father was more interested in

12. *Ibid.*, 62.
13. *Ibid.*, 71–73, 88.
14. Adams, *John James Audubon*, 365.

fame than family. The fact that Audubon refused to send for his
mother and brother proved to Gifford's satisfaction that his father
was afraid that if Lucy joined him she would find out that his success was more imaginary than real. Even though he sympathized
with his mother, he must have been relieved when the topic of conversation changed from Audubon and his publication to his brother.

For some time Lucy had been aware that Woodhouse' education
was being neglected. She had already written to Audubon asking
that Woodhouse be allowed to go to England alone so that he might
be enrolled in a suitable school, but she had yet to receive an answer.[15] Now, as she saw the boy trailing about after his brother, plying him with questions about his job and his life of independence in
Louisville, and hanging upon Gifford's every word, she realized that
the problem of Woodhouse' education and future had become more
immediate. Anticipating that Audubon's reply might not be favorable, Lucy discussed with Gifford the possibility of sending Woodhouse to school in Louisville. Gifford promised to find out about
tuition rates when he returned, and he also assured his mother that
he would take care of his younger brother in the event that she decided to send him to Louisville.

Lucy wanted Gifford to enjoy his vacation, and so she did not
dwell on serious subjects very long. She usually saw the boys off in
the morning with guns in their hands, anticipating a productive
hunt. On occasion they accompanied her on her morning ride.
Lucy took great pleasure in showing Gifford off to her friends in
West Feliciana. She also noted with some amusement that her son
took every opportunity to swagger about before her attractive female students. For Lucy the days of Gifford's visit went by too
quickly, and all too soon it was January and time for Gifford to return to Louisville.[16] After accompanying him to Bayou Sara, where
he took a steamer upriver, Lucy returned to her classroom, satisfied
that her elder son was developing into a responsible man.

For a few weeks Lucy had been preoccupied with her sons, but
her respite was all too brief, for in February she received news from

---

15. John James Audubon to Lucy Audubon, December 5, 1827, in Audubon Papers,
American Philosophical Society, cited in Ford, *John James Audubon*, 219.
16. Corning (ed.), *Letters of Audubon*, I, 62.

Audubon that caused her fresh worry. John James told her that, because of delays on the part of Mr. Lizars, he had transferred the publication and engraving of his collection to R. Havell and Son in London. It is likely that this simple explanation produced more questions than it answered. Had he lost subscribers? Had he been unable to provide Lizars with the funds needed to continue his work? Was the expense of doing the work in life size too great? Did he need money to keep the work going? Lucy immediately forgot about feeling neglected, picked up paper and pen, and wrote to Audubon for answers. She hoped that she would not receive evasions instead. Even though she had little money to spare, Lucy asked her husband if he was in need of funds, and she offered him her savings to keep the work going.[17] Lucy's reaction to the slightest indication that something might be amiss with the publication of the collection showed that *The Birds of America* was very important to her.

No sooner had Lucy posted her letter than she received another missive from Audubon. Evidently, the gratification of his ambitions was blinding him to the welfare of his younger son, for Audubon seemed to think that any determination of Woodhouse' future could await the "ultimate success" of *The Birds of America*. Now Audubon wrote that he did not wish the boy to join him. Incredibly, Audubon denied ever suggesting that Woodhouse should come to England: "I never dreamed of such a thing, and I love the dear boy too much ever to part him from thee."[18]

Exasperated with her husband, Lucy decided that Woodhouse' education could not await his father's pleasure. She would send the boy to school near Louisville where he would be close to his brother and her family. This would, however, take more money than she had to pay his tuition and provide for his personal needs. Lucy did not ask her husband for assistance. She feared that Audubon would only tell her to wait because all the money he had was being used to keep the publication going or, worse, that he would again caution

17. *Ibid.*, 44, 62, 64, 66.
18. John James Audubon to Lucy Audubon, December 5, 1827, in Audubon Papers, American Philosophical Society, cited in Ford, *John James Audubon*, 219. Lucy believed that her husband was as worried as she about their "boyish" younger son, and so it seemed when in an earlier letter Audubon made it evident that he wanted Woodhouse to join him. See, Ford (ed.), *The 1826 Journal*, 333; Grinnell (ed.), "Some Audubon Letters," 119.

her to be silent about her monetary needs so that he would not be embarrassed. In addition, until Lucy learned whether the transfer of the publication to London meant that Audubon was in financial difficulties, she did not want to add to his problems. Therefore, she swallowed her pride and looked elsewhere for help. Lucy turned to her youngest brother, Will, and asked if he would lend her the amount of Woodhouse' tuition.[19]

William Bakewell responded as Lucy knew he would. He offered to provide the tuition, and in addition, he told Lucy that he would find his nephew a part-time position as an apprentice in his business.[20] Lucy knew that her brother would look after the boy's welfare. William had fond memories of the days he had lived with his sister in Henderson, and he was anxious to help Lucy, who had been more of a mother to him than a sister.

By turning to her brother for help, however, Lucy provided her family with yet another grievance against her husband. Both Nicholas and Will had refused even to answer Audubon's letters—ample indication that they still blamed him for the miserable plight of his family and that they had little confidence in his success. John James had felt Will's silence especially keenly because Lucy's youngest brother had always regarded him highly. Will more than likely informed Eliza and Nicholas of Lucy's request. To her family, Lucy's need for money could only mean either that Audubon's accounts of his success were exaggerated or that he was so preoccupied with his new fortunes that he had abandoned his family. It would seem that Lucy's relatives had no reason to revise the judgment that they had made previously—John James was still an irresponsible scoundrel and Lucy was still "poor Lucy."

Fortunately, since Beech Grove was a long way from Louisville, Lucy was unaware that her request had reinforced her family's conviction that she was to be pitied. Lucy had, in fact, been feeling rather sorry for herself. Audubon's responses to her letters indicate

19. Ford, *John James Audubon*, 229; John James Audubon to Lucy Audubon, November 2, 1828, in Audubon Collection.
20. Ford, *John James Audubon*, 229; John James Audubon to Lucy Audubon, November 2, 1828, in Audubon Collection; Corning (ed.), *Letters of Audubon*, I, 74.

that she was despondent. She continually pressed him for details of the progress of his work and asked repeatedly about when he intended to send for her. Once she decided to borrow his tuition and send Woodhouse to school, her self-pity evaporated. She wrote fewer letters to her husband, and she stopped asking about when she could expect to go to England. Instead, she went to her classroom with the renewed purposes of providing her son with suitable clothes and other necessities and of repaying William's loan. She was no longer merely awaiting a summons from her husband.[21]

In preparation for his sojourn in Louisville, Lucy sent Woodhouse to school in Natchez. She feared that her son's innate dislike for serious study might put him at a disadvantage in Kentucky, and she hoped that a short time in a formal school setting might better prepare him to compete with the students he would meet in the fall of 1828.[22]

Lucy was relieved and delighted to see that Woodhouse was enthusiastic about the arrangements that she had made for him. It had been difficult for her to watch her son's eagerness fade each time she had to tell him that his father was not ready for them to go to England. She knew that she could hardly expect the impatient youth, who idealized his father, to understand why Audubon did not send for him when she herself did not understand. However, when Lucy told him about the plans she had made for him, Woodhouse seemed to forget about England. He enjoyed his sojourn in Natchez, and when he returned to Beech Grove in the summer, it seemed to Lucy that he could talk of nothing but going to Louisville in the fall.[23]

For Lucy the fall came soon enough, and she took Woodhouse to Bayou Sara and watched him board the steamboat. At least for a moment Lucy must have envied her son's ability to forget about being disregarded by his father. When she returned to Beech Grove, Lucy was completely alone for the first time in her life. Still,

21. Corning (ed.), *Letters of Audubon*, I, 41, 42, 55, 57, 72, 66, 67, 74, 77, 78; Herrick, *Audubon, the Naturalist*, I, 409; Ford (ed.), *The 1826 Journal*, 344.

22. Corning (ed.), *Letters of Audubon*, I, 61, 62. Woodhouse' absence from St. Francisville and his sojourn in Natchez correspond to school terms.

23. Corning (ed.), *Letters of Audubon*, I, 72, 74; John James Audubon to Lucy Audubon, November 2, 1828, in Audubon Collection; Herrick, *Audubon, the Naturalist*, I, 409.

she was certain that she had made the right choice in sending Woodhouse to Louisville. Evidently, she herself had decided to remain at Beech Grove only until she could gather enough money to join her sons in Louisville.[24]

Audubon's letters continued to be laced with thoughtless remarks. Typical was the following: "Could I have supposed that my Success would have been what it is I certainly would have had thee with me from the first." She refused to allow herself to be tantalized by her husband's description of what their future life would be like. When Audubon wrote telling her that they would make their home in London and spend each summer in the country, Lucy ignored the message. When he advised her to "sell off" as many of her possessions as possible before she sailed, because when he sent for her she would be refitted in England in a much better style, Lucy disregarded his counsel.[25]

The letters that Lucy wrote to Audubon continued to vacillate between affectionate chitchat and stinging rebukes. Occasionally, she gave him delightful and entertaining accounts of the latest news about family and friends, but all too frequently she condemned his indifference to her and complained because he evaded her questions about the progress of the publication.[26]

Although Lucy's letters no longer mentioned joining Audubon in England, John James continued to explain why he had not sent for her and why it might "appear" that he was neglecting her. John James maintained that her excessive preoccupation with their lack of money had made him too "timid" to send for her. He told Lucy that he was afraid that she had ideas about their style of living in England that might not be in keeping with reality, for as he explained, their income would only be 500 pounds per annum and she should not expect more. These explanations were foolish and unconvincing. Obviously, John James was beginning to feel guilty about ignoring his family, and he was making a lame attempt to cast the blame on her. Of course, Lucy refused to believe that she was in any way at fault, and she determined never again to mention

24. John James Audubon to Lucy Audubon, November 2, 1828, in Audubon Collection.
25. Corning (ed.), *Letters of Audubon*, I, 56.
26. *Ibid.*, 64, 68, 72.

money matters in her letters. She wrote to Audubon less frequently, and the letters she did write became cool and indifferent.[27]

Ironically, Lucy's apathy came at the very time that her husband began to fret over separation from his wife. By 1828 Audubon was beginning to miss Lucy as a wife and a partner. He told her that she could be of great help to him: "When I am forced to absent myself to go after Subscribers or visit some of those whom I already have, thou being on the spot would see that no relaxation did take place in those in my employ, would write to me &c &c &c—Two heads are better than one and I think it would be of great mutual advantage, *the ultimate* success of my Publication." Although Audubon may have been attempting a bit of flattery, it is apparent that he valued Lucy's intelligence. He reminded her that "only 5 Numbers come out per annum and that from the beginning to the last of the full completion of the whole 16 years are wanted, so that certainly my Lucy must come to me sometime." Finally, Audubon told Lucy that his situation would probably be such that by January, 1829, he would be able to send for her, but his pride impelled him to mask his feelings in indifference. He advised Lucy that, if she should "prefer still to remain longer in America through fear of meeting with disappointments" in England, she was "at full liberty to judge and to act for" herself.[28]

If Audubon was trying to lure his wife to England, he surely took the wrong approach. As Lucy saw it, Audubon did not need a wife; he needed a trusted business partner, someone to supervise the work on the publication while he was off swaggering about Europe. It is apparent that John James would have fared better if he had concentrated upon hearts rather than heads in giving Lucy reasons why she should join him. Indeed, the fact that Audubon had chosen the course that he would follow for the next sixteen years while leaving his wife at liberty to do as she pleased only made Lucy harden her attitude toward her husband.

In an acid communication Lucy informed Audubon that she was "*comfortable in the extreme*" at Beech Grove and that she had no in-

27. *Ibid.*, 68, John James Audubon to Lucy Audubon, November 2, 1828, in Audubon Collection; Herrick, *Audubon, the Naturalist*, I, 408–409.
28. Corning (ed.), *Letters of Audubon*, I, 69, 59, 70.

tention of going to England alone.[29] Actually, she was telling her
husband that his summons had come too late. Woodhouse was
comfortably settled in Louisville, enjoying his work with William
and benefiting from the education he was receiving at school. Lucy
advised Audubon that, if she left Beech Grove, she would go to
Louisville. If Audubon wanted her, he would have to leave England, his subscribers, his book, and his wealthy friends. He would
have to come to her and convince her that she was first in his life.

If Lucy expected that her husband would be upset by the news
that she would not join him, she was disappointed. Audubon sent
her a heartless answer: "I wrote this day a very long letter to Victor
which if he receives it will make him open his eyes respecting
my Publication that *you all* seem not to Know any thing correct
about—do my Lucy understand me well—My work will not be
finished for 14 years to come . . . and if it is thy Intention not to
Join me before that time, I think [we] will be better off both of us to
Separate; thou . . . in America and I to Spend my Life most Mis-
erably alone for the remainder of my days." This was bad enough,
but Audubon also accused her and William of taking Woodhouse
from him. She must have observed that her husband was primarily
concerned that he had lost the services that his son could have provided if he had been working for the success of his father's publication: "In the course of another Year I think that it will be impossible for me to do without an assistant and as between thyself, Thy
Brother William & Co My Son is Swept off I must look to an utter
Stranger."[30]

It was apparent that Audubon had convinced himself that Lucy
was more interested in money than she was in her husband. He
vowed that he would never send for her until his pockets were overflowing with cash so that he would be able to give her the "extraordinary comforts without Which it appears my being thy Husband is
of but little Consequence." Curiously, after his sweeping rejection,
Audubon told her that he was sick of being alone, that he needed
her, and that he was capable of supporting her: "Thy means of liv-

29. John James Audubon to Lucy Audubon, November 2, 1828, in Audubon Collection.
30. *Ibid.*

ing at present do not I am sure exceed 5 or 6 hundred Dollars per annum, why not receive that same sum from thy husband and half as much again and be with him—comfort him in times of troubles and sorrows and assist him in his labours?"[31]

Lucy had waited a long time for her husband to be in a position to support her, but now that the time had come, she had to refuse his offer. In three years, too many accusations and cutting words had passed between them, and with the threat of separation and the charge that she had "swept" his son from him, Lucy had had enough. Hurt, lonely, and weary beyond her years, she told Audubon that she was tired of *The Birds of America* and that she preferred the simplicity of her humble style of life to the complexity that affluence and fame had brought to his life.[32] Her attitude was extraordinarily independent. She was willing to risk separation at a time when separation was socially untenable rather than accept what she considered a secondary position in her husband's affections. Her letters became even less frequent and more indifferent in tone. The birds had won, and Lucy was willing to leave John James with his first love.

31. *Ibid.*
32. Herrick, *Audubon, the Naturalist*, I, 409.

CHAPTER X

Concession and Reunion

Audubon, in his self-imposed exile in England, could not understand that his domestic happiness was collapsing. He had overcome innumerable disappointments and obstacles to achieve his goal only to find that the people who were most important to him, Lucy and his sons, were no longer interested in his accomplishments. He concluded that Lucy must be responsible for the transatlantic family fray and that she had aroused family resentment against him, but he conceded that she may not have realized his true situation. He was partially correct in the latter assumption, for his exaggerated accounts of his doings in Europe had not given her an accurate picture of the hard work and the near brushes with failure that had dogged his path.

When John James arrved in Liverpool on July 21, 1826, he was forty-one years old, and he had no illusions that fame and success would be handed him easily. He knew that he would have to create opportunity and seize it wherever it came because it was unlikely that the chance to change his fortune would come again. Audubon's journal reveals that he was convinced that his sojourn in Europe was his last opportunity to prove that he had not wasted his life in a fruitless pursuit. Indeed, his journal entries show that he was consistently obsessed with the haunting fear that he would fail in his quest of fame and fortune.[1] However, Audubon never communicated these fears to Lucy because he was keenly aware that he

---

1. Maria R. Audubon (ed.), *Audubon and His Journals*, I, 81–342 *passim*; Ford (ed.), *The 1826 Journal*, 45, 50.

had failed to fulfill his duties as head of the Audubon family. He knew that she pinned her hopes and dreams on his ability to find a publisher, and he would not send her any news that would have made her think that the European venture was merely another failure in the long line that stretched back to Henderson, Kentucky.

The letters that Audubon sent to Lucy recounting his extraordinary reception were true, but Audubon refrained from describing the misery of his first days in Liverpool. As soon as he arrived, he went to the countinghouse of Gordon & Forrestall to see Alexander Gordon, an old acquaintance who had befriended him during his bleak stay in New Orleans in the early 1820s. In a sense, Gordon was a relative, having married Lucy's youngest sister, Ann, in 1823. In his journal, which he addressed to Lucy, Audubon described his reception:

> I was coldly received. . . . I was asked, when I took my leave (which was not long, I assure thee, after our meeting) if I would not call there again!!!! [Gordon did not then invite Audubon to call at his home; hence, the remarks that follow.] Where is that sweet sister of thine who almost grew [up] by my side, Ann Bakewell that I knew when [she was] a child? She is here in Liverpool, and I shall not see her. It is severe, but it must be endured. Yet what have I done? Ah, that is no riddle, my friend, I *have grown poor*.[2]

After leaving Gordon, Audubon called on a number of persons to whom he carried letters of introduction and who he hoped could help him launch his work. By ill chance, the people that Audubon called upon were not at home. On July 22, John James went to see Gordon a second time: "I saw Mr. G. again. He was much the same. He gave me *his card*, and I now can go to see thy sister, if I feel inclined or think it proper." John James was further annoyed because Gordon sent a mere clerk to accompany him to the Custom House where his "drawings went through a *regular, strict,* and *complete examination*," which resulted in Audubon paying duty fees he believed Gordon could have helped him avoid.[3]

Audubon returned to his lodgings at the Commercial Inn, haunted by the thought that he would be a social outcast in En-

2. Ford (ed.), *The 1826 Journal*, 45; B. G. Bakewell, *The Family Book of Bakewell*, 27.
3. Ford (ed.), *The 1826 Journal*, 47.

gland just as he had been in America and that Liverpool would be
as empty of people who were interested in publishing his work as
Philadelphia had been. After a restless night, John James awoke on
Sunday morning and went on a sight-seeing excursion to Wales,
but the trip did little to lift his depression. Seeking to find an escape, he consumed a considerable amount of port, and by evening
when he sat down to write in his journal he was obviously intoxi-
cated as indicated by the following excerpt:

> Dost thou remember the wife of George Keats, Esq., of London, &c.,
> &c., &c.,? (I will write no more *et ceteras*, these dull my German
> quill.)
> "Remember her? I am surprised thou shouldst put fresh question to
> me" thou sayest.
> Well if I did not see Mrs. Keats, the wife of George Keats of London,
> &c., &c. (confound the &c.'s, I say) I saw, undoubtedly, her ghost in
> Wales this afternoon.
> "Why, is it possible?" thee asks. Yes it is possible, and I will answer
> thee *why* with, "Because it was Sunday." Formerly ghosts walked at
> night. Now they walk on *Sun*-day. Pho! Pho! — what a poor pun. I do
> acknowledge that if I did not see Mrs. George Keats, the wife of George
> Keats, Esq., of London, &c., (damn the &c's), I undoubtedly saw her
> ghost, or a ghost very much like her ghost.[4]

Journal entries on the following day, July 24, show that Audubon's spirits remained low and that by evening he was once again
tipsy. In an unsteady hand he wrote, "Well, I trotted like a horse
that is string-halt, street after street, through alleys and gutters of
streets until I reached—no, I did not reach the desired object. 'Oh,
how is this? What? Could not find Norton Street?' Damn Norton
Street. I could not find the sisterly lips of Ann, to imprint on them
an affectionate, purest kind of kiss."[5] (At a later date Audubon did
find Norton Street and Ann Gordon's home where he was received
kindly by Lucy's sister.)

The misery of Audubon's first days soon ended, though, and he
was able to send Lucy good news. He met a number of wealthy and
influential people, like the Rathbone family and William Roscoe,
who encouraged him and introduced him to Liverpool's elite. He

4. *Ibid.*, 49.
5. *Ibid.*, 52.

placed his drawings on exhibition, and they were well received by the public. Praised as a "most extraordinary man" and courted by people of wealth and affluence, Audubon went from the depths to the heights, from self-denigration to self-praise. His sudden success led him to write those incredibly boastful letters to family, friends, and acquaintances that astonished later readers. Everything in him screamed to let people know that they had been wrong to think him lazy and shiftless. Yet the long years of poverty and disgrace impelled Audubon to seek more than praise. He wanted more than words, he wanted wealth, and in a dogged, even in a ruthless manner, he set out to do whatever had to be done to gain fame and economic respectability.[6]

He learned to dress in a socially acceptable manner, but he realized that certain quirks in his appearance worked to the advantage of an aspiring artist. Thus, Audubon could truthfully say that his long flowing hair did as much for him as his artistic talents. He spent many uneasy and silent moments among his newfound wealthy friends, while he tried to cultivate the manners and social niceties that life on the American frontier had dulled. He succeeded in establishing himself as a talented man of independent means. His quaint accent and his tales about life in the American forests quickly made him a sought after social companion, particularly to the women he met. However, he did not let the glitter of social acceptance interfere with the purpose of his sojourn in England. On one occasion when Audubon saw the great numbers of people who crowded the gallery where his collection was displayed at the Royal Institution in Liverpool, he did not hesitate too long before he decided to charge a shilling admission fee. He put aside the lofty notion that charging admission would make him seem more of a showman than a naturalist.[7]

Although Audubon's letters to Lucy and others in America made it seem that he confused social acceptance and crowded exhibitions with economic success, he knew that he had made only a small be-

6. *Ibid.*, 250.
7. *Ibid.*, 354; John James Audubon to Lucy Audubon, December 9, 1826, in Audubon Collection; Maria R. Audubon (ed.), *Audubon and His Journals*, I, 108, 109, 110, 112, 121, 135, 136, 140.

ginning toward the publication of his work. To earn money that he would put to use when he found a publisher, and to gain recognition as an ornithologist, Audubon traveled to other cities and exhibited his work. He gave Lucy glowing accounts of these journeys, but he never mentioned exhibitions that did not draw crowds or those that left behind only empty tills. When he reached Edinburgh and finally found a publisher, he gave Lucy a full account of his good fortune, but he minimized the numerous obstacles and difficulties that had to be overcome before he could count on success. He insisted upon publishing the work in life size just as he had drawn each specimen, which meant that it would take sixteen years to publish the entire collection and that the expense involved would be enormous.[8] He had to bear the full cost of publication, and he had to count on the funds procured from subscribers to carry on the work. Initially, Audubon did not understand the magnitude of the task that he had undertaken, and it was this lack of understanding that led him to invite Lucy and Woodhouse to come to England to share in his new fortunes.

However, Audubon soon learned that being dependent upon subscribers who changed their minds from one day to the next was a precarious business. Indeed, he quickly realized that the success of the publication depended upon his capacity to work almost constantly. Audubon's social life was, therefore, far more limited than his letters led Lucy to believe. During the day he was most frequently at William Lizars' shop supervising the reproduction of his work. He exhibited his collection to earn funds and to advertise *The Birds of America*. On one occasion, an exhibition in Edinburgh yielded nearly eight hundred dollars in admission fees. Once the first number of his work was completed, he traveled about enlisting subscribers. He was frequently invited to dine out in the evening, and he never missed an opportunity to meet wealthy people whom he regarded as potential subscribers. When he returned to his room at night, he spent his time revising drawings, writing about the habits

8. Maria R. Audubon (ed.), *Audubon and His Journals*, I, 123, 128, 152–64; Corning (ed.), *Letters of Audubon*, I, 59.

of the specimens in his collection, and recording all of his doings in his journal.[9]

While Audubon was busily engaged in all of these activities, he received Lucy's letter informing him that she and Woodhouse intended to join him during the summer of 1827. But he realized that it was too soon for his wife and son to come. He had too much work yet to do, and he was not at all certain that he could secure enough subscribers to ensure the success of the publication. He knew that he had exaggerated the account of his success to Lucy, but he believed that if he had time and the freedom to pursue his objective he would ultimately triumph. The coming of his wife and son would land additional expenses on him, and more alarming, Lucy might be disappointed if she came and found that he had only made a small beginning on a task that would take years of hard work to bring to a successful conclusion. Hence, Audubon wrote asking Lucy to remain in America until he was certain that he could enlist enough subscribers to assure them a comfortable life.[10] John James could not chance having anyone interfere with his work now that he was so close to achieving his goal, not even Lucy and Woodhouse.

Lucy was in part responsible for Audubon's attitude. Had she been a helpless female, dependent upon him to direct her every thought, word, and deed, John James would never have felt free to devote all of his time and energy to the publication. As it was, Audubon knew that Lucy was capable of managing any situation that arose without his help. Ironically, although Audubon appreciated Lucy's independent spirit, it rankled his pride that he had had to depend upon her to earn the family living and that family and friends paid Lucy the respect that should have come to him as head of the Audubon family. The experience of receiving respect and acclaim from strangers made Audubon more conscious of the shabby treatment he had received at the hands of family and friends. In his

9. Ford (ed.), *The 1826 Journal*, 305–316; Corning (ed.), *Letters of Audubon*, 23–24; Maria R. Audubon (ed.), *Audubon and His Journals*, I, 98–342 passim; John James Audubon to Lucy Audubon, June 20, 1827, in Audubon Collection.

10. Corning (ed.), *Letters of Audubon*, I, 14, 25; Ford (ed.), *The 1826 Journal*, 352; John James Audubon to Lucy Audubon, May 15, 1827, in Audubon Collection.

headlong rush to prove his worth as a man, a husband, a father, and a talented artist, John James forgot his wife's dedication to him and his work, and he placed Lucy among that throng of people who had ceased caring about him after he had become poor.[11] Consequently, he avoided telling her about any financial reverses that came his way. He wanted neither advice nor any further financial assistance from Lucy. He was jealously guarding his right to claim full credit for any success he attained, and he did not want either Lucy or Woodhouse with him until he could show them conclusively, in dollars and cents, that he was not a failure.

John James did not tell Lucy how close the whole publication came to collapsing during the summer of 1827. On April 5 of that year, Audubon left Edinburgh for London where he hoped to ex-hibit his work and enlist new subscribers. He took a roundabout course to the capital city, visiting Belfore, Newcastle-upon-Tyne, York, Leeds, Liverpool, and Shrewsbury. In each place he showed his drawings and added subscribers to his growing list. Then, shortly after he arrived in London, Audubon received word from Lizars that the colorists who had been working on *The Birds of America* were striking for higher wages. John James worked frantically paint-ing pictures of otters, partridges, ducks, and rabbits, which he sold for one hundred dollars each, to procure additional funds for the colorists. Despite his labors, he soon learned from Lizars that the money he had sent to Edinburgh was insufficient to get them back to work. Convinced that Lizars could not handle the work, Audu-bon transferred his collection to R. Havell and Son in London. The Havells offered him cheaper terms, just under 115 pounds per num-ber of five prints each, and Audubon soon saw that his new en-graver did work that was superior to that turned out by Lizars.[12]

Having found a publisher and saved his work from disaster, Au-dubon plunged ahead with incredible energy. He haunted the work-rooms of the Havell establishment, frequently criticizing the work

11. John James Audubon to Lucy Audubon, November 2, 1828, in Audubon Collection; Corning (ed.), *Letters of Audubon*, I, 72.
12. Maria R. Audubon (ed.), *Audubon and His Journals*, I, 230, 258; Herrick, *Audubon, the Naturalist*, I, 374–77; 380, 382–88; Ford, *John James Audubon*, 214–15.

of colorists and at times demanding that work be done over. He procured new subscriptions, and he was especially delighted when he learned that George IV had become a subscriber. He also carried on a grueling social life, accepting invitations that would place him among people of wealth and affluence who could further his publication.[13]

By the end of 1827, *The Birds of America* had become a complicated business to manage, as indicated by the following description:

> In addition to being his own artist, his own production manager, and his own salesman, he had to serve as circulation manager, collection agent, and bookkeeper—no small task in an era when the mails were uncertain and the methods of transferring funds still cumbersome. Each subscriber had agreed to take five numbers a year, paying two guineas apiece on delivery. This meant that Audubon had to make certain that each number was received by the subscriber in good condition, the money collected immediately and deposited with a commercial house on which he could draw for funds, and the appropriate records kept. For every hundred subscriptions, therefore, he had to make five hundred deliveries and collections a year. To handle this business, he had established centers at Edinburgh, Newcastle, York, Leeds, Manchester, Liverpool and London, appointing agents who were sometimes friends, sometimes business acquaintances.[14]

Audubon soon realized that his agents were not as energetic as he was and that it was necessary for him to see to the business himself. He noted in his journal, "I attended to my business closely, but my agents neither attended to it nor to my orders to them; and at last, nearly at bay for means to carry on so heavy a business, I decided to make a sortie for the purpose of collecting my dues, and to augment my subscribers."[15] The sortie involved traveling to Manchester, Leeds, York, Newcastle, Edinburgh, Glasgow, Liverpool, and back to London. In each place he collected monies due him, attempted to find new subscribers, and tried to rouse his agents to greater ef-

---

13. Herrick, *Audubon, the Naturalist*, I, 388–97; Maria R. Audubon (ed.), *Audubon and His Journals*, I, 258–80; Ford, *John James Audubon*, 217; Corning (ed.), *Letters of Audubon*, I, 39; John James Audubon to Lucy Audubon, December 9, 1826, in Audubon Collection. It may be that George IV failed to pay.

14. Adams, *John James Audubon*, 326.

15. Quoted in *Ibid.*, 326–27.

forts. By the beginning of 1828, Audubon calculated that he had 144 subscribers, a figure still short of his goal of 200.

While Audubon was busy worrying about keeping his subscribers satisfied, adding new ones to his list, collecting money due him, and paying salaries at the Havell establishment, he was being bombarded with seething complaints from Lucy. Her letters had become increasingly sharp and impatient with what she termed his evasiveness about sending for her and Woodhouse and about his economic situation. Audubon interpreted her plaintive missives to mean that she was badgering him about their lack of money and that she did not appreciate the exhausting work that he was doing to make her life comfortable in the future.[16] Lucy's letters only made Audubon think that he was correct in passing the same judgment upon her that he had passed upon so many members of her family—she had stopped loving him when he became poor. Believing this, Audubon wrote letters to Lucy that were harsh and cruel.

Yet, by the summer of 1828, Audubon's anger and annoyance with his wife turned to worry and depression. He missed Lucy, and believing that he had enough subscribers to ensure her a comfortable existence in England, he wrote asking her to join him. He was completely baffled when he received her letter informing him that she would not come to England and that she awaited the day when he would return to the United States to live a humbler but happier life. John James felt that Lucy was being completely unreasonable. She had been complaining for a year or more that he had grown cold toward her, basing her charge on his refusal to send for her. Now when he finally asked her to join him, she refused. Writing to a friend Audubon lamented:

> I have had sad news from my dear wife this morning, she has positively abandoned her coming to England for some indefinite time, indeed she says that she looks anxiously for the day when tired myself of this country I will return to mine and live although a humbler (Public) Life, a much happier one—her letter has not raised my already despondent spirits in *somethings* and at the very instant I am writing to you it may perhaps be well that no instrument is at hand with which a woeful sin

16. Corning (ed.), *Letters of Audubon*, I, 64, 72; John James Audubon to Lucy Audubon, May 15, June 20, 1827, November 2, 1828, all in Audubon Collection.

might be committed— . . . My two sons are also very much against coming to England. . . . What am I to do?[17]

On September 1, 1828, Audubon took a trip to Paris in search of new subscribers. He was anxious to enlist the royal family. Unfortunately, the trip did not yield the expected success, and John James returned to London where his thoughts turned more and more frequently to Lucy and his sons.

Audubon could not accept the cool indifference of his family, and by the end of 1828, his letters to Gifford were desperate and pathetic. Because there was little else that he could say, John James told his son that he had no objections to the careers that the two boys had chosen. However, Lucy's refusal to come to England was another matter, as he explained to Gifford, "Your Mamma alone is all that I may expect to see and she is not willing to come over until I have acquired a *great fortune*."[18]

In December Audubon wrote to Gifford again, and it was evident that he realized that the bond between Lucy and his eldest son had become stronger in his absence and that Lucy sought and listened to Gifford's opinions. John James attempted to win Gifford over to his side in the conflict that had developed between him and Lucy, and in so doing, he revealed how little he knew about his son and how keenly he felt being ignored by him. He asked Gifford to write to him and to tell him about his life in Louisville, about his likes and dislikes, and about his favorite amusements. In an obvious attempt at flattery, he told Gifford, "I think I see in your present age the mild and interesting turn of mind of your Dear Mother!" Depressed because Nicholas, William, and Tom had not thought enough of his success even to answer his letters, John James asked Gifford for a report on how the Bakewell uncles felt about him.[19]

By January, 1829, Audubon came to the conclusion that his letters to Lucy and Gifford were useless as persuasive literature. He realized that Lucy would never come to him. He would have to go to her. He explained to Lucy, "I had no wish to go there so soon, al-

---

17. Corning (ed.), *Letters of Audubon*, I, 69–70, 72, 74; Herrick, *Audubon, the Naturalist*, I, 409.
18. Corning (ed.), *Letters of Audubon*, I, 72.
19. *Ibid.*, 74–76.

though as I have often repeated to thee [that] I always intended to go on account of my work; but I have decided in doing so *now* with a hope that I can persuade thee to come over here with me and under my care and charge." He told Lucy that he did not intend to go as far as Louisiana but only to Louisville where he expected her to meet him. "I have been induced to come to this firm and decided conclusion because writing is of no avail, thou couldst not understand my Situation in England or my views of the future was I to write 100 pages on it—but will understand me well in one hour's *talk!*"[20]

Having made the decision to go to America, John James sat in his London flat from first light to late at night turning out copies of his drawings that could be sold in various shops in London so that Havell would be assured of regular wages during his absence. Afraid that he would lose subscribers if it became known that he was leaving the country, Audubon decided to travel under an assumed name. He quickly changed his mind, though, and his friend George Children of the British Museum agreed to "watch the going on" of his "*famous* Work."[21] John James selected the drawings needed to keep the work going for twelve months and entrusted them to the younger Havell.

In February, Audubon wrote to Lucy informing her that he would sail for New York on April 1, and although he expressed great delight at the prospect of seeing her and the children, he reminded her that he was a serious artist, and that he would have to spend his time in America drawing new specimens for *The Birds of America.* "When landed I will appraise thee of my plans of operations, but thou knowest I must *draw hard* from Nature *every day* that I am in America, for although I am strong & active I do not expect to make another voyage there except when at last I will retire from *Public Life!* — Of course Lucy will come to England with her husband &c but we will talk of that when again our lips will meet."[22]

Lucy received this letter after Audubon was aboard a vessel

20. *Ibid.*, 77–78.
21. Maria R. Audubon (ed.), *Audubon and His Journals*, I, 342; Corning (ed.), *Letters of Audubon*, I, 79.
22. Corning (ed.), *Letters of Audubon*, I, 80.

bound for New York. Although she was delighted at the prospect of seeing her husband after three years of separation, she found little in his letters to convince her that he was coming to America because she was first in his affections. The letter he had written on February 1 reinforced her doubts. If her husband's primary concern was to see her and to convince her to accompany him to England, why did he not want to come to Beech Grove? Her feelings seemed to be secondary in her husband's decision to come to America. She waited anxiously for news that John James had arrived in New York.

Lucy did not have long to wait. Sometime in June, she received a bulky letter from John James. Her excitement was boundless as she saw that it had been posted in New York, but when she finished reading the letter, her hopes were dashed, and her suspicions confirmed. Audubon's letter, carefully reasoned and divided into six numbered sections, was as cool and impersonal as a lawyer's brief:

> 1. I have come to America to remain as long as consistent with the *safety* of my publication in London without my personal presence. . . .
> 2. I wish to employ and devote every moment of my sojourn in America at Drawing such Birds and Plants as I think necessary to enable me to give my publication *throughout* the degree of perfection that I *am told* exists in that portion already published and now before the Public. . . .
> I intend to remain as *stationary* as possible in such parts of the Country as will afford me most of the subjects, and these parts I know well.

Lucy then read the detailed financial statement that figured prominently in her husband's letter.

> 4. The exact situation of my stock on hand left in Europe I give thee here bona fide copied from the receipt I have on hand and with me here. —

Amount of Debts due me	1st Jany 1829		466.16.4
Value of my Engraved Coppers—	"	"	504. 0.0
Stock of the Work ready for sale	"	"	262. 8.0
Cash in Wam Rathbones hands	"	"	132. 5.0
Sundry Paintings, Frames, Books &c &c			200. 0.0

Sterling £1565. 9.4

about 6,960 dollars.

I have with me 150 pounds 2 copies of my work, $200 plenty of clothes, my watch 100£ Gun 20 pounds &c — The above my dear Lucy

is the present stock of thy husband, raised in the 2 first years of my Publication, the two most difficult years to be encountered.[23]

It seemed incredible to Lucy that her husband was using his financial assets as a basis upon which to issue his ultimatum:

> To my Lucy I now offer myself with my stock, wares and chattels and all
> the devotedness of heart attached to such an enthusiastic being as I
> am. . . . in return for these present offers I wish to receive as *true* and as
> *frank* an answer as *I know my Lucy will give me*, saying whether or no,
> the facts and the prospects, will entice her to join her husband and go
> to Europe with him; . . . the "no" or the "yes" will stamp my future
> years—if a "no" comes *I never will put the question again* and *we probably*
> never will meet again—if a "yes," a kindly "yes" comes bounding from
> thy heart my heart will bound also, and it seems to me that it will give
> me nerve for further exertions![24]

The above passage gave Lucy little taste for reading on, but she
plowed ahead to find that her husband demanded that she make her
decision promptly. In addition, without ever having inquired in
three years about her financial situation, he instructed her to sell all
of her cumbersome possessions and to make certain that she did not
leave debts behind her. Again Audubon emphasized that he could
not come to Louisiana "without running risks incalculable of not
receiving *regular news* from London." He intended to await Lucy's
"yes" or "no" in Philadelphia where he planned to stay for some
time "because the market is good for my purpose and the woods
very diversified in their trees."[25]

To Lucy, Audubon's message was painfully clear. He had been
willing to leave his precious publication and to spend thirty-five
days crossing the Atlantic only so that he could find and draw additional specimens for *The Birds of America*. He was unwilling, in
spite of his protestations of undying love and his lamentations over
three years of separation, to stop drawing and seeking subscribers
for the short time that it would take him to come to Beech Grove
and mend the breach that threatened to destroy their marriage.

At first Lucy could not seriously believe that her husband in-

23. *Ibid.*, 81, 82.
24. *Ibid.*, 82–83.
25. *Ibid.*, 83–84.

tended to remain in Philadelphia. Surely, he was not so smitten by fame and affluence that he would not go to Louisville to see Gifford and Woodhouse. He could not have grown so insensitive as to believe that she would respond favorably to a summons that only deepened the wounds that he had been inflicting upon her since *The Birds of America* had become a reality. Lucy did not realize, any more than Audubon did, that his ultimatum was in a sense a declaration of independence reestablishing John James as head of the Audubon family. Lucy did not understand the extent to which her husband's masculine ego had been threatened by her role as family breadwinner. After all, she had assumed that role reluctantly, and she had lived for years in anxious anticipation of the day that Audubon could provide for the family through his own labors. Nor did Lucy realize that her husband's decision to remain in Philadelphia was as much a matter of pride as it was a matter of drawing birds and seeking subscribers. In effect, Audubon was demanding that his family accept his decisions as final, and that they respect his judgment.[26] He had conceded and come to America, and if his family remained indifferent, his success would be a hollow victory indeed. Even had Lucy understood her husband's needs, it is unlikely that she would have accepted a bruised ego as a sufficient excuse for his callous attitude toward her.

Lucy brooded about Audubon's letter for more than a week before she sat down in her room at Beech Grove to answer his ultimatum. Her letter was brief and terse. She informed him that she would not leave Beech Grove to join him in Philadelphia. She reminded him that she had an obligation to the Johnsons and to her students, that Woodhouse' tuition had taken all of her earnings, and that she was without funds until the end of the fall semester when tuition fees for 1829 were due. However, she made it clear that her lack of funds had little to do with her decision to remain at Beech Grove. Lucy explained that it was Audubon's lack of affection and his coolness toward her that were responsible for her decision. She pointed out that his refusal to come to Beech Grove was sufficient proof that he no longer loved her.[27]

26. *Ibid.*, 88–89.
27. *Ibid.*, 89.

Her decision made, Lucy had to live with it, and that was far more difficult than writing and posting the letter that carried her message to John James. For the first time since she had been at Beech Grove, she could find solace neither in the scenic woods nor in playing her piano nor in her students and friends. As the summer months dragged by, Lucy retreated to the privacy of her room whenever she was not teaching. Sullen and bitter, she hoped to avoid the conversations that invariably left her at a loss to explain why her husband had come to America but had not come to see his wife. Lucy regretted having told their friends in Feliciana that John James was returning to escort her to England.

While Lucy sulked in Feliciana, John James received her emphatic rejection of his demand that she settle her affairs in Feliciana and join him. Exasperated, he wrote to Gifford, hoping that his son would intervene on his behalf with Lucy. Yet his letter to Gifford was a blundering attempt at persuasion since he was almost as angry with his son as he was with his wife. He had been in America almost two months, and Gifford had yet to write to him. Hence he began his letter:

> Not a word from you yet my dear Victor.—where are you? what are you doing? are you as your Mother seems to be *quite* unwilling *to believe* that I am doing all I can for the best for all of us; and in such a case have you abandoned the Idea of ever answering my letters?— . . . it is neither kind as a man or dutifull as a son to keep such an extraordinary silence—Have you thought as your Mother that *although* I wrote that I could not go Westerly or Southerly that I would undoubtedly do so? —if you have? undeceive yourself and believe me I cannot go either to Kentucky or to Louisiana.[28]

After making a great to-do about his financial affluence, Audubon finally asked Gifford to write to Lucy and to urge her to follow her husband's advice.

Understanding and sharing his mother's feelings, Gifford had no intention of assisting his father. It had been five years since he had seen John James, and he believed that Audubon's excuses for not coming to Kentucky were as flimsy as those that he gave for not going to Louisiana. It was obvious that John James did not visit his

28. *Ibid.*, 88.

sons because he feared that he would not be received as a "most extraordinary man" by the Bakewells and the Berthouds. Audubon had admitted as much in his letters: "I probably might have had other inducements to go to Kentucky had I had a friend there besides my Son but at present I know no one in that country by that precious name, and I may safely say that I *paddle my canoe* in the face of the storm, and against strong contrary currents, but no matter." In explaining why he could not go to Louisiana, Audubon confessed to Gifford's satisfaction that *The Birds of America* was more important than Lucy: "*I cannot go to her* because was I to lose my Summer by so doing I would miss the birds that I want and that are not at all to be found *west of the Mountains.*"[29]

Gifford did write to his father, and in an attempt to set him straight about his mother's feelings, he enclosed a portion of one of Lucy's letters. The letter showed that John James was wrong in assuming that her major complaint was that she lacked funds or that his fortune was not great enough to satisfy her or that she feared traveling to Philadelphia alone. Gifford did his best to let his father know that Lucy refused to leave Beech Grove because she would not tolerate being sent for like so much baggage. Evidently, Gifford demanded that his father meet Lucy halfway—in Louisville—in exchange for his help in persuading her to leave Beech Grove. Gifford's strategy worked, and John James replied, "I will merely say that *I will be at Louisville to meet your Mamma* as soon as I hear from her saying that she will have left Bayou Sarah to join me never to part again!"[30]

At the same time that Audubon was being gently prodded to revise his decision about traveling westward, Lucy was also having second thoughts about refusing to leave Beech Grove until John James came to get her. After Gifford obtained Audubon's promise to come as far as Louisville, he probably encouraged his mother to do the same. Whatever the case, by the fall of 1829, Lucy's letters to John James held out the possibility that she might join him in Louisville in early January. She had found a considerable measure

29. Ibid., 91, 89.
30. Ibid., 93.

of independence in Feliciana, and she was not at all certain that she should entrust her continued independence to *The Birds of America* and the whims of subscribers. She was particularly concerned about going to England and leaving her sons in Louisville, fearing that the great distance and the slowness of communication would preclude any chance of her helping them if they should ever be in need.[31] Although these doubts and fears were very real to Lucy, it was her husband who remained at the heart of her indecision. She desperately needed some reassurance that she was first in his life, and she was not at all sure that his concession to travel as far as Louisville was enough.

While Lucy struggled with her doubts, Audubon was busy scurrying about in the woods in the vicinity of Philadelphia. By late October he had completed forty-two new drawings.[32] He had taken it for granted that Lucy would meet him in Louisville, and anxious to begin his westward journey, he worked with all possible speed. In early November, John James arrived in Louisville, and he went immediately to the Berthoud countinghouse to see Gifford. After five years he had difficulty recognizing the tall slender young man who raced to embrace him. The reunion was a happy one, and Gifford soon forgot the many complaints that he had harbored against his father.[33] John James and Gifford then sought out Woodhouse, who was delighted with his father's return, and the boys spent many hours listening as John James told of his adventures in Europe, of his success, and of the elite social circles in which he had moved.

Gifford and Woodhouse lived with William Bakewell and his wife of one year, Alicia Adelaide Matthews. William was the first of Lucy's relatives to give Audubon the warm reception he so desperately wanted, but Nicholas and Eliza also received him warmly. Looking at the bound copies of his work that Audubon presented to them, William and Nicholas quickly realized that the years that John James had spent wandering in the woods and drawing had not

31. *Ibid.*, 97; John James Audubon to Lucy Audubon, November 2, 1828, in Audubon Collection.

32. Corning (ed.), *Letters of Audubon*, I, 96; Ford, *John James Audubon*, 258.

33. Ford, *John James Audubon*, 258; Maria R. Audubon (ed.), *Audubon and His Journals*, I, 62.

been fruitless. For the first time in many years, John James was a welcome guest in the homes of Lucy's relatives, and overnight they stopped referring to Audubon's wife as "poor Lucy." [34]

Although Audubon savored his triumph, he stayed in Louisville only a few days. He knew that if Lucy came it would not be until January, and once in Louisville, he was too close to her merely to await her arrival. Indeed, he finally came to the realization that unless he went to her and reassured her that he needed and loved her, Lucy might remain unconvinced of the deep feelings he held for her. John James wasted little time in catching a steamer downriver to Bayou Sara.

It was near midnight on November 17, when John James arrived in Bayou Sara. He described his arrival and his reunion with Lucy:

> I was aware yellow fever was still raging at St. Francisville, but walked thither to procure a horse. . . . I soon reached it, and entered the open door of a house I knew to be an inn; all was dark and silent. I called and knocked in vain, it was the abode of Death alone! The air was putrid; I went to another house, another, and another . . . doors and windows were all open, but the living had fled. Finally I reached the home of Mr. Nubling, whom I knew. He welcomed me, and lent me his horse, and I went off at a gallop. It was so dark that I soon lost my way, but I cared not, I was about to rejoin my wife, I was in the woods, the woods of Louisiana, my heart was bursting with joy! The first glimpse of dawn set me on my road, at six o'clock I was at Mr. Johnson's house; a servant took the horse, I went at once to my wife's apartment; her door was ajar, already she was dressed and sitting by her piano, on which a young lady was playing. I pronounced her name gently, she saw me, and the next moment I held her in my arms. Her emotion was so great I feared I had acted rashly, but tears relieved our hearts, once more we were together. [35]

Once Lucy was with John James and both of them had apologized for the harsh words that they had aimed at each other for more than two years, Lucy's doubts and fears vanished. Audubon's charm was still irresistible to her, and the fact that he had come to Beech Grove was sufficient to prove that she was loved and needed. Lucy

---

34. Ford, *John James Audubon*, 261–63; Corning (ed.), *Letters of Audubon*, I, 105; Adams, *John James Audubon*, 366–67; Arthur, *Audubon*, 385.
35. Maria R. Audubon (ed.), *Audubon and His Journals*, I, 62–63.

listened for hours as Audubon told her about his life in Europe, about the progress of his work, and about his plans for their future. Lucy was enthusiastic about those plans, and she once again felt that *The Birds of America* belonged to her as well as to her husband. She also let John James know that she was proud of what he had accomplished.

For the remainder of November and throughout the month of December, Lucy and John James enjoyed being together at Beech Grove. While Lucy taught her classes, Audubon plunged into the woods collecting trees, plants, and insects that he shipped to England.[36] In the afternoons and on weekends Lucy and John James visited with friends, and Lucy was delighted that Audubon received something of a hero's welcome from the Johnsons, the Popes, the Bourgeats, the Holls, and the Mathewses.

Audubon's absence, the fact that they had regained economic respectability through his labors, and the prospect of returning to the land of her birth combined to rekindle in Lucy the spirit and enthusiasm that she had had as a young woman. She taught her classes with renewed vigor; she could again enjoy the sights and sounds of the woods and the clear rippling waters of Bayou Sara. However, Lucy and John James had little time to savor the peace that the slow pace of plantation life afforded. Indeed, the Johnson household was in turmoil during the month of December. Mrs. Johnson and her daughters scurried about helping Lucy pack, and in the midst of happy chatter there were probably tears, for Lucy had been a treasured member of the Johnson family since 1827. Lucy's students were similarly affected. They were happy that Mrs. Audubon's husband had returned to Feliciana a famous man, but they shed tears at the news that their teacher was leaving Beech Grove. When classes were over many of the girls would linger on merely to talk to Lucy or to ask if they could help her pack. Many wanted to know who would replace her as their teacher.[37]

Lucy, too, was worried about finding a replacement for her young

36. Corning (ed.), *Letters of Audubon*, I, 101.
37. Herrick, *Audubon, the Naturalist*, I, 433–34.

charges. She spoke to John James about the matter, and he wrote to Robert Havell whose sister was interested in such a position. The Johnsons were grateful for Audubon's assistance, and they authorized him to hire a suitable teacher in England if Havell's sister did not accept the position.[38]

Lucy and John James would probably have stayed at Beech Grove longer had Havell not sent Audubon an urgent warning that he was losing subscribers.[39] Confident that he could recoup all losses when he returned to England, Audubon advised Havell not to worry. He gave Lucy the same advice, but he encouraged her to hurry with the packing.

On January 1, 1830, the Audubons were ready to begin their long journey.[40] In front of the Johnson home they said their final good-byes to the Johnson family. Audubon then assisted Lucy into the waiting carriage and swung into the seat beside her. The carriage rolled down the drive, and when they reached the road, Lucy turned to wave and to look for the last time on the family and the plantation that had given her so much security and happiness.

In Bayou Sara the Audubons boarded a steamer for New Orleans where they spent several pleasant days visiting Anne and William Brand. On January 7, as first-class passengers, Lucy and John James boarded the luxury steamer *Philadelphia* for Louisville.[41] Arriving on board the *Philadelphia* was the closest that Lucy and John James ever came to riding through Louisville in a coach-and-six, but it was close enough for Lucy.

She and Audubon enjoyed William's hospitality, and Lucy had a delightful visit with her sons, her brother, his new wife, her sister, and Nicholas. Like Audubon, Lucy savored the respect that they now gave her husband, and she was especially pleased to note that she was no longer pitied because of him.

On March 7, their visit over, the four Audubons went to the landing where Lucy and John James prepared to board a boat up-

38. *Ibid.*, I, 434–35.
39. *Ibid.*, I, 432.
40. *Ibid.*, I, 435; Maria R. Audubon (ed.), *Audubon and His Journals*, I, 63.
41. Herrick, *Audubon, the Naturalist*, I, 435; Lucy Audubon (ed.), *Life of John James Audubon*, 203.

river. It was difficult for Lucy to leave her sons knowing that she would be separated from them by a great distance and not knowing when she would see them again. When the steamer's whistle signaled that it was time for her and Audubon to board, Lucy embraced the boys, both of whom towered over her. She was crying, trying to smile, and giving them instructions to write and to take care of themselves, all at the same time. The boys, in turn, were smiling and trying to reassure her that they were capable of taking care of themselves. It was Audubon's comforting hand on her shoulder reminding her that it was time to board the boat that tore Lucy away from Gifford and Woodhouse. Once on board, Lucy and John James stood at the railing and waved to the boys, and Audubon's closeness and reassuring words convinced Lucy that all would be well. They ascended the Ohio to Cincinnati, and at Wheeling they took a mail coach to Washington.[42]

In Washington, Lucy and John James met Andrew Jackson, and they were befriended by Edward Everett who subscribed to *The Birds of America* in behalf of the Library of Congress. Their reception at the nation's capital was reassuring. It was certainly a long way from the screaming mob in Henderson, the near starvation in Cincinnati, and the bleak days of poverty in New Orleans. By the time she reached New York, Lucy was thoroughly convinced that the Audubons had only bright days before them. She could hardly contain her excitement when, on April 1, 1830, she and John James boarded the ship *Pacific* bound for Liverpool.[43]

Since Lucy had first crossed the Atlantic as a youngster many years before, much had happened in her life. She surely had had her share of heartaches, yet the hard times had given her an incredible strength of character. There can be no doubt that she loved John James. Tension and strife between them was usually the result of prolonged separation. Lucy was able to cope with poverty and a husband who was frequently irresponsible and childish as long as she was certain that she was first in his affections. Watching the

42. Herrick, *Audubon, the Naturalist*, I, 435; Corning (ed.), *Letters of Audubon*, I, 103–105.
43. Herrick, *Audubon, the Naturalist*, I, 437.

skyline of New York disappear, Lucy knew that without her *The Birds of America* could not satisfy Audubon. He needed her as a wife and as a partner in his work, and she anxiously anticipated living a comfortable life with John James—a life enhanced by Audubon's contentment with his work and freedom from the tensions created by poverty.

Epilogue

ᑭᖇᐅ

Lucy's life with Audubon from 1830 until his death in January, 1851, was both full and rewarding. From April, 1830, to August, 1831, she accompanied John James about England and Scotland on his sorties to find new subscribers. She advised him about business matters and became a hard-working partner in a new undertaking.[1]

From the very beginning, John James had planned a set of volumes describing the habits of the birds in his plates. He, Lucy, and William MacGillivray, a young Scottish naturalist and a talented writer, began work on *Ornithological Biography* in October, 1830. Using the notes and journals he had kept, Audubon wrote the narrative of the work, MacGillivray edited the manuscript, and Lucy copied it. It took eight years for all five volumes of *Ornithological Biography* to be completed, and Lucy was delighted to be actively involved in her husband's work.[2]

In August, 1831, Lucy and John James sailed for the United States so that Audubon could draw additional specimens and seek American subscribers for his work. The visit brought its greatest rewards to Lucy and John James when Gifford and Woodhouse became a part of their father's work. Throughout the northeast the four Audubons "traveled by steamer, stage, scow, and cart," united in a family enterprise and enjoying their newfound security. Before

1. Ann Bakewell to Mrs. Gifford, April 4, 1831, Miss M. A. Coltman to Mrs. Gifford, March or May 1838, Lucy Audubon to Mrs. Gifford, November 27, 1834, September 29, 1838, all in Audubon Collection; Ford, *John James Audubon*, 268, 269, 272, 273.
2. Herrick, *Audubon, the Naturalist*, I, 438, 439; Ford, *John James Audubon*, 273.

long John James sent Gifford to England to supervise the publication of *The Birds* and to procure subscribers. Woodhouse, a better
artist than his brother, assisted Audubon in collecting and drawing
specimens.[3]

In 1831 Audubon set out on a bird-gathering expedition to Florida. Lucy visited Will in Louisville where she continued working
for *The Birds*. She wrote regularly to Havell, informing him of Audubon's wishes and receiving in turn progress reports on the publication and the subscription list. To keep interest in her husband's
work alive, Lucy corresponded extensively with his friends and acquaintances in England. In addition, Lucy also proved a capable
saleswoman as she procured a number of subscribers in the Louisville area. Most important, separation no longer prompted criticism
of John James.[4] Instead, a peculiar reversal of attitudes took place.

Lucy sent Audubon press clippings reminding him that "the world
had its eyes upon him" and that family members were praising his
accomplishments. However, she worried that Nicholas might attempt to collect debts left from the Henderson debacle, and she informed Audubon that none of her relatives would be willing to help
them in their American enterprises. Whether because Lucy worried
about business affairs in England or perhaps because, like Elizabeth
Bakewell, Sarah Pears, and Georgiana Keats before her, she found
living with her relatives in Kentucky rough and disagreeable after
her sojourn abroad, she thought of returning to England to await
Audubon. It was Audubon who counseled patience.[5]

After spending the winter of 1832 with John James pursuing new
subscribers in New England, Lucy stayed in New York at the
Berthoud home while Audubon and Woodhouse set out on an expedition to Labrador. She resumed correspondence with Havell,
MacGillivray, and others in England, and she relayed messages
from John James to Gifford. However, she continued to suspect that
Nicholas, who had become Audubon's agent in the United States,

3. Ford, *John James Audubon*, 281, 287, 297–98; Herrick, *Audubon, the Naturalist*, II, 31;
Corning (ed.), *Letters of Audubon*, I, 188, 213, 229.
4. Corning (ed.), *Letters of Audubon*, I, 167–69, 178, 182–83, 185–89.
5. *Ibid.*, 169–70, 174–75, 178–79, 183, 194; Ford, *John James Audubon*, 287–89.

This unfinished portrait of Lucy, of which only a detail is shown here, seems to be the only likeness of his wife that Audubon ever attempted. Courtesy of the Audubon Memorial Museum, Henderson, Kentucky might appropriate funds from newly acquired American subscribers to settle debts never recovered from Audubon.[6]

In the fall of 1833 Audubon returned to New York and shortly afterward he and Lucy set off overland for Charleston and the home of John Bachman, a scientist who had befriended Audubon. In every town and hamlet along the route south the Audubons sought subscribers. Pleased with their success, Lucy and John James had further cause for joy when they arrived in Charleston. They found that Woodhouse, who had traveled south by packet, was much smitten with Bachman's daughter, Maria. The Audubons thought Maria charming and they were delighted when Woodhouse announced his engagement.[7]

However there were few such light moments in the work schedule that Audubon and Lucy set for themselves. John James busily prepared for a new expedition to Florida and the Gulf Coast, and he bombarded Gifford and Havell with letters to find out if all proceeded apace with *The Birds*. Lucy spent long hours transcribing the notes her husband had made on the Florida and Labrador expeditions in preparation for another volume of *Ornithological Biography*. Much to their disappointment the new expedition had to be canceled when Gifford informed his father that he was needed in England. In March, 1834, the Audubons left for New York, and in April they boarded the *North America* for Liverpool.[8]

Woodhouse accompanied his parents and the family had a pleasant reunion with Gifford in London. Audubon returned to a grueling schedule of drawing, writing, and traveling to procure subscribers. Lucy resumed her dawn-to-dusk duties as copyist for *Ornithological Biography*. She copied each letter Audubon wrote, and she found time to mend socks, make shirts, and see to the orderly running of the Audubon household. Woodhouse learned to do portraits in black chalk, and Gifford painted landscapes and assisted with subscribers.[9]

6. Corning (ed.), *Letters of Audubon*, I, 214, 217, 219, 228, 229; Ford, *John James Audubon*, 297–301. Nicholas and Eliza had moved to New York.

7. Corning (ed.), *Letters of Audubon*, I, 243, 258; Ford, *John James Audubon*, 307, 313.

8. Corning (ed.), *Letters of Audubon*, I, 269, 275; II, 3, 21, 27.

9. *Ibid.*, II, 30, 73, 76; Ford, *John James Audubon*, 325; Adams, *John James Audubon*, 425.

In 1836 Audubon and Woodhouse left Lucy and Gifford in England while they returned to the United States to obtain still more specimens. Lucy did not accompany her husband and son because she was too ill to take the long ocean voyage. During this period she was frequently sick, and she was under a physician's care for some time. The nature of her illness is not known, but for weeks at the time, she was unable to walk.[10] Nevertheless, Lucy continued to work as copyist for *Ornithological Biography*, and she helped Gifford to keep account of Havell and *The Birds*.

In the summer of 1837 John James and Woodhouse returned to England. Lucy's health remained poor, but her spirits lifted when she saw that Woodhouse had kept his promise and married Maria Bachman. Shortly after the Audubon family was reunited, Maria gave birth to a little girl, who was named Lucy, and the Audubons had their first grandchild to pamper and spoil. The child was nicknamed Lulu, and Lucy frequently called her the little queen.[11]

In June, 1838, the engraving of four folio volumes of *The Birds of America* was completed. For both Lucy and John James the completion of Audubon's magnificent work was somewhat anticlimactic. Although the work had given the Audubons a certain measure of financial stability, it had been extremely costly to publish. Moreover, many subscribers had become impatient at waiting twelve years and had dropped off the subscription list before they obtained the complete work. Nor had John James enlisted as many subscribers as he had initially planned. Hence, *The Birds* had not brought in the princely profit that he had anticipated. Lucy explained, "It is Strange rather how few complete copies of the 'Birds of America' there will be, everyone believing that afterwards it would be cheaper; and already the mistake is beginning to be felt since the coppers are all put by—in the application of some for a few extra plates which cannot be had even now."[12]

---

10. Miss M. A. Coltman to Mrs. Gifford, March or May, 1838, Lucy Audubon to Mrs. Gifford, September 29, 1838, both in Audubon Collection.
11. Lucy Audubon to Mrs. Gifford, September 29, 1838, in Audubon Collection; B. G. Bakewell, *The Family Book of Bakewell*, 32.
12. Lucy Audubon to Mrs. Gifford, September 29, 1838, in Audubon Collection; Herrick, *Audubon, the Naturalist*, II, 202. Victor Audubon once estimated that only 175 copies of the original number of the *Birds* were in existence.

After the publication of the fifth and final volume of *Ornithological Biography* in May, 1839, the Audubons made a final return to the United States, and the family settled in New York. Hardly had Audubon arrived when he determined to push ahead with plans long entertained for another publication, which would bring additional funds into the Audubon coffers, *Viviparous Quadrupeds of North America*. Writing to Dr. Morton at the Academy of Natural Sciences, he explained, "I hope to be able to present that work to the public at a price which ought to enable me to meet the expenses of such a publication without difficulty. I am also going to publish immediately a new edition of 'The Birds of America,' the figures of which will be reduced from the plates of original drawings of my large work." In these new enterprises Woodhouse was charged with assisting with the art work and supervising the reduction of the original pictures. Audubon's responsibility was to collect and draw specimens and to sell the book. Gifford would act as business manager.[13]

The business of writing, revising, seeking new subscribers, collecting from patrons and delivering materials helped to distract the family from the sorrows that befell the Audubons in 1840 and 1841. In 1840 Maria Audubon died after an illness that had become steadily worse for nearly six months. Lucy did her best to console Woodhouse, and she became a mother to his two infant daughters, Lucy and Harriette. "My own dear little ones," she wrote, "grow so fast and I am kept altering their clothes constantly." The marriage of her elder son to Maria's sister, Mary Eliza Bachman, in December, 1839, helped to lighten the sorrow that had come with her sister's death. Yet in less than twelve months, Lucy was once again consoling a grieving son, for Gifford's wife died in 1841.[14]

In the midst of this personal sorrow and the activity involved in new publications, John James began to look for a tract of land away

13. Corning (ed.), *Letters of Audubon*, II, 221, 229, 242–50; Lucy Audubon to Mrs. Gifford, September 29, 1838, in Audubon Collection; Adams, *John James Audubon*, 445, 447; Ford, *John James Audubon*, 367, 429.
14. B. G. Bakewell, *The Family Book of Bakewell*, 31–32; Corning (ed.), *Letters of Audubon*, II, 250, 265, 269, 275, 226; Ford, *John James Audubon*, 379; Albert Lownes (ed.), "Ten Audubon Letters," *Auk*, N.S., LII (April, 1935), 165. The child's name is at times spelled Harriet.

from the hustle of the "crazy city" where he could build Lucy a
home of her own. In 1841 he purchased a large tract of land on the
Hudson River in Carmansville. The land was well wooded, high,
and rolling, and the Audubons decided to build their home at the
foot of the river bluff amid a cluster of fine oaks, chestnuts, and
evergreens. This location commanded a sweeping view of the river
and the rugged beauty of the cliffs and bluffs on the other side of the
Hudson.[15]

Frequently, Lucy accompanied John James to the building site
where Audubon spent much time supervising the construction. In
April, 1842, Lucy moved into her new, long-awaited home. John
James named the estate Minnie's Land because while they were in
Scotland he had given Lucy the affectionate nickname Minnie. To
Audubon, seeing Lucy established at Minnie's Land was the fulfill-
ment of the promises he had made to her so often over the years.
The beautiful new home was in a sense designed to repay Lucy for
the long years of disappointment, poverty, and loneliness.

John James certainly succeeded in pleasing Lucy with the acquisition of Minnie's Land. She had not known such happiness and
peace since the early Henderson, Kentucky, years. Once again
there were servants to supervise, furnishings to purchase and ar-
range, gardens and orchards to be planted and cared for, and animals to be raised and fed. Secluded from the main road by a thick
stand of hardwoods and a winding drive, the estate consisted of a
spacious wooden three-story home, stables, a dairy house, poultry
yards, and enclosures for deer, elk, wolves, and other wild animals
that Audubon kept to study and draw. A short distance from the
house, perched atop a slope above the main dwelling, John James
built his studio.[16] In her ample spare time, Lucy liked to stroll
through the grounds. When John James was home, they walked to
the banks of the Hudson together, and Lucy frequently accompanied him to his studio and read aloud to him while he drew.

Lucy was never lonely these days. Both of her sons had remar-
ried, and when Audubon left in search of specimens in the wilds

15. Herrick, Audubon, the Naturalist, II, 234; Ford, John James Audubon, 381.
16. Herrick, Audubon, the Naturalist, II, 235–38, 286; Adams, John James Audubon,
464–66; Ford, John James Audubon, 382.

and her sons were off on business, she had her daughters-in-law and her ever-growing number of grandchildren to keep the Audubon estate lively and cheerful. Gifford and his wife, Georgiana Richards Mallory, had six children, while Woodhouse married Caroline Hall and had seven children with her in addition to the two from his previous marriage. Lucy was always ready to respond to their youthful inquiries, to read aloud to them, to guide their fingers over the piano keys, and to arbitrate the little disputes in which the youngsters frequently became involved.

Once the Audubons had regained financial affluence and Lucy was again established in her own household, she proved to be very much a product of her times. That is, she was happy and content with home-centered activities. There is no evidence to indicate that she knew of the Seneca Falls Convention or the fledgling feminist movement of the mid nineteenth century.

Unfortunately, the Audubons' hard-earned peace and tranquility was short-lived. In 1844 Audubon brought his octavo edition of the *Birds* to a close, and after that year he devoted his time exclusively to the *Quadrupeds*. Two years later, after he had completed work on the second folio volume, Audubon's eyesight failed, and he was unable to see well enough to draw. He turned over all the work to his sons. Woodhouse handled the art work and Gifford the business activities. Lucy noted sadly that when he became unable to draw any longer his heart seemed broken.[17]

Lucy had been concerned about her husband's health for some years. He seldom was ill, but his aged appearance indicated that the years of hardship had taken their toll on the Frenchman. At age forty-seven his hair and beard were already gray. By 1846 his hair was snow white, and he looked older than his sixty-one years.[18]

For all too short a time Lucy, John James, and the large Audubon household enjoyed the leisurely days of retirement. Thomas M. Brewer, a valued friend, described the scene at Minnie's Land in 1846:

17. Adams, *John James Audubon*, 466–67; Herrick, *Audubon, the Naturalist*, II, 286; Thomas K. Brewer, "Reminiscences of John James Audubon," *Harper's New Monthly Magazine*, LXI (1880), 675.

18. Brewer, "Reminiscences of Audubon," 675; Herrick, *Audubon, the Naturalist*, II, 237, 258, 286; Ford, *John James Audubon*, 408.

The patriarch, then about sixty-six years old, had greatly changed since I had last seen him. He wore his hair longer, and it now hung in locks of snowy whiteness over his shoulders. His once piercing gray eyes, though still bright, had already begun to fail him. He could no longer paint with his wonted accuracy, and had at last, most reluctantly, been forced to surrender to his sons the task of completing his *Quadrupeds of North America*. Surrounded by his large family, including his devoted wife, his two sons with their wives, and quite a troop of grandchildren, his enjoyment of life seemed to leave to him little to desire. He was very fond of the rising generation, and they were as devoted in their affectionate regards for him. He seemed to enjoy to the utmost each moment of time, content at last to submit to an inevitable and well-earned leisure, and to throw upon his gifted sons his uncompleted tasks. A pleasanter scene or a more interesting household it has never been the writer's good fortune to witness.[19]

The pleasant scene that Brewer described quickly deteriorated to one of sadness for Lucy and the family when in 1847 Audubon suffered a slight stroke. Physically, he was left unimpaired, but mentally, he was never the same again. John Bachman visited Minnie's Land in the spring and left the following account: "I found all well here, as far as health is concerned. Mrs. Audubon is straight as an arrow, and in fine health, but sadly worried. John has just come in from feeding his dogs. Audubon has heard his little song sung in French, and has gone to bed. Alas, my poor friend, Audubon, the outlines of his countenance and his form are there, but his noble mind is all in ruins."[20]

Lucy had much to contend with as her husband's mental state continued to deteriorate. She provided the constant care and attention that he needed, but the pain of seeing her once quick-witted, gay, and charming husband engaging in senseless childish prattle or sunk in a deep morass of empty silence was incredibly hard for her to bear. Lucy's sadness increased with each passing day as John James became "crabbed, uncontrollable," spending his time playing childish pranks about the house. He hid hen eggs, rang the dinner bell at all hours of the day or night, and ordered that the dogs be fed

19. Brewer, "Reminiscences of Audubon," 675; Herrick, *Audubon, the Naturalist*, II, 286–88.
20. Quoted in Herrick, *Audubon, the Naturalist*, II, 289.

at all hours. He constantly badgered Lucy to provide him with "dry shirts" and more food. At night he demanded that she read to him, and that "his little songs in French" be sung. He wanted each of the ladies and the children to kiss him before he would allow Lucy to whisk him off to bed.[21]

Finally there came a day when the pranks were replaced by silence, and John James no longer recognized anyone. Lucy's brother Will evoked Audubon's last response when he came to Minnie's Land to see his ailing brother-in-law. While Will stood beside his bed, Audubon looked at him, and for a moment that characteristic enthusiasm and energy returned. "Yes, yes, Billy," he said. "You go down that side of Long Pond, and I'll go this side, and we'll get the ducks." Duck hunting was of special significance to the two men, for in lighter moments John James called Will the "Duck Killer." Reportedly, these wonderfully appropriate words of hunting and winged creatures were the last Audubon spoke. On January 27, 1851, with Lucy and his two sons at his bedside, Audubon died at Minnie's Land. Quiet and composed, Lucy moved to his side, and gently she reached out to close his eyes.[22] Perhaps she knew then that her husband's rare ability to see natural beauty and his extraordinary talent in capturing and reproducing that beauty for posterity had given him a small corner of immortality.

After Audubon's death, Woodhouse and Gifford, under the leadership of Bachman, brought three accompanying volumes of text for the *Quadrupeds* to completion, and a three-volume miniature edition of *The Quadrupeds of North America* was also offered to subscribers. In 1852 and 1853 Lucy's sons built large homes for their growing famlies at Minnie's Land, and Gifford insisted that his mother rent her home and move in with his family. However, the cost of constructing the new homes took considerable funds from the Audubon coffers. In an attempt to bring in additional monies, Gifford published a second reduced edition of his father's *The Birds of America* in 1856. Shortly afterwards, Gifford was in an accident

---

21. Ford, *John James Audubon,* 418.
22. Note by Maria Dillingham Bakewell, January 30, 1912, cited in Ford, *John James Audubon,* 422; Ford (ed.), *The 1826 Journal,* 344.

that left him an invalid. For three years Lucy assisted in caring for her elder son, and she was at his bedside in 1860 when he died.[23] Thereafter, the burden of caring for the large Audubon family fell upon Woodhouse.

However, Lucy did her part to help the family. In 1857, the year of Gifford's accident, Lucy was in her seventieth year, and still active in mind and body. Indeed, she decided to return to teaching school. Now her students were her numerous grandchildren and a few other youngsters from the neighborhood. She conducted her classes in a large room in Gifford's house, and one observer remarked that "she loved to read, to study, and to teach." Most important, "she knew how to gain the attention of the young, and to fix knowledge in their minds." "If I can hold the mind of a child to a subject for five minutes, he will never forget what I teach him," she once remarked. "And, acting upon this principle, she was as successful, at three score and ten years, in imparting knowledge, as she had been in early life when she taught in Louisiana."[24]

While Lucy was preoccupied with her students, Woodhouse was trying to manage the large estate and the business. Never a good businessman, he became involved in a venture that plunged the Audubon family into financial disaster. In 1859 he invested a considerable sum to published in a single volume 106 double-elephant folio plates of the *Birds*. Most of the subscribers resided in the South, and with the outbreak of the Civil War, the investment was forever lost. One of Lucy's granddaughters explained:

> During this long period of my uncle's illness all the care of both families devolved on my father. Never a 'business man,' saddened by his brother's condition, and utterly unable to manage, at the same time, a fairly large estate, the publication of two illustrated works, every plate of which he felt he must personally examine, the securing of subscribers and the financial condition of everything—what wonder that he rapidly aged, what wonder that the burden was overwhelming! After my uncle's death matters became still more difficult to handle, owing to the unsettled condition of the southern states where most of the sub-

23. Herrick, *Audubon, the Naturalist*, II, 291–96, 300, 406; B. G. Bakewell, *The Family Book of Bakewell*, 31; Ford, *John James Audubon*, 449; Grinnell, "Some Audubon Letters," 119.

24. Herrick, *Audubon, the Naturalist*, II, 300; Grinnell, "Some Audubon Letters," 119.

scribers to Audubon's books resided, and when the open rupture came between north and south, the condition of affairs can hardly be imagined, except by those who lived through similar bitter and painful experiences.[25]

When it became apparent that Woodhouse's enterprise would fail, publishers placed liens upon the Audubon estate. Shortly thereafter, overburdened and exhausted, Woodhouse became ill. On February 18, 1862, Lucy stood quietly by as the last of her family, her youngest son, then only forty-nine years old, died.

In 1863 in order to satisfy the debts incurred by her sons and to secure some funds for the Audubon family, Lucy sold Minnie's Land. In the same year she also sold the original drawings of the plates of *The Birds of America*.[26] Hence, at seventy-five years of age Lucy found herself without husband, children, or fortune. She moved to Washington Heights, where she lived in a boardinghouse with a granddaughter for a number of years. In 1865 in a letter to a relative, Lucy wrote sadly of the loneliness of old age.

> We have passed through a very cold winter which tried both my Granddaughter . . . and myself much. I have hoped until I almost despair that [she] would have a short Holiday so that we could go up to Hudson for a week and see you all and mingle with those who sympathize and care for us, but in a Boarding house, one seems a stranger in the world, and as I pass my days alone generally from breakfast till our dinner hour six o'clock evening when [my granddaughter] comes home from her music Pupils of whom she has now ten, and from that time I am glad when she is invited out to refresh her mind.
>
> I seldom leave home but to go up to see my other Grand Daughter Lucy Williams, but being sixteen miles off we do not go there often. . . .
>
> I have heard from my Sister Gordon lately of Orleans, she has her Son at home! but they are likely to lose all their Property on account of Sister's Son having been engaged in the Confederate War. It does seem to me . . . as if we were a doomed family for all of us are in pecuniary difficulty more or less. As to myself I find it hard to look back patiently upon my great ignorance of business and the want of a wise adviser who I now find could have saved me half the property I have under errour and ignorance sacrificed and have just enough left to keep us but not

25. Herrick, *Audubon, the Naturalist*, II, 295–96; Ford, *John James Audubon*, 447.
26. Ford, *John James Audubon*, 429, 448.

It is clear from this *carte-de-visite* photograph by Bogardus that Lucy remained quite an imposing figure even in old age.

enjoy life by any travelling about in this beautiful World. I sat on Sunday night after Church on the Piazza contemplating the beautiful Moon & its Creator, and I cannot yet say I wish to leave it, notwithstanding all my disappointments and mortifications. Excuse this long detail about myself. I cannot help looking back as well as to the present and future.[27]

When Lucy was in her eighties, she left New York and went to Louisville to live with another of her grandchildren. On the trip south she contrasted the comforts of rail travel with the harrowing experience of crossing the mountains by stagecoach, of traveling down the Ohio by flatboat, or of taking the trip on horseback as she had done as a young woman. Louisville held many memories for her. It was there that she and John James had begun their incredible odyssey. Unfortunately, while she was in Louisville her eyesight began to fail, and she found to her distress that she could no longer read.[28] After that, when she was alone she had only her memories to sustain her.

Lucy spent her last days at the home of her youngest brother Will in Shelbyville, Kentucky, where she died at the age of eighty-seven on June 18, 1874. She was an extraordinary woman possessed of a quiet but imposing dignity, femininity, and strength of character that allowed her to cope with the incredible difficulties that dogged her path. No matter how numerous and varied the hardships she met, Lucy's zest for living remained unabated. Like John James, she saw beauty in nature and found retreat and excitement in the lively silence of the woods. The bright spots in her life were her early years in Henderson, Kentucky, and most especially her score of years at Minnie's Land, where she had enjoyed prosperity and the happiness of being surrounded by her husband, children, and grandchildren. Perhaps her greatest tragedy was that she lived long enough to see all that she and John James had worked so long and hard for lost, and she had neither her youth, her husband, nor her sons to temper the feeling that life had been unjust to the Audubons. Yet, she realized that all had not been in vain, that her

27. Herrick, *Audubon, the Naturalist*, II, 301–302.
28. *Ibid.*, 302; Lucy Audubon to Mrs. Kelly, March 14, 1873, in Miscellaneous Papers, Department of Archives and Manuscripts, Louisiana State University, Baton Rouge.

husband's name and fame had become an important part of the history and culture of the land she had come to as a girl, and that she had earned a share in whatever immortality posterity chose to grant to the Audubons.

Bibliography

PRIMARY SOURCES

MANUSCRIPTS

Audubon, John James Collection. Princeton University Library. Princeton, N.J.
Audubon, John James, Journal, May 23, 24, 31, June 1, 1821. In John James Audubon Papers, American Philosophical Society Library, Philadelphia.
Audubon, John James, Papers, 1807–1827. Department of Archives, Tulane University Library, New Orleans.
Bakewell, William, Journal. MS in possession of Susan Lewis Shaffer, Cincinnati.
Barrow, Bennet H., Diary. Department of Archives and Manuscripts, Louisiana State University, Baton Rouge.
Bradford Family Papers. Department of Archives and Manuscripts, Louisiana State University, Baton Rouge.
Browder, Frederick, Journal. In Department of Archives and Manuscripts, Louisiana State University, Baton Rouge.
Clore, Julia Alves. "Genealogy of the Audubon and Bakewell Families." In Family Files, Henderson Public Library, Henderson, Ky.
Combs, John P., Ledger. In Department of Archives and Manuscripts, Louisiana State University, Baton Rouge.
Hamilton, William S. P., Papers, Department of Archives and Manuscripts, Louisiana State University, Baton Rouge.
Henderson Public Library Files, Henderson, Ky.
Kilbourne Collection. In possession of Mrs. Stephen Dart, St. Francisville, La.
Lytle, William, Papers. The Cincinnati Historical Society.
Miscellaneous Papers. Department of Archives and Manuscripts, Louisiana State University, Baton Rouge.

Nuebling, Max, Letter Book. In Department of Archives and Manuscripts, Louisiana State University, Baton Rouge.

Pears, Thomas, Papers. In possession of Thomas Pears III, Pittsburgh.

Rozier, Ferdinand, Diary. In possession of Welton A. Rozier, St. Louis.

Swift, John, Account Books. In Department of Archives and Manuscripts, Louisiana State University, Baton Rouge.

Turnipseed and Babcock Ledger, 1827–28. Department of Archives and Manuscripts, Louisiana State University, Baton Rouge.

Walsh, Antonio Patrick, Papers. Department of Archives and Manuscripts, Louisiana State University, Baton Rouge.

Weeks, David and Family Papers. Weeks-Hall Memorial Collection, 1782–1894. Department of Archives and Manuscripts, Louisiana State University, Baton Rouge.

AUDUBON'S PUBLISHED WORKS, CORRESPONDENCE, AND JOURNALS

Audubon, John James. *Delineations of American Scenery and Character.* New York: G. A. Baker, 1926.

———. "Four Audubon Letters," *Cardinal,* IV, No. 7 (January, 1938), 167–73.

———. *Ornithological Biography; or, An Account of the Habits of the Birds of the United States of America; Accompanied by Descriptions of the Objects Represented in the Work Entitled "The Birds of America," and Interspersed with Delineations of American Scenery and Manners.* 5 vols. Edinburgh: A. Black, 1831–39.

Audubon, Maria R., ed. *Audubon and His Journals.* 2 vols. New York: Dover, 1960.

———, ed. "Audubon's Story of His Youth," *Scribner's Magazine,* XIII, No. 3 (March, 1893), 267–89.

Corning, Howard, ed. *Journal of John James Audubon Made During His Trip to New Orleans in 1820–1821.* Boston: Club of Odd Volumes, 1929.

———, ed. *The Letters of John James Audubon, 1826–1840.* 2 vols. Boston: Club of Odd Volumes, 1930.

Deane, Ruthven, ed.. "Extracts from an Unpublished Journal of John James Audubon," *Auk* (1904), 334–38.

———, ed. "William Swainson to John James Audubon (A Hitherto Unpublished Letter)," *Auk,* XXII (January, 1905), 31–34.

Dwight, Edward H., ed. "The Autobiographical Writings of John James Audubon," *Bulletin of the Missouri Historical Society,* XIX (October, 1962), 26–35.

Ford, Alice, ed. *Audubon, by Himself: A Profile of John James Audubon.* Garden City, N.Y.: Natural History Press, 1969.

———, ed. *The 1826 Journal of John James Audubon*. Norman: University of Oklahoma Press, 1967.

Grinnell, George B., ed. "Some Audubon Letters," *Auk*, XXXIII (1916), 119–30.

Lownes, Albert E., ed. "Ten Audubon Letters," *Auk*, N.S. LII (April, 1935), 154–68.

McDermott, John Francis, ed. *Audubon in the West*. Norman: University of Oklahoma Press, 1965.

Peattie, Donald C., ed. *Audubon's America: The Narratives and Experiences of John James Audubon*. Boston: Houghton Mifflin, 1940.

OTHER PUBLISHED CORRESPONDENCE, JOURNALS, AND DIARIES

Bakewell, Thomas, W., "Audubon & Bakewell, Partners: Sketch of the Life of Thomas Woodhouse Bakewell Written by Himself," *Cardinal*, IV, No. 2 (1935), 34–42.

Birkbeck, Morris. *Notes on a Journey in America*. Ann Arbor, Mich.: University Microfilms, 1966.

Bradbury, John. *Travels in the Interior of America in the Years 1809, 1810, and 1811*. Liverpool: Smith and Galway, 1817.

Brown, Samuel R. *The Western Gazetteer*. Rpr. New York: Arno Press & the New York Times, 1971.

Bullock, W. "Sketch of a Journey Through the Western States of North America, from New Orleans, by the Mississippi, Ohio, City of Cincinnati, and Falls of Niagara, to New York, in 1827," in Reuben G. Thwaites, ed. *Early Western Travels, 1748–1846*. 32 vols. Cleveland: A. H. Clark, 1904–1907. Vol. XIX, 119–54.

Clifford, James L., ed. *Dr. Campbell's Diary of a Visit to England in 1775*. Cambridge: Cambridge University Press, 1947.

Cuming, Fortescue. "Sketches of a Tour to the Western Country Through the States of Ohio and Kentucky; a Voyage Down the Ohio and Mississippi Rivers, and a Trip Through the Mississippi Territory, and Part of West Florida. Commenced at Philadelphia in the Winter of 1807, and Concluded in 1809," in Reuben G. Thwaites, ed. *Early Western Travels, 1748–1846*. 32 vols. Cleveland: A. H. Clark, 1904–1907. Vol. IV.

Davis, Edwin, ed. *Plantation Life in the Florida Parishes of Louisiana, 1836–1846, as Reflected in the Diary of Bennet H. Barrow*. New York: Columbia University Press, 1943.

Dwight, Margaret Van Horn. *A Journey to Ohio in 1810 as Recorded in the Journal of Margaret Van Horn Dwight*. Ed. Max Farrand. New Haven: Yale University Press, 1920.

Fearon, Henry Bradshaw. *Sketches of America: A Narrative of a Journey of*

Five Thousand Miles Through the Eastern and Western States. Benjamin Blom, 1969.

Flagg, Edmund. "The Far West; or, A Tour Beyond the Mountains. Embracing Outlines of Western Life and Scenery; Sketches of the Prairies, Rivers, Ancient Mounds, Early Settlements of the French, etc., etc.," Part I, in Reuben G. Thwaites, ed. *Early Western Travels, 1748–1846.* 32 vols. Cleveland: A. H. Clark, 1904–1907. Vol. XXVI.

Flagg, Gershom. "Pioneer Letters of Gershom Flagg," Illinois State Historical Society *Transactions,* 1910.

Flint, James. "Letters from America, Containing Observations on the Climate and Agriculture of the Western States, the Manners of the People, the Prospects of Emigrants, &c., &c.," in Reuben G. Thwaites, ed. *Early Western Travels, 1748–1846.* 32 vols. Cleveland: A. H. Clark, 1904–1907. Vol. IX.

Flint, Timothy. *Recollections of the Last Ten Years in the Valley of the Mississippi.* Ed. George R. Brooks. Carbondale: Southern Illinois University Press, 1968.

Forman, Maurice B., ed. *The Letters of John Keats.* 3rd ed. New York: Oxford University Press, 1947.

Hall, Basil. *Travels in North America in the Years 1827 and 1828.* 3 vols., New York: Arno Press, 1974.

Hall, Frederick, *Letters from the East and from the West.* Baltimore: F. Lucas, 1840.

Hulme, Thomas. "A Journal Made During a Tour in the Western Countries of America, September 30, 1818–August 8, 1819," in Reuben G. Thwaites, ed. *Early Western Travels, 1748–1846.* 32 vols. Cleveland: A. H. Clark, 1904–1907. Vol. X, 19–84.

Latrobe, Charles Joseph. *The Rambler in North America, 1832–1833.* 2 vols. London: R. B. Seeley and W. Burnside, 1836.

Longstreet, Augustus B. *Georgia Scenes, Characters, Incidents, &c, &c., in the First Half Century of the Republic.* 2nd ed. New York: Harper and Brothers, 1854.

McDermott, John F., ed. *Up the Missouri with Audubon: The Journal of Edward Harris.* Norman: University of Oklahoma Press, 1951.

Mathews, William, ed. *The Diary of Dudley Ryder, 1715–1716.* London: Methuen, 1939.

Michaux, François André. "Travels to the West of the Alleghany Mountains in the States of Ohio, Kentucky, and Tennessea [sic], and Back to Charleston, by the Upper Carolines; Comprising the Most Interesting Details on the Present State of Agriculture, and the Natural Produce of Those Countries: Together with Particulars Relative to the Commerce That Exists Between the Above Mentioned States, and Those Situated East of the Mountains and Low Louisiana, Undertaken in the Year

1802, Under the Auspices of His Excellency M. Chaptal, Minister of Interior." In Reuben G. Thwaites, ed. *Early Western Travels, 1748–1846.* 32 vols. Cleveland: A. H. Clark, 1904–1907. Vol. III, 105–306.

Murray, Charles Augustus. *Travels in North America During the Years 1834, 1835, and 1836 Including a Summer Residence with the Pawnee Tribe of Indians and a Visit to Cuba and the Azore Islands.* 2 vols. New York: DaCapo Press, 1974.

Nolte, Vincent. *Fifty Years in Both Hemispheres; or, Reminiscences of the Life of a Former Merchant.* New York: Redfield, 1854.

Nuttall, Thomas. "Journal of Travels into the Arkansa [sic] Territory, During the Year 1819, with Occasional Observations on the Manners of the Aborigines," in Reuben G. Thwaites, ed. *Early Western Travels, 1748–1846.* 32 vols. Cleveland: A. H. Clark, 1904–1907. Vol. XIII.

Padgett, James A., ed. "The West Florida Revolution of 1810, as Told in the Letters of John Rhea, Fulwar Skipwith, Reuben Kemper, and Others," *Louisiana Historical Quarterly,* XXI (January, 1938), 76–202.

Pope-Hennessy, Una, ed. *The Aristocratic Journey: Being the Outspoken Letters of Mrs. Basil Hall Written on a Fourteen Months Sojourn in America, 1827–1828.* New York: G. P. Putnam's Sons, 1931.

Speed, John Gilmer, ed. *The Letters and Poems of John Keats.* 3 vols. New York: Dodd, Mead, 1883.

Thwaites, Reuben G., ed. *Early Western Travels, 1748–1846.* 32 vols. Cleveland: A. J. Clark, 1904–1907.

Torrington, John Byng. *The Torrington Diaries, Containing the Tours Through England and Wales of John Byng (Later Fifth Viscount Torrington) Between the Years 1781 and 1794.* Ed. E. C. Bruyn Andrews. 4 vols. New York: Barnes and Noble, 1970.

Trollope, Frances. *Domestic Manners of the Americans; edited, with a History of Mrs. Trollope's Adventures in America.* Ed. Donald Smalley. New York: A. A. Knopf, 1949.

OFFICIAL DOCUMENTS

Aggregate Amount of Persons Within the United States in the Year 1810. Washington, D.C.: Luther M. Cornwell, 1811.

Census For 1820. Book I. Washington: Gales & Seaton, 1801.

Deed Books C, D, E. Court of the Chancery, Henderson, Ky.

East Feliciana Parish Police Jury Minutes, vol. 2, July 22, 1818–July 25, 1822. Department of Archives and Manuscripts, Louisiana State University, Baton Rouge.

Fifth Census; or, Enumeration of the Inhabitants of the United States, 1830. Washington, D.C.: n.p., 1832.

Padgett, James A., ed. "Official Records of the West Florida Revolution and Republic," *Louisiana Historical Quarterly*, XXI (July, 1938), 685–805.

Population Schedules of the Fourth Census of the United States, 1820. Microcopy Collection 33. 142 rolls. Washington, D.C.: National Archives Microfilm Publications, 1958–1959. Vol. 9, roll 24, Vol. 2, roll 31.

Return of the Whole Number of Persons Within the Several Districts of the United States, According to "An Act Providing for the Second Census or Enumeration of the Inhabitants of the United States," Passed February 28, 1800. Washington: William Duane and Son, 1801.

Succession Records of John Hamilton. Box 41, 1829. St. Francisville Court House. St. Francisville, La.

Succession Records of Robert Percy. Box 82, 1819. St. Francisville Court House. St. Francisville, La.

Succession Records of Stephen Swayze. Box 92, 1828. St. Francisville Court House. St. Francisville, La.

Succession Records of William Garrett and Judith Johnson, Box 143, 1869. St. Francisville Court House. St. Francisville, La.

SECONDARY
SOURCES

BOOKS

Adams, Alexander, B. *John James Audubon: A Biography.* New York: G. P. Putnam's Sons, 1966.

Arnett, Maralea. *The Annals and Scandals of Henderson County, Kentucky, 1775–1975.* Croydon, Ky.: Fremar, 1976.

Arthur, Stanley Clisby. *Audubon: An Intimate Life of the American Woodsman.* New Orleans: Harmanson, 1937.

Arthur, Stanley Clisby and George de Kernion. *Old Families of Louisiana.* Baton Rouge: Claitor's Publishing Division, 1971.

Audubon, Lucy, ed. *The Life of John James Audubon, the Naturalist.* New York: G. P. Putnam's Sons, 1869.

Bakewell, B. G. *The Family Book of Bakewell, Page, Campbell.* Pittsburgh: Wm. G. Johnston, 1896.

Baldwin, Leland. *The Keelboat Age on the Western Waters.* Pittsburgh: University of Pittsburgh Press, 1941.

Benson, Mary Sumner. *Women in Eighteenth Century America: A Study of Opinion and Social Usage.* New York: Columbia University Press, London: P. S. King and Son, 1935.

Bradford, Mary Fluker. *Audubon.* New Orleans: Graham and Sons, 1897.

Brannon, Peter A. *Edward Harris, Friend of Audubon.* New York: Newcomen Society of England, American Branch, 1947.

Buchanan Robert. *Life and Adventures of Audubon, the Naturalist.* New York: E. P. Dutton, 1924.

Burroughs, John. *John James Audubon.* Boston: Small, Maynard, 1902.

Butterworth, Hezekiah. *In the Days of Audubon; a Tale of the "Protector of Birds," with an Appendix on the Formation of Audubon Societies.* New York: D. Appleton, 1901.

Cantwell, Robert. *Alexander Wilson, Naturalist and Pioneer: A Biography.* Philadelphia: J. B. Lippincott, 1961.

Carter, Hodding. *Lower Mississippi.* New York: Farrar & Rinehart, 1942.

Caughey, John Walton. *Bernardo De Galvez in Louisiana, 1776–1783.* Gretna, La: Pelican, 1972.

Chamberlain, Summerell. *This Was Home.* Chapel Hill: University of North Carolina Press, 1938.

Chancellor, John. *Audubon: A Biography.* New York: Viking Press, 1978.

Clark, Thomas. *Frontier America: The Story of the Westward Movement.* New York: Scribner's Sons, 1959.

———. *The Rampaging Frontier: Manners and Humors of Pioneer Days in the South and Middle West.* New York: Bobbs-Merrill, 1939.

Coleman, Ann. *The Life of John J. Crittendon with Selections from His Correspondence and Speeches.* 2 vols. New York: DaCapo Press, 1970.

Cox, Isaac. *The West Florida Controversy, 1798–1813: A Study in American Diplomacy.* Gloucester, Mass.: Peter Smith, 1967.

Dall, William H. *Spencer Fullerton Baird: A Biography, Including Selections from His Correspondence with Audubon, Agassiz, Dana, and Others.* Philadelphia: J. B. Lippincott, 1915.

Darby, William. *A Geographical Description of the State of Louisiana with an Account of the Character and Manner of the Inhabitants. Being an Accompaniment to the Map of Louisiana.* Philadelphia: John James Melish, 1816.

Deane, Phyllis. *The First Industrial Revolution.* Cambridge: Cambridge University Press, 1969.

Deerr, Noel. *The History of Sugar.* 2 vols. London: Chapman and Hall, 1949–50.

Dexter, Elisabeth. *Career Women in America, 1776–1840.* Francestown, N.H.: M. Jones, 1950.

Dick, Everett. *The Dixie Frontier: A Social History of the Southern Frontier from the First Transmontane Beginnings to the Civil War.* New York: Capricorn Books, 1964.

Ellis, Sarah. *The Women of England: Their Social Duties and Domestic Habits.* New York: D. Appleton, 1839.

Flexner, Eleanor. *Century of Struggle: The Woman's Rights Movement in the United States.* Cambridge: Belknap Press of Harvard University Press, 1959.

Ford, Alice. *John James Audubon*. Norman: University of Oklahoma Press, 1964.

Fortier, James, ed. *Audubon, the Creole Naturalist*. A publication of the Louisiana State Museum. New Orleans: T. J. Moran's Sons, 1938.

Fussell, G. E., and K. R. Fussell. *The English Countrywoman: A Farmhouse Social History, A.D. 1500–1900*. New York: B. Blom, 1971.

Gershoy, Leo. *The French Revolution and Napoleon*. New York: Meredith, 1964.

Groves, Ernest. *The American Women: The Feminine Side of a Masculine Civilization*. New York: Emerson Books, 1944.

Harper, Ida Husted. *The Life and Work of Susan B. Anthony; Including Public Addresses, Her Own Letters and Many from Her Contemporaries During Fifty Years*. 3 vols. Indianapolis: Bowen-Merrill, 1898–1908.

Harris, Barbara J. *Beyond Her Sphere: Women and the Professions in American History*. Westport, Conn.: Greenwood Press, 1978.

Herrick, Francis Hobart. *Audubon, the Naturalist: A History of His Life and Time*. 2 vols. New York: Dover, 1968.

Holmes, Jack. *Gayoso: The Life of a Spanish Governor in the Mississippi Valley, 1789–1799*. Baton Rouge: Louisiana State University Press, 1965.

Houghton, Walter E. *The Victorian Frame of Mind, 1830–1870*. New Haven: Yale University Press, 1975.

James, C. L. R. *The Black Jacobins: Toussaint L'Ouverture and the San Domingo Revolution*. New York: Dial Press, 1938.

Keating, L. Clark. *Audubon: The Kentucky Years*. Lexington: University of Kentucky Press, 1976.

Kirkpatrick, John Erwin. *Timothy Flint, Pioneer, Missionary, Author, Editor, 1780–1840: the Story of His Life Among the Pioneers and Frontiersmen in the Ohio and Mississippi Valley and in New England and the South*. Ohio: Arthur H. Clark, 1911.

Kraditor, Aileen S., ed. *Up From the Pedestal: Selected Writings in the History of American Feminism*. New York: Quadrangle Books, 1968.

Lerner, Gerda, ed. *The Female Experience: An American Documentary*. Indianapolis: Bobbs-Merrill, 1977.

Lewis, Samuel. *A Topographical Dictionary of England, Comprising the Several Counties, Cities, Boroughs, Corporate and Market Towns, Parishes, and Townships, and the Islands of Guernsey, Jersey, and Man, with Historical and Statistical Descriptions: Engravings of the Arms of the Cities, Bishoprics, Universities, Colleges, Corporate Towns, and Boroughs, and of the Seals of the Various Municipal Corporations*. 5th ed. 4 vols. London: S. Lewis, 1844.

Merrill, Boyton J. *Jefferson's Nephews: A Frontier Tragedy*. Princeton: Princeton University Press, 1976.

Muschamp, Edward A. *Auducious Audubon: The Story of a Great Pioneer,*

Artist, Naturalist, and Man. New York: Brentano's, 1929.

Newcomer, James. *Maria Edgeworth, the Novelist, 1767–1849: A Bicentennial Study*. Fort Worth, Tex.: Texas Christian University Press, 1967.

Peattie, Donald. *Green Laurels: The Lives and Achievements of the Naturalists*. New York: Garden City, 1938.

————. *Singing in the Wilderness: A Salute to John James Audubon*. New York: G. P. Putnam's Sons, 1935.

Peirce, Bradford. *Audubon's Adventures; or, Life in the Woods*. Cincinnati: Cranston & Stowe, New York: Hunt & Eaton, 1889.

Percy, John Hereford. *The Percy Family of Mississippi and Louisiana, 1776–1943*. Baton Rouge: Printed by J. E. Ortlieb, 1943.

Philbrick, Francis S. *The Rise of the West, 1754–1830*. New York: Harper & Row, 1965.

Phillips, Margaret, and William S. Tomkinson. *English Women in Life and Letters*. London: Oxford University Press, 1927.

Reeves, Miriam. *The Felicianas of Louisiana*. Baton Rouge: Claitor's, 1967.

Rourke, Constance. *Audubon*. New York: Harcourt, Brace, 1936.

Rozier, F. A. *Rozier's History of the Early Settlement of the Mississippi Valley*. St. Louis: G. A. Pierrot & Son, 1890.

St. John, Mrs. Horace. *Audubon, the Naturalist of the New World: His Adventures and Discoveries*. New York: C. S. Francis, 1856.

Scott, Anne F., and Andrew M. Scott. *One Half the People: The Fight for Woman Suffrage*. Philadelphia: J. B. Lippincott, 1975.

Scott, Anne Firor. *The Southern Lady: From Pedestal to Politics, 1830–1930*. Chicago: University of Chicago Press, 1970.

Simon, Charlie May. *Joseph Mason: Apprentice to Audubon*. New York: E. P. Dutton, 1946.

Sinclair, Andrew. *The Emancipation of the American Woman*. New York: Harper & Row, 1966.

Smith, Page. *Daughters of the Promised Land: Women in American History, Being an Examination of the Strange History of the Female Sex from the Beginning to the Present with Special Attention to the Women of America, Illustrated by Curious Ancedotes and Quotations by Divers Authors, Ancient and Modern*. Boston, Little, Brown, 1970.

Staars, David. *The English Woman: Studies in Her Psychic Evolution*. Trans. and abr. J. M. E. Brownlow. London: Smith, Ekler, 1909.

Starling, Edmund L. *History of Henderson County, Kentucky, Comprising History of County and City, Precincts, Education, Churches, Secret Societies, Leading Enterprises, Sketches and Recollections, and Biographies of the Living and Dead*. Henderson: n.p., 1887.

Stenton, Doris Mary. *The English Women in History*. New York: Macmillan, 1957.

Taylor, Harrison. *Ohio County, Kentucky, in the Olden Days: A Series of Old*

Newspaper Sketches of Fragmentary History. Louisville: J. P. Morton, 1926.

Taylor, William. *Cavalier and Yankee: The Old South and American National Character.* London: W. H. Allen, 1963.

Towles, Susan Starling. *John James Audubon in Henderson, Kentucky: A Sketch.* Louisville: John P. Morton, 1925.

Townsend, Charles Wendell. *In Audubon's Labrador.* Boston: Houghton Mifflin, 1918.

Welter, Barbara. *The Woman Question in American History.* Hinsdale, Ill.: Dryden Press, 1973.

Wollstonecraft, Mary. *Thoughts on the Education of Daughters with Reflections on Female Conduct in the Important Duties of Life.* New York: Garland, 1974.

Woody, Thomas. *A History of Woman's Education in the United States.* 2 vols. New York: Octagon Books, 1966.

Workers of the Writers' Program of the Work Projects Administration in the State of Kentucky, comps. *Henderson: A Guide to Audubon's Home Town in Kentucky.* New York: Bacon, Percy, and Daggett, 1941.

ARTICLES

Aucoin, Sidney Joseph. "The Political Career of Isaac Johnson, Governor of Louisiana, 1846–1850," *Louisiana Historical Quarterly,* XXVIII (July, 1945), 941–89.

Audubon, Maria R. "Reminiscences of Audubon by a Granddaughter," *Scribner's Magazine,* XII (1876), 333–36.

Bakewell, Rev. Gordon. "Reminiscences of John James Audubon," *Publications of Louisiana Historical Society,* V (1911), 31–41.

Brewer, Thomas K. "Reminiscences of John James Audubon," *Harper's New Monthly Magazine,* LXI (1880), 665–75.

Butler, Louise. "West Feliciana: A Glimpse of Its History," *Louisiana Historical Quarterly,* VII (January, 1924), 90–120.

Demos, John. "The American Family in Past Time," *America Scholar,* XLIII (Summer, 1974), 422–46.

Fries, Waldemar H. "Some Remarks on Audubon's Writings," *Princeton University Library Chronicle,* XXI (1959–60), 1–7.

Gillespie, Dorothy. "John James Audubon: Relations of the Naturalist with the Western Museum at Cincinnati," *Ornithology Leaflet* No. 2. Cincinnati Society of Natural History (February 26, 1937), 1–4.

Jordon, David Starr. "Rafinesque," *Popular Science Monthly,* XXIX (1886), 212–21.

Postell, Paul Everett. "John Hampden Randolph: A Louisiana Planter," *Louisiana Historical Quarterly,* XXV (January, 1942), 149–223.

Rice, Howard C., Jr. "Mr. Audubon's Lucy," Princeton University Library
    Chronicle, XXIV (1963), 128–34.
Rickels, Milton. "Thomas Bangs Thorpe in the Felicianas, 1836–42,"
    Louisiana Historical Quarterly, XXXIX (April, 1956), 169–97.
Stirling, Sarah Turnbull. "Audubon in West Feliciana," *Americana*, VII
    (July, 1912), 631–40.

NEWSPAPERS

Baton Rouge *Gazette*, August 31, 1833.
Florida Gazette, June 27, 1829.
Norristown, Pa., *Weekly Register*, April 6, 1808.
St. Francisville *Louisiana Journal*, February 5, March 4, May 27, 1824,
    February 5, March 24, 31, April 14, 15, 23, 28, 19, June 2, October 15,
    22, November 5, 1825, July 28, 1827, April 19, October 4, 18, 1828.
Phoenix, September 7, 1833.
Asylum and Feliciana Advertiser, November 15, 1821.
St. Francisville *Asylum*, January 29, 1825.
Crisis, November 22, 1828.
Louisianian, May 8, 22, 29, June 5, 12, 26, July 10, 17, October 9, 1819.
Time Piece, May 9, 16, 23, 1811; May 7, June 25, August 8, September
    12, October 10, 14, 1812; September 30. October 3, 8, 1813.
New Orleans *Times-Picayune*, May 2, 1915; August 6, 1916.

Index